ISSUES IN
COMMUNITY
EDUCATION

ISSUES IN COMMUNITY EDUCATION

Edited and introduced by
Colin Fletcher &
Neil Thompson

 The Falmer Press

ISBN 0 905273 08 7 paperback
     0 905273 09 5 cased

Jacket Design by Leonard Williams

Printed and bound in Hong Kong

for
The Falmer Press
Falmer House
Barcombe
Lewes Sussex
BN8 5DL

Contents

Introduction: The Shape and Purpose of the Book

Colin Fletcher and Neil Thompson

Despite some fifty years of activity in community education there are remarkably few readily accessible writings. This is in part because it is a minority commitment, partly because its practitioners have devoted most, if not all, of their energies to the tasks in hand and partly because as a movement most of what has been written has had a limited circulation. Thus, the first two conferences, held at Sutton Centre in 1977 and Stanton-bury Campus in 1978, which led to the formation of the Association of Community Schools, Colleges and Centres gave the impetus and material needed to enable the discussions to reach a wider public.

Contributors were asked to write upon the theoretical and practical issues which they faced. They were also asked to give as much detail and substance as their concern warranted. Consequently the book serves as a source for descriptions of recent developments as well as showing the broad diversity of opinion and beliefs about what constitutes an issue.

The four sections are not intended to compartmentalize too tightly but rather describe the main drift of their contents, opening with an important if obvious concern, namely that community education exists in a particular climate and is seen to be in part an answer to basic material problems.

The second section, which is concerned with tensions in development, is addressed to issues which have already loomed large, whilst the third concentrates on current practice. Finally, and optimistically, the section on projections looks at some of the plans and attempts to achieve the next stage.

Undeniably the full story of community education is multi-dimensional but this book is largely concerned with developments in the areas of secondary and adult education. So, too, it concentrates upon education within 'the system' rather than upon alternative projects. We see a key issue as being what is possible within the state system when the term 'system' itself is usually understood as favouring control at the expense of creativity.

Both editors are committed to community education in their jobs, one professes whilst the other practices and we have been united by the will to ensure that the academic and the activist learn with and from each other rather than grow fruitlessly apart. Most of the authors here are first and foremost practitioners for whom the ambiguities of community education are less important than opportunities for single-minded effort. We believe that what commends this book to you, the reader, is that all contributors are authorities in their chosen arenas of action.

On behalf of the Association we would like to thank the contributors

1

for giving half of their royalties to the furtherance of its work. We would also like to thank Malcolm Clarkson of The Falmer Press for his encouragement and Sandra Hufton for expertly typing the book in its present form.

Sutton Centre and
Abraham Moss Centre
April 1979

1

THE CONTEXT

Introduction

The five papers chosen to set the scene do so from contrasting perspectives and indicate the two main strands of developments in community education this decade. The earlier emanates from the work of the Director for Education in Cambridgeshire, Henry Morris; the other stems from a change of focus in the early 1960s when attempts were initiated to find solutions to many societal problems in the community rather than in the individual.

Colin Fletcher's brief history touches upon developments in state secondary education, adult education and the work of charitable bodies. These are seen as having a common concern with what would now be called approaches to deprivation and with a community having rights and responsibilities which, when recognized, change rather than alter that which is called education. To some there may be obvious attractions whilst for others the commitment to community education can come from a rejection of other 'solutions' which do not, and will not, work. Community education is therefore pictured as a direct challenge rather than a collection of achievements.

In a paper read at the RIBA in 1956, and reprinted here by kind permission of the RIBA Journal, Henry Morris argues forcefully for an enlightened approach to architectural design. He sees architecture as the great public art in an age when technology is killing the culture and links industrialism with the disintegration of the visual environment. With startling insight, he further stresses that with increasing free time at our disposal the need is for an 'active, sensuous and emotional experience' rather than for 'passive amusement'. Schools and colleges are well placed to be the focal points for neighbourhoods which should be full of life and vitality. The aim should not be simply to relieve boredom but to positively create civilized communities. Although the task is formidable, Morris states that modern architecture must 'nourish humanist values' and he will not contemplate failure.

Peter Boulter is concerned with the lesson learned by one authority and usefully discusses a range of activities and problems associated with three schools in Cumbria. His conviction is partly that community education is worth doing and partly that much depends upon where the focus is put, how the school is run and by whom it is staffed. In particular if community education is to be described as a system then it is important that it functions by participation rather than paternalism for then the context is part of the solution rather than part of the problem. He therefore acknowledges and confronts the problems which experience tells us are inevitable.

Eric Batten's paper is of a different order. He locates community education as part of the response to ecological issues. He sees community education as a chance beginning, even historically necessary but also probably a response to the demand for participation by which the demand itself is then contained. He argues that only a humanist, socialist ideology is clear about how community education tackles inequalities within and between countries. He casts community education as a feature in a combative creed.

Keith Jackson makes at least five telling points against ambiguity and lack of clear purpose. The term community, he says, 'is used to avoid the discomfort of being understood exactly'. Although challenging some forms of traditional education, community education can also mean a rejection of traditional workers' education. It can be a means of reinforcing class oppression by being supposed to be a cure for all ills; distracting the local working class from the material problems they face and the common cause they have with other localities. Community education workers who are not clear about where they stand in relation to the working–class movement are well placed to obstruct its progress. There is both the possibility of rejection and the probability of misdirection.

Nevertheless, Jackson shows how community education 'may sharpen up the meaning of education in some contexts' and argues for different kinds of education to be openly discussed. His most fruitful contribution to this discussion is to clarify the concept and the contrasting 'forms of solidarity' to which it refers.

Keith Jackson, in effect, introduces, in this book at least, relevant texts in the social sciences that have yet to be worked through by many educationalists. Community Studies have much to offer theoretically, descriptively and practically although many explore conflict rather than harmony. Thus, writing from within adult education Keith Jackson suggests a central tension for all those within community education; a contemporary version of the age-old 'us and them' and the folly of pretending otherwise.

Developments in Community Education: A Current Account

Colin Fletcher

At present community education takes a potentially bewildering variety of forms. It also attracts a host of critical views from orthodox and radical educationalists alike. And yet day by day more authorities and headmasters, adult education tutors and charities are tempted to make an experiment in what may be the only growth zone within their territories. Thus community education may actually be a point of departure even though in practically every sphere of education—except those who educate the educators—it has already achieved some sort of presence.

In fact, the miscellany is probably as much responsible for antagonisms as the actual activities which the term describes. It is undoubtedly true that the term means different things to different people and even that it is a cover for commiting educational resources precisely at the point at which there may be politically sensitive change. But despite the range and risks community education is now something of a peculiarly British movement—as though traditional ad hocery has once again allowed the evolution of a genuine and worthwhile form to which some can be completely committed. Now the interest of foreign educationalists is so intense that it causes embarrassment to those called upon to explain what is happening. Their questions usually go right to the heart of the matter, is community education more than a collection of codes? Does it add up to a charter? What has it really got to do with all these enormous centres built in such contrasting locations?

To begin with the answer depends upon which sector of education is in focus for both secondary and adult education have sought alternatives in community education. State education has had the advantages of salaries and sustained resources, which have allowed experience to develop. Community development workers and charities, in contrast, have struggled with being under-resourced and short-term. So, for the moment, no common history would immediately suggest itself even though in practice features such as outreach work; devoting printing facilities to local groups; becoming places where people can meet on their own terms and encouraging 'classes' with adults and children can all be found in most instances. For the time being educationalists seem to want to emphasize their differences rather than their common dilemmas and even the most intrepid of explorers may despair of ever being given a map. Yet even ad hocery gives the chance of hind-sight and it is just possible to see where community education has come from even if its ultimate goal remains something of a mystery.

5

In 1924 Henry Morris, Director of Education in Cambridgeshire, completed a pamphlet on his proposals for village colleges. On Christmas Eve he cycled round to his councillors' homes and posted them their copies. Here was a man in love. Harry Ree's book *Educator Extraordinaire* contains the full pamphlet reprinted and shows what a tour de force passion and charm can be. The idea might have been defensively expressed: how do we prevent village schools from being forced to close by the depopulation of a depression?

Instead the ideal becomes that of transforming the school into a cultural centre, an actual growth point for morale. Shared libraries and shared halls were the social needs that would naturally become economic benefits. Above all Henry Morris was a man of culture and so to him educational good sense would be graced not by savings but the benefits of broader use. In this pamphlet, then, there were three principles that could actually become tawdry, separate and given undue emphasis. First, let all the villagers come to their place; bring them in. Second, let education be informed by where it is found; be relevant. Third, let facilities be shared; save money.

Morris was successful in persuading his councillors. During the 1930s some thirty colleges were created. He even had Gropius design Impington College, a mini-monastry for renaissance man. His enthusiasm inspired his juniors and architects alike because he was actually marking a different route. He made musical analogies rather than mental arithmetic and, as with many 'open' homosexuals, he attracted young men and women equally.

Cambridgeshire contained the idea in the sense that because of the county's circumstances it probably appeared as a special solution to the intractable problem of a dispersed rural population. The men who had learned from Morris were not yet in positions of power and were still working steadily up hierarchies throughout the shire counties. Harry Rée has plotted a family tree of deputy and chief education officers who have pushed forward community colleges and who began with junior positions in Cambridgeshire. He has also plotted a second generation of influence which shows a network almost as extensive as the 109 education authorities.

Leicestershire and Cumberland were the next counties to create colleges. The emphasis was now a little less on shared halls and libraries and more upon shared premises for a secondary school, adult education and youth work. The Leicestershire 'solution' proved acceptable because it avoided the problems of comprehensive education when it was just a whisper in the Fabian Society members' ears. Again there was the scattering of small towns and villages; some had secondary modern schools and the older prestigeous grammar schools commanded a heady loyalty. The secondary modern schools became middle schools for the eleven- to fourteen-year olds and the grammar schools had been relieved of the peak of adolescence and were to expand as virtual sixth-form colleges. Cumberland, with a much smaller budget built a model college at Egremont (Wyndham College) and both authorities set about learning a new generation of lessons.

It is a truism that those who make a new animal also find that they eventually make a new cage. The head of a village college is not only responsible for more services, he is also meant to be responsible to the local people whose wishes he comes to serve. He has power over more entities but less power within them. There are questions of management and government that enter into every detail and the consequence of this for the authority is the beginnings of a lively independence. Colleges seek control over their budgets. The more successful they become in managing their own affairs the more there is talk not of self-financing but of paying a proportion to the authority and spending the rest of the revenue on whatever they see fit.

So, too, there are educational innovations as the school in the college seeks to be the school in the community. It is as though an opportunity to rethink all has been created from curriculum to culture. Many young staff are attracted to the freedoms relative to other schools. Informality, creative learning and the absence of uniform and corporal punishment are not just attractive notions. Those who work in such conditions find they lead to yet further changes in coursework. By this time the college may have left its host community breathless and confused. When community education comes to mean community school it may mean that early in its life there will be intense public debate and in-depth enquiries, as at Countesthorpe College and Sutton Centre, even before they have had a full generation of pupils. The details of these matters are often of intricate concern in the secondary education sector and so the point is often missed. The keystone would seem to be that the school is part of something larger and is taking a critical stance in its setting. No community school yet has taken its role to be that of child containment. Conformity in any sense is not a hallmark of community education.

It is, however, the spread of secondary education to other settings that is central to any account of the development. In this way it is possible to understand why the community education label came to apply not to colleges plus culture but centres plus leisure. Morris's vision had attracted architects partly because it meant a better use of 'educational plant' and partly because a design for people could be more imaginative and attractive. But the scale was barely that of a modern primary school let alone a big comprehensive.

Then a comparatively obscure circular was jointly published by the Department of the Environment and the Department of Education and Science in 1966. This said, quite simply, that they would welcome plans and enable funds for buildings built to be shared. The author, Eric Pearson, became a friend to those who approached him and a new era began.

The circular had coincided with a number of features which made construction quicker than it might otherwise have been. Comprehensive education in many areas meant that small secondary schools could not be

7

enlarged to meet the size requirements. Inner city and urban problems had moved from being matters of blight to ones of acute social malaise. Little, if any, had been spent for so long that a programme of compensation or positive discrimination was called for. In effect, the decay in Victorian terraced streets was to be arrested and reversed by Educational Priority Areas (for primary school expenditure), General Improvement Areas (for housing) and sometimes this was to be followed through with a community education complex as at Abraham Moss Centre, Manchester and Sidney Stringer School and Community College, Coventry.

Even local government reorganization played a part because, again for the briefest of moments, authorities were prepared to borrow and spend large sums. Between 1968 and 1974, therefore the ferment in three sectors, comprehensive education, urban aid and local government reorganization made it possible for Labour and Conservative Councils alike to invest in community education complexes. The final achievement was often made possible by the Sports Council who made grants for the leisure facilities to be used by the public. The Sports Council's job was to encourage recreation when there were few places in which it was possible. Community education complexes came to resemble, in financial terms, a unit trust for an host of institutional investors.

Perhaps the cramming in of everything possible gave too much importance to collecting revenue and becoming, in Colin Ball's telling phrase, 'hypermarkets of corporate life'. What is clear is that community education was moving into a near commercial phase, that management would preoccupy the Head or Principal and that the links of some activities to education would be tenuous in the extreme. Some who failed to understand these creations called them 'schools with knobs on'. Others realized that the school and its statutory responsibilities could be swamped by a voluntary atmosphere. As in the beginning the problems associated with community education had to do with the atmosphere within. Outside, until it came inside, was something of a secondary problem.

These new urban centres did have at least one feature in common with the village colleges; they were put in settings of known human life. The community itself was not in question, be it actually a densely packed neighbourhood or nestling northern town. The settings were described as working-class, conservative with a little c, friendly and full of families. There was effectively a 'capital' to be drawn upon, it was to be regenerated and so enlarged by a community resource with educational purposes.

At this point it would seem that there could be no further developments of Morris's ideas, unless of course community education could put a heart where a hole was; could bring a focus to the ghastly rash of post-war new towns. It was already too late to reverse the new town resettlement policy but it was not too late to give new schools an essentially social task. Milton Keynes has Stantonbury Campus, Peterborough The Cressett, Telford has Madeley Court and at Livingston there is Deans Community High

School. These complexes are not necessarily an administrative after-thought or founded upon official guilt. There are instances of an explicit attempt to initiate a process of identification and self-reliance and at this point they have a lot in common with what community education means in adult education.

Although Colin Kirkwood has argued that the roots of community education with and for adults go back to African colonial experience it is hardly the case that the beginnings are actually as clear as this. Instead community education is a relatively recent phenomenon and is generally recognized as taking its meaning from the work of Lovett and his colleagues in central Liverpool. At the same time as Eric Midwinter was enlivening primary education in the city ('Priority Education') the local WEA and University were working gradually at the point of people's concerns and with those people who would not ordinarily attend their classes. Many unkind things were said, then and since, about 'taking politics into the pubs' and 'the adult education that reaches parts which the others cannot reach'. Radicals cried 'tokenism' and reactionaries claimed the work was the misuse of public funds. For what was obvious to both was that small groups of local people were being helped to express and publicise their problems and in some cases emerge into an articulate opposition of the authorities and especially 'the planners'. Just as many Community Development Projects had crystallized the low status of those in public housing, the Community Education Projects gave voice and courage to those in sub-standard private housing. Lovett's writings were explicit: 'it's not a matter of getting them in but of getting ourselves out there'. The community education tutor, in this view, is a mobile resource, the by-now clichéd solution in search of a problem who ought to realize that his problem is to reach out to other people's solutions. Obviously, the work would be less tangible and of poor quality in patches. There was no big building to be looked at nor were there actually many workers on the ground. Instead there was a challenge to extra-mural tutors and WEA tutors to recast their roles much as community schools cast a question for those in comprehensive schools.

Work similar to that of Lovett's then (and at present in Londonderry) has been extensively undertaken by charitable bodies throughout the country and most is so immediate and local that it goes unnoticed altogether. Some major fund-finders such as Ed Berman's 'Interaction' refer to their community art and town centre farms as community education. 'Centreprise' in London's East End has attracted a lot of interest because it combines coffee house, book shop and publishing devoted to Hackney matters. 'The National Elfrida Rathbone Society' virtually specializes in inner-city projects during the schools' summer holidays. Significantly this light infantry of community education is often very critical of their expensive counterparts' inability to function throughout the year and their criticisms go to the heart of the matter.

The Context

Community education develops largely to the degree to which its educational and economic gains can be bought by or sold to authorities. The latter may then feel a little cheated if the expertise recruited turns out to be devoted to political activism. They may feel that they bought the package and that the contents were concealed from them. Of course this is not always the case but it happens often enough to make one realize that those who would forsake the neat contractual obligations of the minimal requirements, for the frontline risks with children, their parents and their neighbours, are likely to be imbued with a keen sense of social concern. Specifically they may well see the tensions in their own jobs between being social worker, youth worker and teacher as just tolerable if education is a vehicle for change as a consequence. As they become virtually shift workers there can be problems of adequate recognition by their unions. Observation certainly suggests that teachers in community education take risks, and have problems with, virtually all of their traditional contacts.

But not all community education investments proved to be hot-beds of radicalism. Some complexes are more or less thwarted by the day to day management issues and others are determined to settle into their neighbourhood as part-time community centres. Schools are used for under one sixth of a year and maintained for all of it. The public use, organized and spontaneous, does bring life into the buildings, spreading the sense of belonging and protection when schools are all too often sitting targets for reprisal raids. Some enlightened authorities also reason that comprehensive schools have virtually become forms without content and that becoming a community school helps all, as it were, because it virtually recreates (or sustains) the close bonds now largely associated with primary schools. Teachers, too, have often no wish to be so distant and meeting parents only on stage-managed occasions or when some crisis has occurred. In effect, community education suggests itself to some because it is away from that which holds little promise. This was Henry Morris's perspective fifty-four years ago at the onset of the last major depression and it does not make one a doom watcher to say that similar conditions are to be found today. The question may be posed differently: not why did community education develop but why did it develop to such a limited extent?

Architecture, Humanism and the Local Community*

Henry Morris

The age of industrialism and democracy has brought to an end most of the great cultural traditions of Europe, and not least that of architecture. In the contemporary world in which the majority are half-educated and not many even a quarter educated, and in which large fortunes and enormous power can be obtained by exploiting ignorance and appetite, there is a vast cultural breakdown which, as we approach universal literacy, will stretch from America to Europe and from Europe to the East. One effect of the breakdown to which I refer is to be seen in the disintegration of the visual environment in highly civilized countries in Europe with a long tradition of humanized landscape occupied by villages and towns of architectural character, sometimes of moving beauty. The march of squalor proceeds from the Eastern hemisphere to Africa and then to the West. In its grimmest and most cruel form it is to be found in industrialised countries, for instance in large parts of the United States.

The kind of visual environment which upholds and dignifies the episode of man is being destroyed in old countries like our own, and it is simply not being created in countries all over the world which are now being, or are about to be, industrialized. I do not stop to diagnose the reasons for this collapse and failure or discuss what the remedies may be. I hasten to point out that we are about to be confronted with another disabling deprivation in our surroundings. Let me first point out the extent to which the quantitative, the impersonal, the non-human is becoming almost wholly the condition of existence in a society whose main instrument is applied science and technology. This impersonal mechanical element is invading and dominating all spheres, the economic, the political and the social. I need only to mention nuclear science, automation, electronics, the monolithic state, giant industrial combines, speed, noise, the enormous proliferation of administration. (Up to 1916 the British Cabinet, which was engaged in governing not only these islands but the Empire, met regularly without an agenda and kept no minutes of its proceedings.) We are only at the beginning of this revolution in the life of man. Before long the whole of humanity on this planet will have passed from an agricultural and hand-craft civilization to a highly industrialized technological civilization.

I ought at this point to explain that I mean by architecture the ordering of the whole of our visual environment, and in architecture thus conceived

*Read at the RIBA 15 May 1956 and reproduced here by kind permission of the editor of the RIBA journal.)

The Context

I include not only the architect, the engineer and the craftsman, but also the sculptor, the painter and the landscapist. One of the main functions of architecture in high civilization has been to give significance to man's physical environment, either in terms of feeling through awe and the numinous (the sense of what is hallowed and sacred) or in terms of the human body and its manifold physical states—all of these being humane values of great importance and efficiency in the psychological, emotional and physical life of man. As Geoffrey Scott has said, we transcribe ourselves into terms of architecture: also, we transcribe architecture into terms of ourselves. The whole of architecture is in fact unconsciously invested by us with human movement and human moods. This is the humanism of architecture.

I am referring to all that in Well Building forms part of the quality and condition of *delight*.

What all this has meant in the life of man by giving it meaning and the wonder of an ubiquitous humane incarnation is not to be expressed, except perhaps in an utterance which itself would be a work of art. I trench here on the supreme importance of architecture in the life of man because of its public character. It is our subtlest form of compulsory aesthetic education.

I stand before you this evening as one convinced intellectually, technically and aesthetically not only of the inevitability of new forms of modern architecture, but eager and enthusiastic to embrace this chance of a new beginning. In this case the inevitable must not merely be accepted; it must be embraced. Such realism has always been a condition of an original flowering of art forms. The conjugation of the forms of architecture that have been traditional for some three thousand years has become feeble and dies in the presence of the new possibilities of structure and material now available to us. The functional and stylistic revolution of architecture has begun and will become universal. I will refer later to the changes in the social scene which have relevance for architecture. What I would like now to say as a layman is that modern architecture has made great advances in structural originality and in interior functional efficiency and aesthetic efficacy. It has not yet fully developed that external function of delight which the architecture of Europe has performed and which has to be replaced. I am thinking not only of the serving of humane values which Greek and Roman Renaissance architecture and the classically informed architecture of England has performed down to Regency times. I am thinking also of the spatial arrangements that constitute the precinct in its various geometrical forms which have given delight and security to man's daily life.

Not only has modern architecture, I suggest, not yet begun to perform what I should call its external service to the local community. One gets the impression that architects are not sufficiently aware of this service as an imperative and a necessity. I have mentioned those states of psychological and physical pleasure which in the past it has been the external function of architecture to evoke. Modern architects have to search and experiment to

12

find out how far the structural possibilities of modern materials are capable of performing externally this humane, sensuous, and aesthetic function. It is difficult for a layman to see how modern architecture may throw up decorative themes which are but discarded functional devices. Time alone, I suppose, can show that. What is crystal clear is that the expression of humane values in architecture depends more than ever on the architect continuing to be an artist as well as an engineer co-operating with other artists—painters, sculptors, designers of tapestry, and craftsmen. And the creation of these conditions of delight can be quite separate from structural forms and additional to such structural forms as may be found to have aesthetic and humane value.

I would venture to urge that modern architecture should not hesitate to use the geometrical forms that create the local precinct, the square, the three-sided court, the circle, the crescent, and that in doing so it will not involve itself in the futility of imitation. These forms have a continuing social use and convenience as well as aesthetic influence. There may be, awaiting discovery, other forms of capturing and organizing space for the pleasure of man.

It is obvious too that the elaboration of external texture both as to form and colour will continue to be a method of giving humane values to architecture. I have spoken of the condition of *delight* in Well Building. I hasten to note, with emphasis, that it is still within the power of architects to invest modern structures, both within and without, with the sense of awe and the numinous which is the essential character of religious architecture. I believe that Mr. Basil Spence will create a cathedral at Coventry which internally and externally will be invested with these qualities of the awesome and of the numinous as intense and moving as those to be found in the greatest of existing churches.

Again, in this world of increasing impersonality and sameness we must hold before our minds and imaginations the humane value in architecture of the unique work of art, the unique work of sculpture, whether fixed or free, the unique mural decoration, the unique fixed painting or tapestry, the aesthetic use of water in the unique fountain.

I sum up in a sentence the main contention I have tried to make. It is a profound necessity for civilization that modern architecture should discharge its external function of ennobling and giving significance to our environment and to do so in terms of humanist values.

I pass on now to another aspect of the problem of creating and preserving in our environment the individual, the idiosyncratic, the idiomatic, the humane, in a world in which the anonymous and the impersonal increasingly envelop us. I am thinking of something physical, the *locality* (the creation and design of which is the architect's gift to us), and of something social, the *local community*.

Up to almost half-way through the nineteenth century only the governing minorities of societies were literate. Now not only Europe and North

13

America but the whole planet is becoming literate. It is safe to assume that by the end of the twentieth century everyone, except the mentally defective, will be able to read and write. At the same time, science and technology are being applied to all the processes of life. It is in this circumstance that our civilisation, both of the masses and of the minorities, differs from all previous civilizations. Applied science will bring food, clothing, health and conveniences to the undeveloped countries, as it has brought those benefits to existing industrialized countries. But technology and industrialism not only revolutionize agriculture—they kill the culture and the magical art which in rural societies sprang up side by side with agriculture. Where the victory of technology is complete, as in North America, the numinous is never created, and the numinous is a major condition of creative art in the experience of our race so far. In old countries like China and India the conditions of the numinous are being destroyed on a rapid and enormous scale; in countries like England, France and Italy the numinous is evaporating. Urban man, whether he lives in garden cities or the industrial slums, loses natural religion, his songs, music and legends, and the ritual dance.

What happens to industrialized man? He kills leisure time with amusement and, be it noted, amusement mainly passive and largely commercialized —professional sport, the cinema, the radio, television, football pools, gambling, newspaper reading, etc.—which excites and distracts but seldom or never recreates or gives instinctive satisfaction or happiness. 'Small wonder that Monsieur Bergson has called ours an "aphrodisiac civilization". But the epithet is not quite just. It is not that we worship Aphrodite. If we did, we should fear these make-believes as a too probable cause of her wrath. An aphrodisiac is taken with a view to action: photographs of bathing girls are taken as a substitute for it. The truth may rather be that these things reveal a society in which sexual passion has so far decayed as to have become no longer a god, as for the Greeks, or a devil, as for the early Christians, but a toy: a society where the instinctive desire to propagate has been weakened by a sense that life, as we have made it, is not worth living, and where our deepest wish is to have no posterity.' (Collingwood: *The Principles of Art*.)

Is it possible in any way to counter this habit of passive amusement which envelops man everywhere, and to give him the opportunity for activity of body and mind, and active mental, sensuous and emotional experience?

Our species, in solving the problem of poverty and overwork, is in fact moving forward to a more difficult and perilous stage in its history. For what is called social progress, we have now learned, is not a movement towards a static perfection; it is the exchanging of one set of solved problems for a new and more significant set of problems making greater demands on human originality and energy. The solution of the economic problem awaits no longer so much on knowledge as on an effort of political will and administration. Universal comfort, with wealth and repletion and with large margins of free time, is the next great problem of *homo sapiens*. The human house will indeed be swept and garnished for a fresh fate. Words cannot do justice to the urgency and the wisdom of thinking out now new institutions to enable communities to face this new situation. To do this we must arm ourselves with two conceptions which are, in fact, complementary. First, adult education is the major part of education. The centre of gravity in the public system of education should reside in that part which provides for youth and maturity. Secondly, the fundamental principle and the *final* object of all future community planning everywhere, whether urban or rural, should be cultural.

Planning is almost universally conceived of in terms mainly of the reorganization of the economic and instrumental services of community life—industry, transport, housing, sanitation, water, light and amenities. Planning must provide, not only for the economic and instrumental order, but also for the cultural and social life of the community conceived in its widest sense. Apart from the programme of the schools up to the age of eighteen, those cultural objects are religion, the practice of mental and physical health, adult education, science and the humanities, social and physical recreation in community centres, and the consumption and practice of all the arts by adults whether in groups or individually. The most fruitful and far-reaching development of education in our generation will come as a result of conceiving of it not only as a matter of psychology but also as the core of social and political philosophy; and of regarding education as the fundamental principle, and educational institutions as the essential material of concrete social organization. The organization of communities around their educational institutions is capable of universal application in any society and at any stage of culture. It is also the ultimate form of social organization. It is the only method of escape from the impasse of modern society, in which some unity of communal life is necessary, but in which, by the operation of freedom of thought, a multiplicity of autonomous associations has grown up side by side with the State and replaced a single dominant view of life. A pluralistic society has taken the place of a monistic society, and architecture, both in the invisible hierarchy of values and in the visual order of our environment, is difficult or impossible to achieve. Some method for the integration of the life of the community with vital relevance to modern conditions is the prime social necessity of our age. The unity of social and spiritual life with its institutional and civic expression in architecture and organization which was characteristic of the mediaeval town and the parish church and manor of the country-side has gone for ever. But the effect, in modern times, of pluralism of associations and beliefs has been one of social disintegration, less evident in the village than in the contemporary town with its social fissiparousness and resultant architectural chaos. Since the breakdown of the mediaeval civilization we have, so far as the social expression of values in communal living is concerned, been living on credit, consisting of the legacies of the forms of the Middle Ages and of the brief and brilliant, but morally impossible, eighteenth century.

15

Today we have to find a principle of integration which will allow unity of communal life and architectural expression and at the same time give free development to that pluralism of associations on which growth and freedom depend. In mediaeval Europe a common organization for communal living was made possible by a system of common values and beliefs. In our time that element of unity in the life of society which is essential will be attained by the organization of communities around their educational and cultural institutions. It is by some such synthesis that modern communities can again become organic, that the decay of civic life and architecture could be arrested, and the planning of modern towns on lines of imaginative significance surpassing the achievements of the past, be made possible.

The development, therefore, everywhere and for everybody, of a fully articulated system of adult education is the most important of all the tasks that lie before us. Such a development of adult education would include activities at a number of levels, intellectual, aesthetic, and recreative, with extensive provision for corporate life.

This prompts me to dwell with eagerness on certain implications which I believe have a profound bearing on the community pattern in this or any country. The locality or neighbourhood in which we spend our daily lives and the local community to which we belong form the cell of society. It is of supreme importance that the neighbourhood should be full of life and vitality and have significance and meaning for all those who live in it. But vastly increased transport and opportunities for amusement have weakened the local group and its personal and corporate activities. This has happened as much in the cities as elsewhere. How is this vitality to be realized—this activity of body and mind, of emotion and feeling, both personally and in groups, that is the precious essence and core of culture at any level? It comes about when teacher and student, student and student, young and old meet face to face in lecture and debate, in song and dance; or in orchestras, choirs and plays. I have seen groups absorbed in workshops, laboratories, studios, libraries. And there are the virtues of eating and drinking together and conversation in the common room, and all that happens in games and on the playing fields and running track. A community that has these things enjoys the deepest satisfactions, which nothing can replace. It has an antidote to one of the greatest dangers of modern life, the pursuit of all kinds of passive mass amusements which kill time rather than recreate.

Adult education and recreation of the kind I have described are as necessary to everybody as food and air. So are the *active* practice and enjoyment of all the arts. I reiterate the belief I formed thirty-four years ago which has become stronger than ever: it is that the centre of gravity in education and the culture it transmits should be in that part that provides for youth and maturity. How is this to be brought about in the countryside and the cities? One main means to this end is to group our local communities round their colleges and secondary schools. It is plain common sense and wisdom

16

to do this in the new housing estates, the new towns, and the expanded towns which are now being talked about. And it should be done not merely to avoid frustration, loneliness, and boredom, but with the positive intention of creating civilized communities able to live the good life. These colleges and secondary schools are an entirely new thing in our history. They cost vast sums. For instance, in a new town of 60,000 the secondary schools alone cost £1,500,000. In no other country in the world are such magnificent schools now being built. Let us, as the Minister of Education suggests, attach community wings to such colleges and schools so that, with their wealth of facilities, their accommodation and equipment, they can become part of the community pattern and centres of community life.

Such a pattern is valid for the countryside and city in any country at whatever level of culture. All over the world, and especially in Africa and the East, science and technology are being used to abolish poverty, to bring about better food supplies and housing, health and a longer life, and thus to leave behind the life that is nasty, brutish, and short. This is one of the biggest changes taking place in the world today. Nothing can stop it. As Robert Bridges has said, 'They have seen the electric light i' the West' (electricity symbolising the new world of technical invention) as we in the West once saw the star of Christianity in the East. But the application of science to material welfare should take place with a constant regard for human values. I believe that one of the surest ways of doing this, and one ready to hand, is to group communities physically round their cultural institutions so that these can form part of daily life and habit. We must all earn our living and proper training for that is a necessity; but it is also a desperate necessity, and not a luxury, that the satisfaction of the cultural and recreative needs of the local community should be a major aim in town and country everywhere.

I have dealt with the need of men and women in the local community everywhere for institutions to which they can repair to carry on that active personal culture and creative life of body, mind and feeling, which is life at its best and most real.

I return to the physical aspect of the locality. The creation of the locality with its precinctual character is a major task of architecture, but it has been completely forgotten in the speculative building and in the housing estates of the past half-century. Even today the precinctual locality is not provided for in the expansion of existing towns by local authorities. In the conglomeration of long meaningless streets with no social, religious or cultural significance, architecture becomes non-existent. The bus conductor at the terminus of a Birmingham housing estate cries out *Sahara*, and it is indeed in such social deserts that one feels the full impact of the exclamation of the poet, 'Ah, what a dusty answer gets the soul. . . .' I can make my view more explicit by referring to what has been happening in the New Towns.

We can no longer achieve in them the grandeur and impressiveness of domestic architecture such as characterises for instance Bath, Regent's

Park and Bloomsbury. If we are to give our new towns and the housing estates architectural significance and a civic sense we are bound to use our educational and cultural buildings as focal points. This involves the imaginative location of colleges, schools, libraries, community centres, art galleries. I am glad to say that in most of the new towns the college of adult education has been placed in the town centre so that it is given a cultural as well as an administrative and commercial character. There may be a theatre and a cinema, a hotel, cafés, restaurants and the open market. Thus the town's central square by day and night may be alive like St. Mark's Square in Venice. This blend of daily life and civic administration with the main cultural buildings is irresistible as a conception and in practice, and continues an ancient tradition of European civilization.

Likewise the neighbourhood centres, each serving a portion of the town, are spacious precincts for shopping, with an inn, a community centre or hall, the branch library with the large secondary school adjacent or near at hand. Thus, in the new towns, cultural buildings, which are the largest public buildings, have been deliberately located to create an atmosphere of civic significance. In one new town, its nine large secondary schools have been located in groups of three, on three large sites or campuses, lying between the centre and the circumference of the town. Each campus and its buildings, gardens and playing fields is a cultural focal point, lending dignity to the surrounding streets and housing. Even infant and junior schools can be and have been sited so that they are grouped significantly with the surrounding houses.

The majority of our new educational buildings are being built in modern and not traditional terms. It is impossible to overstate the need that such educational buildings should, through their external form, composition and texture, contribute significance to their surroundings. To the extent to which a school building does not serve these humane values it is to that extent an architectural and aesthetic failure in an external world that is becoming increasingly impersonal and mechanized. I should like to observe that we may fail to create this humane function in modern architecture if we are too much influenced or dominated by considerations of speed. It is the techniques of rapid building that have done as much as anything to lead architects to sacrifice the humane external function of school buildings. In a decade or two the bad effects of an unnecessary and doctrinaire worship of speed in school buildings will become painfully obvious.

It is with such a policy, it seems to me, that town and country planning and architecture can enable a town or a group of villages to provide not only an environment, but a way of life, in which the personal, the intimate, the humane are given full expression, and where architecture as an art can make its fullest impact on young and old daily and throughout life.

Here let me state a belief which arises out of a working life spent in public education, from the beginning of which I was seized with the vital importance of architecture. That belief is that architecture, as the great

18

public art present to us all during the whole of our waking lives, is part of the essence of education. Architecture, the understanding and particularly the appreciation of it, should occupy as important a part in education at school and in adult life as our English mother tongue and literature.

Let me try to sum up in a sentence or two the views that I have expounded.

We are living in a world dominated by applied science and technology. The necessity for the artist, who sustains humane and personal values, is greater than ever. Certain creations of the artist, such as music, literature and painting, we are able to obtain and enjoy in our private capacities. But architecture as the great public art to whose influence all are subject can only be provided by Society, and be it noted at the hands of the architect who is an artist. Modern architecture, which is the result of new structural principles and materials with a mechanical logic of their own, is confronted with an imperative which it must obey. This is that, in addition to its practical utilitarian functions, modern architecture must nourish humanist values, especially in its external service of expressing the significance of man's activities, of giving nobility to his environment, and ministering to his delight and appetite for beauty. It is not to be contemplated that modern architecture will fail to do this.

The task is indeed formidable. Already we see that the new textures, for the most part, are unresponsive to the unimaginable touch of Time. There are those who fear that the new mechanics of structure and the new materials may defeat the artist. Such is the challenge to modern architecture and such is its creative opportunity.

Size, Site and Systems

Peter Boulter

Writing in the *New Ideals Quarterly* of March 1926, Henry Morris summed up his philosophy as follows:

> We should abolish the barriers which separate education from all those activities which make up adult living . . . it should be the first duty of education to concern itself with the ultimate goals of education . . . It is the life the adult will lead, the working philosophy by which he will live, the politics of the community which he will serve in his maturity that should be the main concern of education.

This is the Morris view, so novel in those days, which caused him to seek to reconstruct the concept of education 'so that it will be coterminous with life'. It is a view which is now widely accepted but not so widely practised, and it does bring with it in its implementation some very uncomfortable moments as the participatory takes over from the paternal model.

If Morris had not been an educationist he could perhaps well have been an outstanding architect. Certainly he believed passionately in the union of architecture and education so that the former could express the intent of the latter. In the previous paper he said:

> Today we have to find a principle of integration which will allow unity of communal life and architectural expression and at the same time give free development to that pluralism of associations on which growth and freedom depend . . . In our time that element of unity in the life of society, which is essential will be attained by the organization of communities around their educational and cultural institutions.

This concept of the model of a community school may find its philosophy in the rejection of the thesis that education can be regarded as a finite 'once for all' experience. It should also find its adherents amongst those who search quite properly for an economic solution to educational and social objectives. I fear, however, that, although we may give lip service to these objectives and although by now we have many fine practical examples, we have not, as a nation, managed to make the transition to all that is implied by the community school. I write of course with a background experience,

21

somewhat limited geographically to the shire counties, but I have a suspicion that even in more affluent areas there may be a need for another great leap forward. Still we find the traditional confines of our thinking limited by the major needs of a secondary school or the traditional courses of a further education college, although the latter have almost by accident sometimes developed in most interesting ways. We are also limited by finance or by our unwillingness as a community to embrace the consequences of our own aspirations. Thus, in times of financial restrictions, the 'community' aspects of the education service suffers, fees rise, facilities are not so readily available, the cost of heating, of paying the caretaker and so on, assume mammoth proportions quite out of perspective with their relatively minor roles as aspects of the education budget as a whole.

We have had, in the counties at any rate and perhaps elsewhere, three bad years during which those of us who believe that the future belongs to the community school or college have kept our heads down, tried to stifle or muzzle our less inhibited colleagues, worked to maintain the fabric—some would say the skeleton—of the idea, and looked anxiously for the light at the end of the tunnel.

That it has survived and is now showing signs of emergence with new vigour says much for the strength of the community concept. Unfortunately, some aspects of central and local government thinking, as well as local misconceptions and prejudices, do not always help. In counties, District Councils have powers in the area of recreation and leisure, and while the school may seem to be the ideal site for community provision, the thought of making provision which could be part of an education complex, run by someone who works for the education committee, is almost like asking the impossible.

These are logistical, if practical and human, problems, which must be met and resolved. The central thesis, that the school or college is likely to be the major resource which, if sensibly sited, imaginatively designed, sensitively led and well staffed is the likeliest model for community fulfilment, still holds good as an idea as it did for Morris in 1926. The breadth of provision has however greatly broadened from Morris' mainly cultural model.

We can examine the community school in management terms as an 'open' as opposed to a 'closed' systems model. Social pressures are in any event at work in our schools, which can no longer regard themselves as purveyors of knowledge to the grateful young. We can examine the inputs and the outputs of a community school system and see how they interact. The ideal will envisage the whole of the community involved, believing the system to be theirs whether they are pre-school play groups or retirement associations, groups of children going out into the community or industrialists coming into school.

The successful schools of the future will be those where the staff and governors take notice of social and political forces which bear upon educational life, who attempt to understand the nature of these forces and who respond by devising management structures sufficiently responsive and flexible to satisfy their demands. Many school staffs and governing bodies still do not understand these changes and their experiences will be increasingly painful.

The function, therefore, of the community school is to promote educational, recreational and social development of the community through all the age and ability ranges in a partnership between the professional and the consumer. The siting and design of the facilities can either be an aid or a deterrent and sadly too often they are the latter. Many chances were lost in the building era following the 1944 Act but we must remember that in those days educationalists still expected the fulfilment of the promised community colleges.

Many schools fulfil a community role with minimal specialist accommodation and there is no doubt that a willing spirit will triumph in spite of physical problems. It is worth examining ideal modes and some examples which perhaps approach the ideal.

In a shire county the District Council offers possibilities of resources and cooperation—by the same token it can offer rivalry and competition. Increasingly, we should aim to pool scarce resources, not only here but in the provision of health centres, social services facilities, play groups, libraries, swimming and other sports areas. Patterns of use, management control and financial cooperation and coordination can be resolved but often only with great difficulty and by virtue of personalities strong enough to triumph, often over adversity.

It is interesting, I think, to study the changing patterns of provision— the advent of basic education as a creditable area of the curriculum, following the promising work on the literacy programme. The image of adult education and recreational activities is changing. Leisure opportunities in recreation and the arts are vitally important but will retain their credibility only if the community accepts and is willing to support the whole programme.

Design Note 5 'The School and the Community' and Building Bulletin forty-nine: Abraham Moss Centre Manchester, are two DES publications worthy of study. The former concentrating as it does upon our own Cumbrian school, Wyndham in Egremont, speaks of a 1964 design which has now no doubt been much improved upon. Certain basic concepts remain very relevant:

1   the site in the town as part of the town—integrated to a surprising extent;

2   the community aspect is at the heart of the buildings; the entrance, the maxim 'this school is dedicated to the open mind and the open door', the dual use of craft, common room, the dining room, the library, the youth centre, drama and music, the swimming pool and the sports facilities are accessible and designed with all the uses in mind—not with adult use

regarded as an adjunct to the primary purpose of the school. A useful addition has been the resources centre as part of the library which is geared to the needs of the small feeder primary schools over a wide area.

A primary school itself is often most appropriately regarded as part of the total provision in an area. As a satellite to a main centre it can draw from and feed the larger unit, gaining strength in the process. However, a community primary school is by no means a novel or an impracticable idea. The village school has for many years been, to some extent, a community focal point. In Frizington, Cumbria an urbanized, ex-mining village, we used the opportunity of a remodelling to design a small community school— the most interesting feature of which is the library linked with a community lounge/coffee bar area. Pre-school work has also flourished with a nursery unit, an active play group and a children's playground as part of a community playing space.

As I have already indicated, the success or failure of a community school will depend more upon attitudes and enthusiasm than upon anything and more upon management systems than upon physical magnificence—and here I may be somewhat at odds with the Morris concept. I do believe that the running of a community school offers a magnificent opportunity to practise what we preach. The present general practice in my own area is to enlarge the governing body to include representatives of adult education interests. While this is no longer sufficient—if it ever was—it has led to the creation of Further Education Users' Committees which have the right to representation on the governing body. These Committees, if properly nurtured, can be a most effective community influence both ways for the school.

The governing body can easily adopt a position of inertia in the community idea. One method of energising the situation has been adopted at Milnthorpe Community College. The governing body has been restyled the 'Governing Council' with twenty members who sub-divide into management committees of Finance, School and Community. This concept has been given an additional boost by the adoption of a nett budgeting system of finance—derived I believe from Leicestershire's target budgeting, whereby the College undertakes to return to the authority a proportion of the operating costs. Beyond this, all excess income generated by the community activities can be recycled. This calls for a great sense of dedication as well as skill by the Head or Principal and by the staff. The governors feel (and are) more involved and relate both to the college and the community.

This is very new for us in Cumbria. We are monitoring it closely and I have great hopes for the future. I prefer it to our more traditional financing which offers a good deal to the customer by the centre membership scheme, currently running at £4.50 per term, but which has certain other rigidities— a disincentive to the once and for all student; a staff/student ratio of 1 : 12

over all the centre which has regrettably proved a dysfunction following recent price rises when it was intended to help to support small groups. One very welcome development, however, is the growth of the free standing group, arising from a class or tutorial group—mountaineering, badminton, music, drama, chess, do-it-yourself, car maintenance, bridge and travel. These societies and clubs pay an affiliation fee and organize their own programmes. In one of our rural centres supporting a day school population of 650 there are 800 students in tutorial classes, in the main centre or in one of its eight satellites; ten youth clubs look to the centre for support; twenty-three affiliated societies use the facilities with a total membership of 900. This represents a considerable community involvement.

The staffing of a community school is, of course, critical. Personally, I believe strongly that the whole of the staff should be involved in the whole of the enterprise but some colleagues will have specialist skills to contribute. The importance of the specialist community staff being seen as part of the whole school can be effectively ensured by involving them in the teaching programme of the school. Their spheres of influence are thus very wide.

In the management of a large school or college the respective responsibilities of the head and the senior deputies and the senior administrative officer should be clearly delineated. This model illustrates the status of the community role. Last, but by no means least, the level and responsibilities of the non-teaching staff must never be under-rated. The expectations, the rewards and the commitment must be clearly understood. The scheme must not founder on the caretaker.

In conclusion, the size and site location of a community education provision will be determined largely by history, by compromise and by trying to adapt these to strive towards an idea. We are still, in spite of all that has gone before, at an early stage of development. We have suffered many setbacks and frustrations, but while there remain so many dedicated, energetic and able enthusiasts, I am convinced that here is a field of educational and social development which can offer a complete community service in the future.

Community Education and Ideology: A Case for Radicalism

Eric Batten

Notions of community education are not new; Plato, Thomas More, Bacon, Luther each developed their own versions of the concept. During the eighteenth, nineteenth and twentieth centuries, versions of community education were being developed in Switzerland, Denmark, the United States and Great Britain. The 52nd Year Book of the National Society for the Study of Education published in 1953 is entirely devoted to the discussion of community education. It refers to projects then taking place in Thailand, Haiti, India, Mexico, the Philippines. Since then community projects have been developed in the Republic of Ireland, Netherlands, France, Kenya, Tanzania, the People's Republic of China and Israel. Very recently agencies concerned with the transcontinental coordination of community education development in South America and Australia have been set up.

As might perhaps have been anticipated it is the United States with its considerable resources and its particular urban problems that has taken a leading role in developing and funding community education projects both at home and in the low-income countries. In 1975 there were at least eight American Universities offering PhD programmes in Community Education and more than twenty offering masters courses specifically designed to enable teachers to take on community education development roles.

In conception and practice there is no single community education phenomena. Community education developments are to be found in countries representing the whole spectrum of political and economic organization. Between countries and often even within countries there is no general organizing theory of community education. It is fair to suggest that community education projects are at best piecemeal and pragmatic responses to externally defined local problems. They are more likely to be limited curriculum responses by teachers to what they define as educational problems; responses which may be seen by reason of their superficiality as naive or disingenuous or both.

The traditional reluctance of educationists to acknowledge the political nature of their task has lead to the acceptance of superifical, tokenistic gestures in community education. This accounts for the characteristic evanescence of many community education programmes which may only be sustained for a time by the idealistic fervour and drive of a few self-sacrificing individuals before they burn out or drop out. With others, unwillingness to acknowledge the 'social engineering' role of education whilst insisting upon the development of community education programmes taking place within a framework of assumptions about the nature of man as a fallen being (and traditional assumptions about the role of formal education in his moral and economic socialization) is to ensure that community education is but a new name for old practice.

Community education programmes will not cope with the local symptoms of externally defined educational and social breakdown to which they are seen as a response. This is because such programmes seek to deal with 'symptoms' without apparent concern for causes. There is a general inclination to take the view that 'problems' are the product of dissidents, deviants, and minority group agitation. Such local symptoms are however surfacing manifestations not of new problems but of the inadequacy of old explanations. The symptoms of alienation were always there, explanations of social cohesion and coherence have always been inadequate, but in the past the power of those who imposed such explanations remained relatively unchallenged.

There are two aspects to this challenge. Firstly, there is the political challenge implicit in the range of profound ecological problems that we must face within the next decade. In particular this political challenge is given substance by the phenomenon of urbanization.

Secondly, there is the challenge of relativism. By this I mean that as societies shift their concern from an emphasis upon finding truth or absolutes, to an emphasis upon the conditional, the limiting circumstances of knowledge and the boundaries of expertise; then the challenge to the traditional heirarchical views of authority and knowledge distribution must grow. The combined influences of expanding tertiary education, particularly in the social and human sciences, the explosion of communication technology; the evident inadequacies of governmental agencies for social engineering and bureaucratized caring, have each served to create scepticism about the competence and motives of traditional knowledge controlling elites.

The practical considerations brought into focus by current ecological problems and the gradual diffusion of sceptical understanding into formal education content and popular culture make a common cause: experiences and theory are combining to form a critical mass. The resultant pressures of these influences have extensive implications for the ways in which social control, and of course formal education which is an instrument in that control, may be practically conducted in the future.

I should say that my notion of what is practical is rooted in what I see as the logic of the development to which I have pointed. This seems to me to indicate a powerful justification for the implementation of a humanist socialist ideology; the order of emphasis is deliberate. Through applying humanism to education and social processes we may perhaps more reasonably aspire to forms of socialism with a human face at the societal level.

Our increasing acceptance of relativism, our growing appreciation of the methodological problems and the ideological implications of applying positivistic approaches to the analysis of human behaviour and the development of social policy, make the case more or less explicitly for an education which I will call humanistic. Such an education helps us to understand the limits of logic, rationality, and critical tests and the extent to which politics and power determine what counts as knowledge. It requires the recognition of the role of value involvement, self interest and power in the defining of social facts. It also confronts us with our own potential for tyranny.

Humanism is an ethical viewpoint which requires our acceptance of personal accountability and of the role of evidence as the moral justification in determining actions involving the freedom of others. Within humanism a corollary of our claims to the right to be respected as individuals is our acceptance of our duty to support the same right for others. The socialist aspect of the ideological framework is implied because the problems which we face are such that a socialist approach is the only means by which we may reasonably hope to come to a humane ordering of priorities through which we may determine the distribution of the world's limited resources.

My notion then of what is a practical approach to social and educational control does not allow for the practicalities of 'the final solution' techniques of authoritarian states or for the chaotic and capricious subjugation of the weak and under-privileged to the amorality of supposedly free market forces.

This is not to say that I am hopeful that humanist socialist solutions will emerge—the pressure of ecological problems is growing so rapidly; the power of self-interested elites is so entrenched that the views I hold must be regarded as somewhat romantic. Freire says 'We need to have dreams because without them we cannot change.' One man's dreams or ideals are another man's impracticalities: it is in the interpretation of 'social facts' or institutionalized values that arguments about what is practical repose and we must recognize the role of power in determining that interpretation.

In this paper it is suggested that the universal development of community education is, despite the diversity and general superficiality of the response, a reflection of two developments of universal consequence. These are firstly the development of intense ecological problems and secondly a growing sophistication in the understanding of the self-interest component in determining 'expert' knowledge. These developments create a serious challenge to the political practicality and the theoretical justification of hierarchical social control or authority. One response has been a series of gestures in carefully controlled popular participation in the proceedings of a range of governmental agencies. In education we have witnessed the burgeoning of community education.

I argue that what is required is the development of a social response based on an ethic that embodies a continuous sceptical challenge to claims of authority through its demand for accountability in evidential and political

29

terms. This I have described as the humanist socialist approach.

There is little to evidence the emergence of this perspective in social or educational forms so far. However, we may note in some low-income countries the development of community education responses which reflect a pragmatic approach to a scarcity of resources and also sometimes a socialist ideology. In Tanzania there is emerging in rural areas a system of education in which great emphasis is placed upon self-sufficiency and where the development of academic education for the consumption of an elite is being resisted.

Urbanization is a rapidly developing feature of low-income countries and an established feature of advanced industrialized societies. Urbanization, especially when accompanied by high technology, poses particular problems for social control. The effects of processes of attrition upon the industrial and social life of high technology society must place a high premium on governments which rather than resort to violence as a means of control seek instead to persuade, negotiate and covertly manipulate their populations. The capacity of individuals and small groups to resist attempts to impose controls in such society even when such attempts at control might be widely regarded as justified is greatly enhanced.

In the face of growing scepticism about the knowledge bases and physical power capacities of controlling elites, pressures for participation and decentralization grow and are acceded to. Community education responses are one form of this development although as in other areas of social administration the responses so far are more of form than substance. Community education development is likely to be tolerated only when it does not significantly affect elite control over knowledge accreditation and distribution; whilst it remains a ghetto activity. We may observe also that participation is by no means always a radical influence indeed until the debate is joined about the humanist socialist ethic in education, and even then if it is not acted upon in the spirit as well as in the letter, community education will be an authoritarian conservative influence.

Community education will remain impotent until it develops its theory and matches it with practice. In order to develop, community education requires that the ideological assumptions underlying the definition of problems to which it is intended as a response are made explicit.

For community education to be more than a passing fancy we need to promote an understanding of the knowledge basis of authority; to encourage the development of a discussion of the relationship of knowledge to control; and to elaborate publicly the limiting circumstances in which we may be justified in controlling an individual's access to knowledge which may be used as a means of arguing legitimate control over him. Such a position requires a shift of emphasis from our thinking of others in terms of a societal viewpoint to one which embraces their individuality. This can only be done at all comfortably if we envisage individuality as being defined through cooperation rather than through competition. It represents a brotherhood rather than a jungle-animal view of man.

The polarities outlined should not be taken as evidence of an extremist stance on my part but viewed as an attempt to clarify a complex argument. Given the scale of the topic addressed polar positions must be presented. Others can shade in the detail. Within the bounds of the ideology that I seek to elucidate an extremist position is not acceptable. As Fromm says:

'Because humanists believe in the unity of humanity and have faith in the future of man they have never been fanatics.'

So far as the balance between social requirements and individual freedom is concerned we seem to have the capacity as individuals to emphasize the importance of our own individual freedom and its compatability with the social requirement in our own case, whilst we reverse emphasis when considering the freedom of others. Our own actions, though often so individualistic as to be in danger of being characterized as officially deviant by an external observer playing the societal role, should be interpreted in terms of our claimed intentions, motives and attitudes. In other words we seek the freedom to interpret for ourselves the facts of our actions in terms of criteria which may not be directly observed by an external observer. At the same time we impute a claim for the regulation of others by our willingness to interpret their actions in terms of assumed societal norms for the meaning of behaviour.

The extent to which a society, through its constitution and laws and through the agencies of government, seeks to sustain its major emphasis upon either 'society as given' or upon individual freedom to negotiate, provides an index of its dominant ideology; its position on an authoritarian-radical scale. The humanist influence within a society will be concerned with asserting the knowledge basis of the case for the individual's freedom to negotiate his relationship with society. Within education humanism will involve considering ways of encouraging the development of capacities for negotiation, the appreciation of the criteria of knowledge accreditation and the limited role of knowledge in negotiation. The socialist influence evidences itself within society by the acceptance of its duty to seek praxis, that is, to create institutions that aspire to match humanist ideals and intentions with practical outcomes.

Within education this socialist influence implies seeking to minimize the inhibitions upon negotiation created through differential access to formal power. It involves also, bearing in mind the humanist aspect, developing an approach to education which aspires to equity, that is meeting individual educational needs, something more difficult to administer than equality.

These ideological considerations have clear implications for the development of a radical approach to community education. It will significantly affect our view of curriculum. With the authoritarian, 'society as given'

31

emphasis then, curriculum is to be viewed also as 'given', a matter of factual content so self-evidently useful or functional for society that negotiation is not required. With a radical view then, curriculum is to be viewed as a total process in which the procedure of determining the curriculum or what counts as knowledge and how it is managed is shared by the educationally relevant community.

The traditional conservative view of education is that the curriculum is content not process, that for most of those to be educated the emphasis is upon facts not ideas, upon received wisdom and not upon how we come to accord the status of fact with its assumed prescriptive power.

The conservatism of this view is self-evident. It does not help us to understand the stresses and strains within the society or the education system. It encourages the automatic assumption that dissidents are unsocialized or anti-socialized and leads to an emphasis upon more effective techniques of social control. From such characteristics we derive a model of society and of its curriculum with a highly authoritarian potential, clearly political in its implication. The radical view of curriculum has as its principal the politics of openness, it is one in which curriculum is seen as a total process, where processes of administration and knowledge management are themselves the subject of determination, observation and evaluation by those involved, where a clearer understanding of the limits of evaluation procedures is developed and an explicit acknowledgement of the role of power in determining the constraints upon what we do is made.

Education is surely not concerned with the acquisition of 'facts' so called; or indeed with training in reading, writing, numeracy or other technical skills as ends in themselves. Such techniques are intended as means through which we may enhance capacity for understanding how 'facts' come to be regarded as such. Unless the criteria of fact making are understood, or unless the facts themselves are experienced in some nontheoretical form then no growth or educational relationship can develop between the individual involved and the 'facts'.

Furthermore, even within the conservative 'received knowledge' model we find that the academic education provided mainly for a social elite is supposed to be one which equips that elite for knowledge development and evaluation. The academic as a member of the elite is supposedly disinterested and dedicated to knowledge production (regardless of considerations of preferment); he provides the 'facts' without fear or favour or apparently social responsibility, to be filtered for mass consumption by other elite members more directly concerned with knowledge management.

Two major difficulties are usually indicated when it is proposed that we should try and apply the knowledge creating 'academic ideal' to the education of the mass. The first, the commonest and the popularly accepted argument is that the resources required for what amounts to a much more individualized approach to the provision of education are simply not available except for small minorities who may be selected on the basis of their cleverness and virtue. I take the view that the resources argument is false. I believe that the emphasis upon the need for considerable resources external to the individual stems from the fact that we have failed to motivate individuals to develop their personal resources. In the overwhelming majority of cases we do not succeed in creating the will to be educated in those for whom we are concerned. Given an individual passion for education, then even at present overall levels of material provision, there can be few significant obstacles to attainment. I am not so naive as to miss the apparent justification for the elitist viewpoints that this argument gives. I will confine myself here to saying that passions for education are stifled because those social inducements which are assumed to motivate a minority to high attainment cannot be credible for the majority. Advantages through education can only be gained by the minority at the expense of the majority. For most, access to advantage through education never appears to be a realistic possibility. Further, the investment view of education carries within it the seeds of alienation.

So far as the provision of more resources may be a factor in determining educational attainments through making possible a more individualized knowledge-developing education, I would argue that resources are to be found within the community. The community is a considerable reservoir of human and material resources which we have seldom sought to involve in the creation of its own education.

A second argument made against providing the educationally valuable characteristics of elite opportunity for all is usually stated publicly in practical and pseudo-scientific terms, although underlying the public argument which we have been conditioned to accept is the covert argument of elite protectionism. The elitist educational argument is essentially based upon notions of qualitative differences in thinking capacity, that a significant proportion of children are not capable of coping with abstractions, cannot manipulate symbols and so on. This represents a contemporary version of traditional leadership myth, now expressed in psychological terms and with inadequate reference to the effects of the environmental influences upon motivation. The underlying, not usually expressed argument is precisely that to do with leadership, some are born to lead others to be led, the elite will distribute knowledge to sustain this relationship.

Clearly, if we seek to develop a form of education which fosters a sense of individuality and creates a sceptical approach to facts through directly involving the community in the difficulties of knowledge-making as curriculum or social policy, then there is a considerable challenge posed to traditional elite interest.

I suggest that the current universal phenomena of community education development reflects not a shift from a conservative to a radical view of society and curriculum—it would be nonsense to make such a claim—but community education does reflect a preceding stage in this development. It represents a stage at which gestures are being made without any clear understanding of why, but simply as *ad hoc* responses.

Ironically, it may be argued that the rigourous knowledge-developing techniques of the scientist and his technologist counterpart have by reason of their rigour induced 'tunnel vision' and as a consequence have been a significant agency in provoking the problems that we are experiencing. Claims to disinterestedness and concern for discipline integrity have led the modern 'problem solvers' to develop answers which have signally failed to take account of human, social and material resource considerations. Thus the claim to expertise, authority and the right to control on the basis of more rational and demonstrable criteria, is itself becoming suspect.

This is at a time when we are witnessing the remarkable phenomena of unprecedented urban population growth with its explosive political potential. In 1900 fifteen per cent of the world population lived in urban areas. During the next seventy-five years this percentage increased to thirty-six per cent. From 1975 until the end of the century, that is within the early adult life of most of our children, this percentage is expected to approximately double again to seventy per cent. Further, it seems likely that by the year 2000 the population will double and as each expanding generation leaves an even larger base for the next expansion we may on the basis of even optimistic forecasts anticipate that well within the lifetime of our children say, 2020, the world population will triple. This 'optimistic' forecast assumes stabilization with average family size of two children and a world population of eleven billion, which is widely held to be the limit for a reasonably well-fed and healthy but by no means luxurious life for all the world's peoples. What presupposes stabilization, of course, is that we can in the meantime secure a politically acceptable method of redistributing resources.

In this regard we should note the highly exploitive relationship that developed countries presently have with the rest, in terms for instance of their consumption of energy and other raw materials and their exportation of pollution. We can observe the accelerating gap between rich and poor countries. Even between the rich and richer countries of the EEC the gap grows. The EEC is itself an economic union designed in increasingly difficult times to sustain the living standards of its members by more effective exploitation of low-income countries.

Within wealthy countries, including the richest, we see increasing signs of an inability to effectively fund the social services that their internal inequalities make politically necessary. To a large extent this ineffectiveness stems from the inflationary growth of self-entrenching professional bureaucracies. Members of such bureaucracies, their families and friends have, through control over the distribution of resources for the services involved either in terms of salaries, pensions or access through superior knowledge, subverted the officially-stated welfare intent. Too often resources collected through revenue in small amounts from the poor and less well off are re-distributed as services, salaries and pensions to the better off. This phenomena is to be observed in rich and poor societies and is accepted by politicians who will pay well to keep a barrier between themselves and the disadvantaged and to sustain a self-interested conservative electorate.

It may be that the problems of recruitment to management in industrial and commercial bureaucracies and the preference for work in governmental agencies which is to be observed in many societies, represents a growing awareness of the vulnerability of managers and their interests in a commercial setting to the pressures of organized labour and political intervention. It is a nice matter of political calculation to determine how far it is practical for politician to attack the privileges of their bureaucrats who symbolize official munificence and represent a loyal electorate for conservative regimes. Herein perhaps lies the growing attraction of public service in societies more or less willingly following policies of resource redistribution.

It is interesting to note that like academics, bureaucrats officially espouse disinterestedness, they often seek anonymity as well. Such a search for non-responsibility can only ever act as a conservatives influence. Disinterestedness by knowledge providers, bureaucrats or academics must reduce the pressures upon those who have the power to re-act to the new knowledge unless it reinforces that which they already accept. Anonymity extends only to those outside trying to redress grievance, it cannot operate inside the bureaucracy where the power of hierarchy may be applied in its own favour.

In the light of the considerable complex of problems, pressures and interests for which I have provided the briefest glossary, we can only speculate on the political and social tensions that may occur if any serious attempt is made within society to allow greater participation of the people in decision-making.

It is by no means certain that the rich countries of the world will be able through the development of more responsive political and educational systems to persuade their community to trade-in historically based advantages of living standards for the benefit of global society.

It certainly seems more plausible to argue that selfish and short term considerations will lead to the neglect of long-term consequences. Yet this is an unacceptable view. It derives from a fixed and pessimistic notion of man—a hereditarian and conservative view, the logic of which justifies the acceptance of control as the social emphasis and the subjugation of men not only through the exploitation of one nation by another but also within societies. It can only encourage the authoritarian and regimes which are likely to resist equitable redistribution of resources within or between societies.

At an entirely practical level I would argue that the consequences of ignoring the problem of the equitable distribution of the world's scarce resources, and political power will be experienced not in the distant future but certainly in our children's lifetime and probably within ours. Further, the longer we leave our attempt to involve individuals and to invoke their sense of moral responsibility then the more likely we are to be faced with expedient inhuman solutions and with the sanctioning of authoritarian governments.

As educationists we are obliged to be optimists; pessimism allows no way forward and realism is the conservative excuse for trying to maintain the status quo. As educationists we are bound to educate not for acceptance of closed or closing societies, for the acceptance of a fixed or 'given knowledge' view but for the widest participation of the community in the knowledge-making and policy-determining practices of schools and their societies. Open society, open curriculum may not come about but for the educationist it is the point and purpose of community education.

The received knowledge curriculum, justified by the educational investment viewpoint has not served to motivate the educational attainment of the majority of our pupils. We may regard them as being alienated from their product because it is too often without use, because it is not of their creation, it is not their property but the outcome of product–fetishism. The pupil is regarded as an investment resource and not as an individual. We can develop the analogy and see the teachers in existing stratified knowledge-distributing systems as managers, as members of a boss class.

Paulo Friere writes graphically of the relationship between the colonials and the imperialists. He points to the external control of appropriate knowledge in colonial times and he calls for a radicalization of education as a liberating force. There are considerable parallels between the knowledge-controlling exploitive relationships implied by colonial imperialism, and now by its economic forms and those which exist between teachers and taught in traditional hierarchical systems.

Since there is little creative in the formal expectations of the educational (schooling) relationship, acquiescence in minimal necessary involvement is widely accepted in mutual silent conspiracy by teacher and taught. Too often the relationship depends upon power, the obsession is with control and the evidence of the ineffectuality of formal schooling piles up.

Freire argues for praxis the articulation of theory and practice. In terms of what has been said, this involves seeking to implement more widely an education which if practised at all is presently part of the educational experience of elites. Praxis involves treating curriculum as the total process of knowledge-making and defining, not as content alone. Any serious attempt at attaining educational goals must of necessity involve all educationally relevant members of the community in the determination of those goals and the criteria by which their attainment may be assessed.

Only through community involvement may we hope for the development of 'conscientization' or involvement in a truly educational activity which is seldom, at present, to be found. The community becomes central to our thinking in such a process because it shares in the determination of the goals and it is recruited as an aid to their achievement. We are, I believe, reaching the stage when as the result of a constellation of global problems, both practical and theoretical, a radical approach to community education becomes appropriate and in my view essential if we are to have even the slightest hope of avoiding the pressures to dehumanization which many of these problems represent. We are reaching a stage in global development when we must seek to ameliorate much more effectively than hitherto the conditions which generate the political and economic potential for disruption of rapidly growing population especially in urban areas.

Even accepting that the technology of control is feasible and ignoring the moral questions raised by our sanctioning authoritarian societies, then pragmatically the economic and political outcome of backing a process of attrition and the practice of repression is unsound. Economic complexity is such that the standard of living is bound to be seriously affected even for elite supporters in circumstances of repression with its attendant strife. Initially at least the sanctioned elite would be in a position to steadily reduce the circumstances of its own supporters in order to try and sustain its own advantages.

We can realistically envisage a near future in which a large proportion of the population of low income countries will be living underfed and illiterate in urban areas. Population growth and economic forms are creating accelerating pressures on material resources. Low-income countries by reason of their own domestic hardship are likely to seek to redress the impoverishment that they have experienced at the hands of more advanced societies. We can witness the emergence of such processes already.

Within societies the effective administration of a more equitable distribution of resources seems to depend upon finding ways in which the entrenchment of bourgeois bureaucracy may be avoided. There are further a considerable range of ecological problems which raise critical questions about the scale and nature of desirable economic and political forms.

Apart from concern about the adequacy of exisiting economic and political practices with their traditional reliance upon self-perpetuating elites, we are also driven to question the limitation of their knowledge base. To question how far the expert can separate his knowledge from his self-interest is increasingly regarded as a legitimate activity. Within academia the steady development of radical theoretical perspectives provides another questioning dimension to reinforce relativisim and radicalism rather than absolutism and authoritarianism. The remarkable explosion of communication technology also makes it increasingly difficult to restrict knowledge distribution.

All these influences give some substance to the view that it becomes increasingly difficult to justify, practically or theoretically, and to implement politically, social and education organizations which deprive the majority of their members from access to the processes by which the knowledge affecting them is arrived at.

I believe that within education the only response which we may hope to prove a counteracting force to the pressures that we are facing, is one which I have called community education. Further I believe that the community education response which I have tried to indicate is justified not simply by the practical problems that I have outlined but also by our developing understanding of the role which power plays in the defining and distribution of knowledge and the influence which involvement in those activities has upon educational motivation. Richard Shaull writes:

> There is no such thing as a neutral educational process. Education either functions as an instrument which is used to facilitate the integration of the younger generation into the logic of the present system and bring about conformity to it, or it becomes 'the practise of freedom', the means by which men and women deal critically and creatively with reality and discover how to participate in the transformation of their worlds.

Foreword to *The Pedagogy of the Oppressed*
Paulo Freire (1972)

Some Fallacies in Community Education and Their Consequences in Working-class Areas.[1]

Keith Jackson

Ideas do not exist in isolation. Ideas about the nature of society contend with each other. So do ideas about what society should be like. The choice of one set of explanations requires the rejection of another set. Ideas have meaning largely through this process of discrimination. At no time is this more significant than when ideas are used to justify social policies.

A central feature of the concept of 'community' is that it is used to avoid the discomfort of being understood exactly. Raymond Williams (1976) has summed up the situation admirably.

> Community can be the warmly persuasive word to describe an existing set of relationships, or the warmly persuasive word to describe an alternative set of relationships. What is most important, perhaps, is that unlike all other terms of social organisation it seems never to be used unfavourably, and never to be given any positive, opposing or distinguishing term.[2]

So what about 'community education'? Inevitably the ambiguity remains and so do the 'advantages' of not being pinned down which are enjoyed by those who use the concept. And yet the very combination of the idea of education with that of community may sharpen up the meaning in some contexts.

For example community education is used to challenge the strong institutional bias of education which has led critics to describe the educational system as 'schooling'.[3] Community education is used in this context as a respectable version of radical de-schooling proposals. Educational institutions, it is argued, should be opened up to the people at large. The rigid separation of opportunities to learn between age groups and different sections of the population should be replaced by more flexible arrangements. Why shouldn't parents learn maths with their children? Why shouldn't community activists share facilities with students in polytechnics and universities?

Equally, educational institutions should go out to the people. Resources should be decentralized. Detached workers in the youth service and in further or adult education are employed to this end.

So community education is set against more traditional notions of education. It is resisted by those whose immediate interests or peace of mind are threatened and community educationists are readily prepared to accept that there is an opposition—to stand up and be counted.

The use of the term is relatively straightforward. It is clear what is being talked about. Reforms are proposed which require political[4] support, the introduction of more flexible administrative arrangements, and also imaginative thinking on behalf of professional staff. Some of the papers herein, notably the description of the Rowlinson School campus in Sheffield,[5] show what can be done. In themselves policies of this kind could bring benefit to working-class areas because they seek the maximum use of public resources in those areas. But equally such policies are by no means enough. Working-class men and women have to be convinced that there are real benefits from education, for more than a tiny minority.

Some advocates of community education have recognized this and made no bones about it. They have concentrated their attention on working-class areas and identified an 'educational problem' which results from working-class alienation from the educational system, particularly in areas with low wages or low income from state benefits and with high unemployment. As evidence of this they point to lack of motivation and learning difficulties among children in schools, and also to non-participation by adults in the educational programmes which are available.

Here those who advocate community education do not merely propose changes in institutional arrangements. They turn to the purposes and content of education. The key questions are different: Why do people learn? What do they want to learn? What do they learn for? The answers, it is argued, may be found in practice by making the content and purposes of education 'relevant to the community' For this purpose the term community has to be given much greater weight than in the 'deschooling' proposals. Communities are said to exist to which educationists must respond.

Now while community education in the sense we have just examined, stands opposed to much that is narrow, segregating, and inflexible in the traditional schooling system, community education in the more positive sense opposes some features in that system but also rejects another educational tradition when it concentrates on working-class areas. For there is a tradition of 'workers' education' which contains many characteristics claimed by community educationists as their special contribution. Naturally those who have engaged in workers' education[6] have developed content and methods directly relevant to working-class 'communities'. And here the vagueness of 'community' ideas, along with their universal acceptability which Williams noted, is used to disguise the fact that this alternative exists. Community educationists are not prepared to stand up and be counted; they sit on the fence. It is from this standpoint that I should like to examine some fallacies in community education when it is regarded as a radical and positive step forward.

The argument for community education becoming 'relevant to working-class communities' has been given most emphasis by the Educational Priority Area projects set up following the Plowden Report. The Liverpool

EPA took the lead in pressing the case. Dr Eric Midwinter (1972) summed up the starting point as follows:

> Assuredly, a decision, nationally taken by the EPA projects, to consider the EPA school in its communal setting was a wise one, and the Plowden Committee had been well-advised to recommend that community schools should be developed in all areas but especially in EPAs.[7]

Noting that, 'Twice over Plowden decreed that EPA schools should be as good as the best in the land', the EPA projects, wrote Midwinter, decided that this was a misleading view and 'wondered whether an alternative explanation was worthy of consideration. Perhaps different sorts of areas required different educational systems.'[8]

It is here that community educationists suddenly become coy. If education is to take different forms what should be the basis of difference? To put it another way: What actually is the difference between an EPA area and a prosperous suburb? To say they are different kinds of communities begs the whole question. If the differentiating factor is the kind of life possible in the two kinds of areas at the present time, and it is argued that education should be tailored accordingly, consider the implication. Community education in 'EPA' areas must reinforce the consequences of the oppression which has created them whatever its radical rhetoric. This is an educational version of Catch twenty-two which has permeated a great deal of educational, and adult educational, thinking as one passage in the Russell Report (1973) readily illustrates:

> There is no reason to expect any reduction in the demands from the two groups in the population who now seek adult education related to the home and the family; that is, those whose earnings permit them to take seriously the graces of life, like foreign travel, or connoisseurship, or entertaining, and those who need to learn how to apply their own time and skill to the improvement of the home, and the material standard of living of the family.
>
> The needs of the affluent and the better educated are more likely to emerge as spontaneous demand, than those of the low earners. For the latter a number of special needs can be envisaged, some of which are found in present provision but not on anything like the scale required; at a simple level, skills in doing and making and maintenance about the home; at another level access to creative and recreative pursuits that bring personal fulfilment and counter the dehumanizing effects of a deprived environment; at yet another, knowledge about welfare and rights and sources of help or advice; or again, access to skills that may open the way to earning.[9]

A few of the detailed points in this statement need not be questioned.

41

What must be challenged is its quietism; its acceptance of the circumstances it describes to which adult education must adjust. The concept of community has always been used in social policy to divert such a challenge.

For this is by no means the first time this has happened by deliberate intent or by failing to recognize the consequences of an apparently harmless policy. Not long before community work and community education became the fashion there was the town planners' attempt to realize the dream of neighbourhood communities in new towns and housing estates during the 1940s and 1950s. Asking, in an important critical analysis of these policies[10] whether they were either desirable or practicable Norman Dennis (1968) concluded that 'the usefulness of the idea was not commensurate with its popularity' going on to ask 'why should such an idea succeed in pushing itself into prominence in a particular society at a particular time?'

The first part of his answer took into account a prevalent nostalgia for the rural community of the past but also insisted that the idea of community does have a limited 'reality component':

> The point of view that the restoration of the locality community would diminish the volume of social problems of various kinds can be supported by reference to various studies. It is interesting to see that the benefits of locality interaction and solidarity—the feeling of belonging and mutual enrichment—are now increasingly sought by well to do Americans and not just prescribed as a good thing for despised neighbourhoods.[11]

But there is obviously a great deal of difference between being part of a pleasant, cosy, residential neighbourhood where one can be certain that everyone will be socially acceptable and being a community organized by professional social workers.[12] Again the idea of community obscures the most important social and economic relationships involved. Even the 'reality component' of the neighbourhood community isn't all that real. Local social relationships are important to people but the nature and strength of those relationships are determined by factors beyond the locality. Surely adult education should recognize this and be organized accordingly?

Summarizing a wide range of community studies Raymond Pahl (1970) indicates what can be the only valid use of the term community in modern society. In his book *Patterns of Urban Life* he demonstrates that the apparent single meaning of the word is totally misleading. There are, he argues, communities of 'limited liability' (owner occupiers with a major interest in keeping up the market value of the neighbourhood), communities 'as defence against external threat' (against airports, motorways etc.) and communities of 'common deprivation' (exploited coal mining villages or inner city areas). In every case community describes a form of solidarity between people depending first on their political and economic situation and only secondly on living in the same place.[13] Therefore, if it can be argued that education in one *place* should be different from education in another, why can't it be argued equally in the open that education for the *working class* might be very different from education for the *middle class* on and in working-class terms, not those of the local community defined parochially?

This brings us to Norman Dennis's (1968) second reason for the popularity of the neighbourhood community idea: that it plays a very important ideological function. He argued, as have many others, that the idea of community based on locality is an important myth, and he used the word in a very specific sense, i.e. that it is not totally invalid but is believed for other reasons than its validity.

One reason is that the idea of neighbourhood community concentrates attention on the part local factors play in determining the nature of social and personal problems while diverting attention from criticism of fundamental political and economic institutions or dominant social beliefs. In the same vein C. Wright Mills, the American writer, criticised the professional ideology of those who identify social problems in the United States noting that by stressing community welfare the locality sets the scope of 'problematicization and concern'. More positively, to speak of community, with its warm overtones, promotes the idea that both local and national society is organized on the basis of a harmony of interests; the solution to local problems is only a matter of time and effort within existing political and economic arrangements—the eventual solution is certain. There are many people in working-class neighbourhoods and the working-class movement who would reject this view outright and this brings us to Dennis's third main reason why community policies have found favour. They provide a convenient guise for active forms of political and social control. Again this is by no means new as many historians have pointed out. In John Westergaard's (1973) words:

> I am always reminded on this point of the Thomas Chalmers who in his book *The Civic and Christian Economy of Large Towns* in the 1820s advocated a system of 'localism', to break down the working-class districts of the big cities into small units. His purpose was in part to restore—or to introduce—Christianity to the working class; but it was also to do so for one particular reason, the reason so many Victorian commentators had in mind when they wanted to Christianise the working class: that was to stifle any rebellious tendency. His argument was precisely that if working-class interests could be turned inwards into the locality, then workers would be prevented from forming alliances and loyalties across the restraining boundaries of the locality; and social order would be safeguarded. Divide and rule.[14]

Norman Dennis (1968) also recalls the ideas of men like Chalmers and picks out the Settlement movement, introduced into the 'EPA areas' of the late nineteenth century by public schools and universities, as an example of the policy put into practice. The Settlements were of course, direct precursors of community work and community education in Britain today and intended, in the words of one of their founders to

> give to the poorest and most densely populated working-class districts the benefit of a resident gentry such as, in the clergyman, and squire, is generally commanded in rural parishes . . . If the people had wise counsellors whom they trusted, the trade unionists would gladly accept their cooperation . . . and selfish agitators would probably disappear.[15]

There may still be those who would agree with Chalmers and the Settlement sponsors, and they must say so. But those who refuse to take part in educational developments on these terms, or anything like them, are entitled to say so also. Indeed a commitment to democracy and freedom of thought demands that they do so, in order that present developments do not become latter-day versions of the Settlement movement.

Many community associations and community activities into which people are drawn may not be founded in precisely the same spirit of political control as the Settlements but they still serve to divert political imagination and harness energies away from the key political and economic processes which determine many local problems, by consuming the time of the most active people in an area.

It is a matter of democracy and freedom of thought because the debate on these matters must be open and clear to everyone. Only then will the people who live in working-class neighbourhoods, especially those who play uncertain hosts to community projects, be able to join in the debate themselves. When the level of social and political activity is high, as in Northern Ireland, public servants and professionals are forced to open up the debate. These are the reasons why people who are associated with community education should make it clear where *they* stand regarding the various elements in the working-class movement and the rich tradition of workers' education associated with that movement, not in order that we might indulge in academic arguments about the meaning of the word community.

For many of the ideas and practices now promoted by advocates of community education can be found also in association with significant sections of the working-class movement, in the past and in the present, in Britain and across the world. They are harnessed however, to a different concept of 'relevance'. The key issues of political and economic power beyond the local community are considered of primary not secondary relevance, determining incidentally the economics and politics of adult education itself along with much more important aspects of life. And so the purposes for which adult education is sought differ too in this tradition.

The simplest way of summarizing these purposes is to recall the words of Robert Owen[16] who himself made a major contribution to workers' education. Harold Silver (1965) has shown how they contrasted, in the nineteenth century, with the ideas of many opponents:

> When others outside the working class preached charity or the need for a 'kinder language' and 'sympathy with their necessities, which fall though it often times may on unimpressible hearts, never fails to find some that it comforts, and many that it softens', Owenite energies made men aware of the alternative to such argument from charity. While spelling, reading, writing and arithmetic were being given in homoeopathic doses Owen was telling the working man that he had a right to learn what he is in relation to past ages, to the period in which he lives, to the circumstances in which he is placed, to the individuals around him, and to future events.[17]

Many of the words have changed but have the meanings behind them and the actions they justify? We should seek to clarify the matter by examining what happens in the practice of community education with great care.

Notes

[1] My main concern is with adult education as it reflects 'community education' notions.

[2] RAYMOND WILLIAMS (1976) *Key-words* Fontana, p. 66.

[3] See for example IVAN ILLICH (1971) *Deschooling Society*. Calder and Boyers.

[4] I am using the term here in the widest sense, not referring merely to the support of elected politicians.

[5] It is interesting that Sylvia Coupe found no need to describe Rowlinson's imaginative approach to adult education in terms of any 'community education' theory.

[6] I am not of course referring specifically to the Workers' Educational Association although its contribution has been, and still is in many areas, more important than current debates tend to allow. Indeed it is an irony of the last few years that WEA Districts have contributed to the community education bandwagon in such a way that the WEA's other more important contributions have been given far too little attention.

[7] ERIC MIDWINTER (1972) *Priority Education*, Penguin Books, p. 12.

[8] ERIC MIDWINTER, *op. cit.* pp. 12–13.

[9] Department of Education and Science. (1973) Adult Education: 'A Plan for Development' (The Russell Report) HMSO, pp. 9–10.

[10] NORMAN DENNIS (1968) 'The Popularity of the Neighbourhood Community Idea' in R.E. PAHL *Readings in Urban Sociology*, Pergamon.

[11] DENNIS *op. cit.*

[12] I am not suggesting that all local community organizations are the product of community work, or that if they are they have no value.

[13] R.E. PAHL (1970) *Patterns of Urban Life*, Longmans.

[14] J.H. WESTERGAARD (1973) 'Radical Class Consciousness'. A comment in MARTIN BULMER ed. *Working Class Images of Society* Routledge and Kegan Paul, p. 252.

[15] DENNIS *op. cit.*

[16] As usual in the nineteenth century even men of radical imagination failed to make the necessary step and include working women.

[17] HAROLD SILVER (1965) *The Concept of Popular Education* MacGibbon and Kee, pp. 236–237.

2

TENSIONS IN DEVELOPMENT

Introduction

Community education has an host of critics, many of whom dislike the principles and practices and regard them as a threat to their own philosophies and styles. Here, however, the papers are not concerned with criticism from a traditional standpoint but from within the movement itself. To change things does require that numbers of people cooperate and their self-criticism is all the more interesting as a result. The following papers have in common the recognition of the strengths of the opposition and the defects which have to be overcome if development is to lead to real change and tangible benefits. They may also be seen as a progression: from research into classroom practice (Delamont), through the development of community education (Williams and Robins), leading to largely unsupported developmental work in central Nottingham (Simpson and Williams) and finally to community education in a local education authority supported environment, where community action was already established (Jones).

Sara Delamont's view depends upon the fact that to date, classroom research, like many other branches of educational research, has not been concerned with community education. She sees some aspects as challenging and points out that having adults and children in the same class would alter the research methods. Even so, for Dr Delamont, the concluding issue is that community education is not a respectable topic in the academic world and research into its development is likely to be at the researcher's own expense if not also to the detriment of his or her career.

The section continues with a contribution of a different nature; with observations on the Californian Case. Williams and Robins summarize the background to some thirty Community Schools in San Diego county. They distinguish between a programme—which is what people set out to do, and a process in which the community school is a moving part. Significantly one of their observations is all too easy to overlook. Community schools in the United States have begun in primary schools and are intended to spread to secondary schools. This pragmatism is also part of a process being actively encouraged by a major charitable foundation. Williams and Robins conclude by anticipating the issue of relating community education to community action.

Introduction

Alan Simpson and Wyn Williams recall a three-way 'conscientization' process in central Nottingham. They give a full and frank account of working with students, school pupils and residents as part of a community development activity. Their conclusions make disturbing reading because the process had limited success with all three groups and demonstrates how far everyone had to go to get anywhere at all.

Arfon Jones begins with the stated aims of Sidney Stringer School and Community College and contrasts them with the open questions of who controls the enterprise and who makes the decisions? Although the article does not stress the fact, Sidney Stringer was built in an area already developed by the Community Development Programme with a significant amount of resulting community action. This offers a marked contrast to the area described by Simpson and Williams in the previous paper. Despite the prepared ground, Jones is emphatic that from the beginning there were difficulties and the community was hostile or reluctant. Four initiatives were made as part of a participation strategy to overcome objections; a mothers' group, the far reaching responsibilities of the house-head, a $16+$ group and the formation of a School and Community Association. But power did not pass to the masses. Instead key individuals supported by small groups became powerful. This gives a further perspective on points made by John Watts in a later paper: the teacher as a professional can be made yet more powerful by so-called democratic rights rather than less. He or she can speak from two mutually enhancing platforms.

Classroom Research and Community Education

Sara Delamont

The late nineteen sixties and early seventies saw an increased interest in the study of what actually goes on inside classrooms. This interest has shown itself in the publication of newsletters, books and articles, in conferences and workshops, in taught courses for students and serving teachers, and in funding from government and independent institutions. Careers have been built on classroom research and there is a daunting pile of literature for the uninitiated to wade through. However, the burden of this paper is that, so far, classroom researchers have not been concerned with community education.

This paper is designed to do two things: set out the basic features of the classroom research movement and then to discuss ways in which classroom studies and community education may be interrelated in the future. Both classroom research and community education are wide-ranging terms which cover a variety of theories and practices, and I am more expert in the scope of the former than the latter, but I hope the arguments will be of interest to those expert in community education.

Classroom research in Britain has been multi-disciplinary from its earliest days, and has used a wide variety of theoretical viewpoints and practical techniques. This means that there are no clear links between the different researchers and their findings, because, all too frequently, they have nothing in common but a belief in studying what actually happens inside classrooms. So far no genuinely inter-disciplinary studies have been carried out, and few attempts have been made to synthesize findings or generate theory. Classrooms have been studied by researchers with backgrounds in experimental psychology, social psychology, sociology, anthropology, linguistics and ethology, and by those involved in teacher training, whose own education may have been in history, modern languages or chemistry. The type of research conducted, and the conclusions drawn, are likely to be very different in these various cases: for example, linguists are interested in the use of language, while the ethologist may concentrate on non-verbal behaviour. Similarly, sociologists are likely to emphasize the social context in which the classroom is embedded, while an experimental psychologist is likely to want precise measures of behaviour.

The research methods used in classrooms can be divided into three broad categories: schedule-based observation, ethnographic observation and permanent recording. Schedule-based observation is probably the commonest. The researcher goes into the classroom with a set of categories into which salient aspects of the interaction are coded. Thus, someone has decided what is worth observing and has systematized how it will be recorded. This method produces reliable and valid codings of classroom events which can usually be reduced to numbers, and hence handled by computer to produce statistical findings. Ethnographic observation involves the researcher behaving like an anthropologist, immersing herself in the world of the teacher and pupils, to find out what they consider important, significant or noteworthy about classroom events. This method relies on field-notes: the verbatim record of events with formal and informal interviewing. Permanent recording can take various forms, of which the most usual are sound tapes, tape-slide sequences, stop-frame filming, video tape and film. Of these, film is so expensive that researchers have hardly used it while the other techniques have been used a good deal. Linguists obviously need sound tapes to preserve their data, while tape-slides, stop-frame and video have been used by researchers from a variety of disciplines for several different types of project. Permanent recordings tend to be expensive, compared with observers, and the problems of coding the interactions later are often under-estimated! Combinations of the different methods have been used in particular projects, and Walker and Adelman have argued strongly for a combination of permanent record and observation: a technique they call 'participant recording' which is described in their book *A Guide to Classroom Observation*.

British classroom research, therefore, uses a range of techniques and looks to different disciplines for its theories. There is a recent collection of papers (Chanan and Delamont, 1975) which sets out the varying approaches up to that time. In the rest of this paper I want to examine how far classroom research has examined any topics of relevance to those in community education, and how far the development of community involvement in education may affect classroom research.

Classroom Research on Community Education

The term community education is used to cover a multitude of different beliefs and practices, so I have concentrated on a few ideas which seem to feature in many different schemes. In one sense this is hardly necessary for the first part of my exercise, because most classroom research has not examined any of the possible themes in the term community education! Most classroom research has not been carried out in the institutions which call themselves community schools, colleges or centres. A good deal of the work has been done in primary schools and the eleven to sixteen range of secondary schools, often very conventional ones. Adults, sixth-forms, further education, and classes in practical subjects like metalwork and home economics have not been studied.

Community education is often used to mean offering adults in the neighbourhood either special classes of interest and/or attendance at ordinary lessons for 'O' and 'A' level. Classroom research has neglected adult education—at least a research worker at the Open University has been unable to find any extant—and so there is no data on classroom interaction in adult classes. Similarly, there is no published classroom research on the differences, if any, which result from adding adults to classes of school students. Research could certainly be done with profit comparing 'A' level classes of ordinary pupils with those containing adults, looking for such things as differences in discussion patterns in subjects like history, sociology and economics. Commonsense suggests that there might be considerable differences, but research has not examined this.

Another aspect of adult attendance at classes is often a creche run by senior pupils to care for small children while parents study. Researchers interested in nursery-level classrooms might profitably compare behaviour of staff, school pupils and children in these creches with behaviour in more orthodox day care settings. To my knowledge none of the current projects on pre-school interactions have looked at creches in community schools. In community education adults may be involved in the teaching processes as guest lecturers/aides/resources people and so forth. Study of the classroom processes when a non-teacher is 'teaching' or when other adults are present in a teacher's room would be profitable but has not been done very often. There is work on aides at primary level but not the wide variety of roles performed by local adults in schools such as the Sutton Centre. It would be interesting to know how the teaching styles of laypeople compare with those of established teachers, and how the presence of other adults affects classroom dynamics.

Community education can also mean community control over the educational institution, or community participation in the running of such institutions. So far, classroom researchers have not paid much attention to how this might affect their access to classrooms because in general the head and the individual teachers decide whether research can be done. It may be that in future the community will have the power to allow or prevent access to classroom interactions and this may determine the form of classroom research. This could mean that attention is paid to the problems outlined above which have been neglected, but it could be the community—whatever that means—would pose quite different problems.

The Open School?

One common correlate of community education is a commitment to 'open' education: whether by open-plan architecture, or by democratic interpersonal relationships, or both. Of course there are community schools in old buildings with separate classrooms, and people running community schools with traditional hierarchical teacher-pupil relationships, but in many cases the ideas of community involvement go hand in hand with purpose-built institutions and more egalitarian relationships. Thus many institutions involved in community education are built on an open model, with integrated areas (rather than boxes), carpets, easy chairs and cafeterias, plus flexible halls, sports facilities and resources. Pupils are likely to be taught in a humanities area rather than an English room, and to share that area with many other pupils rather than just thirty to forty. Associated with the architecture may be a philosophy of democracy and egalitarianism, in which pupils have a voice in running the institutions and the mode of learning, discipline and working are individual rather than group-based.

Classroom research has yet to come to terms with either open architecture or individualized, integrated pupil regimes and egalitarian relationships. Researchers at primary level have had to come to terms with informal junior classrooms, but so far most researchers at secondary level have not. Most of the secondary school research assumes that one teacher and thirty to forty pupils are shut in a box covering one topic all at the same time by chalk and talk. Thus the schedules assume only one person talks at once, that the teacher is the dominant force, and the pupils are engaged on the same activity at the same time. The results of the research can be illuminating for those teaching in conventional classrooms but is not helpful to those trying to manage very different learning contexts. However, as more schools become architecturally or sociologically open, classroom research is going to adapt, and it is these adaptions to which I now turn.

Will Community Education Change Classroom Research?

Changes in schools are bound to change classroom research because it is one type of research which, because it involves the researcher in school life, cannot ossify in the way that other approaches can. I am, therefore, hopeful that the growth of community involvement in education and the spread of sociologically and architecturally open schools will alter classroom research in the seventies to make it more useful to teachers, although this may be at the cost of its academic respectability and its funding from public sources.

I see, firstly, a switch from schedule-based observation towards ethnographic observation and participant recording. Schedules are not very well suited to large, open areas in which many students and staff are milling about, noise levels are high, movement frequent, and boundaries unclear. Also, as educational philosophies are crucial to the management of such settings, interviewing participants will be more important than in conventional schools. Researchers will turn, I expect, to participant recording as pioneered by Walker and Adelman, and to ethnographic observation of the types described by Stubbs and Delamont (1976).

Secondly, I think that the ideology of community education is likely to affect classroom research in important respects. However the precise details of pupil roles and community participation and control work out in any particular institution, there is a clear message from community schools and colleges about the worth of the individual. This belief in the uniqueness and value of every individual, whether child, parent, cleaner, caretaker or teacher, is hard to reconcile with conventional research ideology. Conventional social science has the researcher as expert: the scientist in the white coat who is objective, knowledgable and wise: while the 'subjects' are passive, ignorant beings who are to be manipulated. This philosophy allows researchers studying classrooms to code behaviour without understanding motives, and even to manipulate the teachers and pupils in the name of science. The schedule-using observer is meant to be a 'fly on the wall' coding like a machine without human contacts. Once ideas about individual worth and importance are accepted this research model seems untenable: it will have to be replaced by research methods in which teachers, pupils and others are partners, participants or colleagues.

Arnold Morrison has spelt out some of the implications of this in his contribution to the collection edited by Chanan and Delamont (1975) and many of the possibilities have been explored by Walker, Adelman and Elliott. There is, however, a serious implication for the researchers in adopting the partnership model of research both in terms of the usefulness of the findings and their career prospects.

There seems to be an incipient conflict at present between research on classrooms which is interesting and useful to practising teachers and research which meets the approval of the research community. At present research which suits academic journals and funding bodies often involves numbers and the scientific model, while that which I have found appealing to teachers is not acceptable to journals and often appals academic audiences. This may be an inevitable clash of interests, but I see no solution, and the growth of community schools will only accentuate it.

References

CHANAN, G. and DELAMONT S. (Eds) (1975) *Frontiers of Classroom Research*. Slough: NFER.
STUBBS, M. and DELAMONT S. (Eds) (1976) *Exploration in Classroom Observation*. Chichester: Wiley.
WALKER, R. and ADELMAN C. (1975) *A Guide to Classroom Observation*. London: Methuen.

Community Education: Observations on the Californian Case

Wyn Williams and Wayne R. Robins

The constitution of the United States places the responsibility of education in the hands of the states. For the past twenty years the federal government has taken a more active role, mainly through federal grants for categorical aid. This federal intervention has produced more and more controls and restrictions. Although the federal government is spending nearly four billion dollars annually, this amount is a minor portion of total educational costs. Federal monies generally go to State Departments of Education (SEAs) with categorical restrictions for distribution to Local School Districts (LEAs). In some cases monies go directly to LEAs from the United States Office of Education (USOE).

At the state level, the authority for operating the public schools is in the hands of the state legislature. This authority, through the education code, is given by the legislature to the state department of education for implementation. The state department of education in California is headed by a state superintendent who is an elected official. The state board of education is appointed by the governor of the state, approved by the legislature, and is responsible for formulating policies. Within the education code, the authority of the state is partially delegated to local school boards. Local boards are elected by the communities they serve and are responsible for specific policies in the operation of that district. (see figure 1).

In San Diego County, there are forty-nine separate school districts each with a local board of directors and a superintendent. These districts vary in size and structure. Some are K-6 districts; that is for the 'primary' years of classes one to six. Other districts are of (classes) six to twelve; (classes) eight to twelve and (classes) thirteen to fourteen. Thirteen to fourteen districts are commonly called community college districts. It is important to realize that 'catchment areas' vary according to class years in San Diego County. Some districts also operate pre-school and/or adult programs and/or community education programs.

The Concept as Expressed in the United States

Community Education is a systematic way of looking at people and their problems. It is based upon the premise that education can be made relevant to people's needs and that the people affected by education should be involved in decisions about educational programs. It assumes that education should have an impact upon the society it serves.

Figure 1

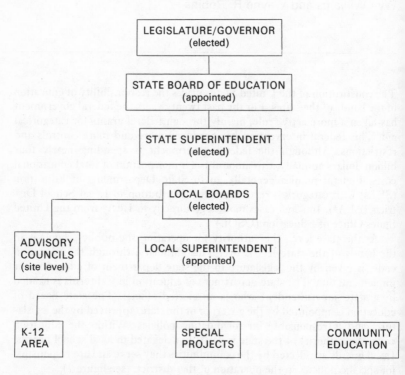

CALIFORNIA

LEGISLATURE/GOVERNOR
(elected)

STATE BOARD OF EDUCATION
(appointed)

STATE SUPERINTENDENT
(elected)

LOCAL BOARDS
(elected)

ADVISORY
COUNCILS
(site level)

LOCAL SUPERINTENDENT
(appointed)

K-12
AREA

SPECIAL
PROJECTS

COMMUNITY
EDUCATION

Community Education encourages maximum use of school facilities, study and assistance in the solution of community problems, cooperation among agencies serving people, community planning, and reinforcing the family unit through shared activities. It also develops a concern for meeting human needs, utilizing community resources, and promotes community leadership and decision-making in the educational process.

Community Education is a direction in education involving two major aspects: a *process* and *resulting programs*. Many people consider only the Community Education program. This is probably due to the high visibility of those activities which results from the developmental process which precedes operating programs. The idea of Community Education, however, first addresses itself to the involvement of the community—all of its people, with all of their points of view—determining its wants and needs, and then determining avenues to satisfy those needs, not only educational needs, but economic, social, and political needs as well.

The idea of Community Education then becomes an instrument for change—a change in community climate which often results in a change in home environment, student and adult attitudes, and ultimately a positive change in student achievement. Through the expansion of community services, the coordination of existing agencies, maximizing the use of school facilities, and the involvement of people of all ages at all times, the process of developing a Community Education program strives toward the development of a 'Sense of Community', people working together to solve their own problems, needs, and wants.

Origin of Community Education in the United States

Community Education is not a fad or passing fancy. It is not even new. It is an eclectic philosophy that combines many desirable features of educational movements of the past and present into a concept of education that is sound and permanent. This conception of education is built upon a conscious choice between a number of educational and social changes. (Daker, 1972.)

The beginnings of Community Education have many roots. In 1845, Henry Barnard wrote the 'Report on Conditions of Improvement of Public Schools in Rhode Island' and discussed the role of the school in improving community and individual living. John Dewey is credited with the progressive education movement which was the basic beginning of community education. The two philosophies/concepts have at least the following principles in common:

1 Establishing their goals and objectives out of the interests, needs, and problems of the people.

2 Using a wide variety of community, human, physical, and financial resources in developing programs and activities.

3 Promoting and practising democracy in all activities within the school and the community.

In the first book written on the subject Everett (1938) stated:

Education is part and parcel of the very fact of living ... The social nature of the individual is but testimony to how the learning process is at the same time the process of becoming. We learn what we live, and what we thus learn is through the very process of living built into the structure of one's being, there to form the foundation for behaviour.

The Alfred P. Sloan Foundation, in the 1940s, carried on several experiments related to school and community economics and family living. The Community Education concept took on a more local thrust through the efforts of Frank Manley of Flint, Michigan, and Charles Stewart Mott, a wealthy industrialist. The Mott Foundation became the financial force which led to the expansion of the concept as a national effort. Community education programs spread throughout Michigan and the mid-west in the 1950s and early 60s. Centers for Community Education, numbering seventy-five in 1976, were established through partial funding by the Mott Foundation throughout the United States. The major goals of the Centers include:

1 the dissemination of the community education concept,

2 to assist interested schools and communities in establishing community schools,

3 to provide various inservice, preservice, and university training programs.

As a national network, the Centers are the moving force in the implementation of community schools. There are now over 4,000 community schools in the United States, 160 in the state of California, and 30 in San Diego County.

The Developmental Process

Prior to establishing a community school, it is extremely important that a developmental process be followed. Community, agency, and school people should have a basic understanding of the process and be a part of the decision to implement the concept. Following a developmental process gives those involved a feeling of personal ownership rather than the visual process of a small group of administrators making the decision and imposing it upon the community.

To explain and to discuss the Community Education concept to the people in a given area, the staff of the Center for Community Education and other community educators make presentations to at least the following groups:

1 Representative groups of people within the community.

2 The school board.

3 Existing school-based council, PTA, etc.

4 The administrative council.

5 School-site personnel.

58

6 Local service organizations and social service agencies.

Implementation of the Process

Each community expresses the community education concept in different ways. This is partially dependent upon the socio-economic status, cultural/ethnic make-up, and existing services within the community. Generally there seems to be a progression or level of sophistication which occurs. This can be graphically depicted (see figure 2).

Figure 2

Integrating the total community
with all its functions

Community Development

Citizens Involvement and Participation
in
Leadership—Decision Making—Shared Power

Interagency Coordination, Cooperation,
and Collaboration

Lifelong Learning and Enrichment Activities

Expanded Use of School Facilities,
Community Schools and Community Centers

Various local areas of the country are at various stages of the pyramid. In California, the emphasis is on the 'middle' sections of the pyramid. Thus community education in California is emerging as a means for expanded citizen involvement in decision making and in community development. In San Diego county there are presently thirty schools designated as community schools each with a full-time director. These community schools have been established since 1973 and are in the beginning stages of operation.

The Philosophy and the Reality

The emphasis and thrust has been to develop the process with programs being a 'gimmick' to get people out of their houses and initially involved. Through this step, informed community school personnel strive to develop community leadership and decision-making processes.

In the implementation of these community schools, there is a great difference between schools in relation to their level of operation and future direction. Part of this is due to the *level of expertise* of community school personnel. This includes those who remain comfortable in providing programs and those who are unwilling or unable to take risks, to those who view the concept for its potential and strive toward that end. The thirty community schools, each with a full-time community school director, now in operation in San Diego County, utilize elementary school (K-6) buildings as the vehicle for implementing the concept. Elementary schools are generally more feasible due to the smaller geographical area they serve, thus lending themselves to the development of a sense of community. As structured in the county and nationally, the community schools strive to serve people of all ages and all people of a given community. Stemming from the philosophy that the total environment must be addressed in order to facilitate change and to improve social conditions, the community schools must go beyond service to only parents and youngsters.

The community school advisory council serves as the major force for bridging the gap between school and community. The make-up of the council is representative of each individual community and is selected on the basis of the factors shown in figure 3.

Figure 3

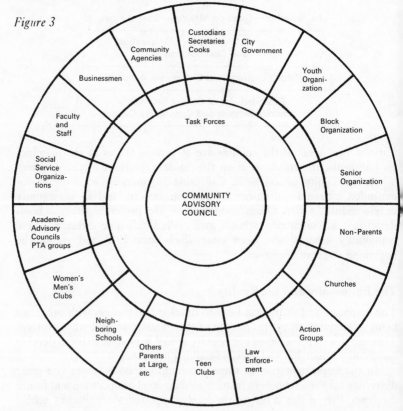

The council in cooperation with the community school director conducts a needs assessment, prioritizes needs, wants, and problems, selects avenues for resolutions, and implements programs and activities. As the council becomes more sophisticated, it develops strategies to involve more community people in the decision-making process and in developing community leadership. One avenue is to organize various task forces to deal with specific issues. This allows more individuals to take leadership roles and to be more directly involved in decisions. The hope then is to take people from the state of being involved in programs and activities to one of being involved in decision-making and leadership development.

Attendance at Programs and Activities, Decision-Making/ Leadership Development

The problem seems to be in getting beyond the center barrier. People are accustomed to having things planned and implemented for them and consequently do not have the process skill to develop beyond that point. As a result, people feel frustrated and react by being apathetic. Assessments have shown that people want to be involved but are frustrated by:

1   not knowing how and/or,

2   not being given the opportunity

The community education process addresses this issue.

Exploring a continuum, (see figure 4) we see that programs and activities are important and necessary but should serve as a means to reaching the objectives at the lower end of the continuum. Programs are necessary and viable, but the potential of community education can only be reached by striving for those items listed below the point of reference.

The Present and the Future

The concept of Community Education has developed in various patterns throughout the United States. The major differences seem to be the emphasis on program or process. There is still a heavy emphasis on programs as an end in themselves. The emerging model and one which is beginning to become successful in some parts of the country is the thrust toward participatory democracy and community development; the notion that education is a total process and that isolating the schooling process from the community is detrimental to the resolution of problems within American society. Part of the problem that exists is the lack of agreement and/or consensus of where community education should be going.

It is hard to predict which of these models for explaining social change will predominate in the future or what the consequences would be for

61

Figure 4   COMMUNITY EDUCATION CONTINUUM

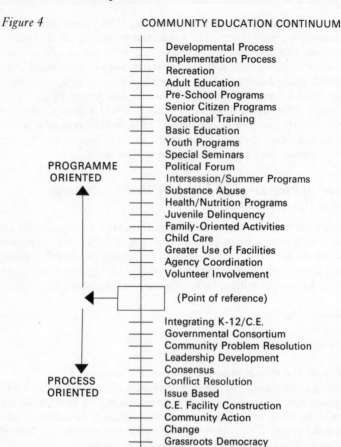

community education if one did come to predominate. Let us rather indicate our own preference. Community education ought to be intimately linked to community action. That action is geared to securing a greater degree of local community control over the bureaucratic system that delivers services and a greater say in the definition of what needs those services should be meeting. The concept is concerned with greater community involvement. It is likely to be linked to movements that see the taking of power by the powerless through class struggle, as a major goal.

References

Daker, Larry, (1972) *Foundations of Community Education* Pendell Publishing Co., Michigan: Midland.

Everett, Samuel, (1938) *The Community School.*

Community Education and Community Action

Alan Simpson and Wyn Williams

In this paper we attempt to outline work undertaken with a group of Comprehensive school pupils, a group of students from the Polytechnic and residents from the area of Nottingham known as Raleigh Street. The educational process that we attempted to implement was based upon the belief that community action, to be effective, has to be informed by a spirit of critical awareness on the part of those undertaking it. The theoretical basis for what we tried to do has been derived from Freire's description of education for liberation. Freire insists that education for liberation is the result of a process of 'conscientization'.

This process is characterised by:

1   The recognition by the teacher that there be a 'critical' knowing and working upon the reality of the situation faced by a group of people.

2   The belief that the teacher must help the 'oppressed' work upon themes that they have identified for themselves arising from their own situation.

3   That in the course of doing such an educational activity people become aware of the possibilities of changing things in their own lives that they had previously seen as immutable or 'fated' to happen.

As will become evident from our description of the work that we undertook with pupils, students and residents, there are significant differences between those three groups and the process described above does not work as effectively with all of them. The differences stem from the fact that it was the 'reality' of the residents of Raleigh Street that we started from. It was they who defined the themes and the issues and questions that arose. The pupils and students were asked therefore to work on the overall theme of Redevelopment that was overtaking Raleigh Street residents.

In consequence the effectiveness of 'conscientization' varied significantly from group to group. The variation may be so extreme as to question whether the process described actually works at all with the group of students.

We intend therefore to set out the paper in such a way that we describe what we did with:

1   the student group

63

2   the pupils

3   the residents.

The process was least effective with students, more effective with the pupils and most effective with the residents. Consequently, each group is discussed as a separate section.

Background

Raleigh Street is a run-down working-class area of Nottingham. Statistically it was the most deprived area in the county[1] in 1974. All the work presupposed that such a categorization applied to the area's material conditions and not to the people in it. There is much common ground in the education process involved in the three projects which we outline below, but in evaluating them we attempt to do so from the stand point of the community action 'pay-offs' for the area and its residents. Thus each group worked within the following parameters:

1   it focused around a real issue which affected the local residents.

2   its results needed to be appropriate to an action strategy which was determined by the local community.

3   it contained a commitment on the part of all involved not to ignore or sidestep the political, economic or social consequences of the action strategy being pursued.

As far as residents were concerned this was not an 'educational' process. Had we mentioned the word ninety per cent of the residents would have immediately switched off. Most of the residents, and their children had been far too brutally 'schooled' to see education in terms other than those which Alinsky[2] used as being synonymous with the words academic and irrelevant.

Life in Raleigh Street was about tangibles rather than abstracts. Theory developed out of practical experience. Community action sprang up most readily around issues of clear oppression, exploitation or neglect. Action only developed:

1   'instinctively'—where spontaneous outbursts came as reflex actions to particular intrusions, like the City making a traffic policy which led to motorists using the area as a short-cut route and knocking down children or,

2   'consciously'—where there existed a strong belief by residents in the chances of winning.

64

Community action is concerned fundamentally with dismantling the structural and psychological apparatus which divides people and which labels them as losers. Uniting and winning are the two themes which form the basis of all subsequent action. Education and community action were synonymous and productive where a clear link had been made in people's minds between the power of information and the power of collective action.

Involving Polytechnic Students

Description
We worked for a twelve-week term with a group of fourteen third-year students in the teacher training department of the Polytechnic. They had opted to take Urban Education in term two of their final year. We presented them with a paper in which we outlined the objectives of the course (in itself an action that is contrary to Freire's process). The objectives were:

1 To study what was happening in Raleigh Street in forms of housing, employment and education and attempt to answer questions which would provide information that the residents could use in their struggle to influence and/or control the redevelopment process affecting their lives.

2 To present the information they found in a readable and usable form to residents.

3 To understand the interrelationship between factors like housing, employment, resource allocation and redevelopment, and consider their educational implications.

The challenge to students involved in this approach
We were clear that we were inviting students to challenge their normal way of working. Most of their products previously were in response to demands for assignments laid down for them by tutors, a fundamentally regurgative process. The work we were suggesting involved them in the acquisition and interpretation of information that was not already processed for them.

For them to tackle this work with conviction it was necessary to identify with the residents of Raleigh Street and share our assumption that deprivation in the area was a reference to material conditions not to faults in the residents themselves.

The method of tackling the work
We, acting as intermediaries, devised questions that residents wanted answering in regard to the three critical topics in their lives—housing,

employment and the way resources were allocated—especially social and educational services.

The students were given the choice of topic and worked as groups of four, five and five. They were also free to choose which of the questions within the topic that they wanted to start with. In practice it proved impossible for any group to tackle more than one or two questions out of the six to ten offered. We then discussed with groups how they were going to gather information. We offered them the initial data from the Area Deprivation Study and also a list of sources, both human and literary, that they might need to consult. They began to bring in data and the problems they met with and we helped them with interpretation and analysis.

Problems of Implementation

Motivational

Although students were given the opportunity to choose between this research project and the conventional syllabus laid down on the lines of the Open University course on Urban Education, this choice was no guarantee that they were committed to the basic objectives of our approach. This was exaggerated by their current position in college. As a group they were Certificate rather than Degree students and as such felt themselves to be 'thick' as one of them consistently put it. Their own expectations of themselves were low and so were their ideas on what we, as teachers, could expect of them. Since the job situation was so desperate that year they also had an overwhelming obsession with job prospects.

Skills

Skills of a high order were required for many of the questions to be answered.[3] Students needed to know *where* data could be obtained, *how* it could be obtained, *what* it meant and how it could be presented in a useful form to the Tenants' Association. We found that students had no prior experience of analysing or interpreting data. A long argument took place about the notion of 'social malaise'—and some students continued to the end to believe that the 'problem' of Raleigh Street was the residents own fecklessness and apathy. In other words we were engaged in educating the students who were *not* contributing to the knowledge required by residents.

Problems with local authority departments

The process implied that we would get co-operation from departments within the local authority. In practice this varied enormously. Students were denied information by one department, Housing, only to be given it by another, Technical Services. In other instances we met with flat obstruction. A letter from the Director of Education indicated that he doubted whether we were fit people to receive the information on the number of pupils in the local comprehensive sitting for public exams or the rate of passes. Students experienced the frustration of waiting two months for a reply on the way Educational Priority status actually benefited the neighbourhood. Even when they eventually did get an interview with the Divisional Officer they found that the cut in class size, so proudly remarked on by the Authority, owed most to the Housing department's destruction of old property and the resultant decline in the numbers of children on roll. Classes dropped from an average of thirty-five to seventeen within two years. Again, while this investigation was an excellent experience for students of bureaucracy at work, it slowed down the production of information to the point where the end of term came faster than the information. Its use to residents was therefore limited.

Problems with the Polytechnic
These came in three forms. First the Administration, having cleared the hiring of Alan as a part-time lecturer, suddenly announced that he could not be paid as he was a County Council employee. Apart from the inaccuracy of this observation, it raised the whole question of how far the Polytechnic hierarchy were prepared to back an investigative approach which required collaboration with an outsider—and one which had political implications. In the end Alan was paid—but not without a struggle.

Secondly this type of activity does not fit easily into Polytechnic time-tables. The time spent on a search of County Council Minutes could not fall necessarily within the allotted four hours a week, and interviews could not always be scheduled on the day set aside for the course. Students faced with other demands on their time were not always willing to put in the effort the task demanded—though, of course, there were honourable exceptions to this.

Thirdly the external examiner decided that he could not accept 'Group assignments' as these were not specifically mentioned in the 'Grey Book' which listed all the regulations. The reply that this type of work required group collaboration and that defining individual contributions was a negation of the process was not accepted as points in an argument. Thus, we ended up with work that was non-assessable. Such a situation was only tolerated once—and we were reprimanded for allowing it to happen.

Conclusions

1 Using students who do not come from the neighbourhood and had no commitment to it was a major drawback. Given the pressures from college on them it was probably unrealistic to expect much from them even if they possessed the skills required.

2 In contrast, their view was that they had learnt far more about the

realities of living in an EPA and the inter-relationship between social, economic and educational factors than they had done on the whole of the rest of their three-year course. They also felt that a direct meeting with tenants to hear their views of critical issues would have been better than Alan and I demarcating questions that needed answering.

3   The information we did get back from the groups was enormously varied in quality. One group simply produced a list of housing ownership in the area. This did however, enable them to recognize that deterioration in the standard of property could not be attributed to immigrants as sixty per cent of the housing belonged to trusts, the Church or the Council. On the other hand a group found out that the nature of work available in the area was changing dramatically as the inner city lost jobs—a finding in line with the Planning and Transportation Department's own survey of Nottinghamshire. They were able to use this information to question the suitability of careers advice offered to youngsters in the area.

4   The biggest problem was the time-scale involved. Students were beginning to ask searching questions and reveal information at the very point where the course stopped.

The School Link-up

Following the raising of the school leaving age the local secondary school, like most others, seemed at a loss to know what to do with their non-examination pupils. The community worker made a brief sortie into the school that year but managed principally to get a commitment for a community project to begin the following year. This was to be a two-year project starting with a fourth-year group and linking them up with the local tenants' association. They would help to examine the issues being tackled by the association. In addition the worker and a teacher would help the pupils to look at why or how the associated problems existed, persisted and might be solved. The project covered a morning a week and was based outside the school (in the tenants' association's office). The pupils were 'specially selected' for this option. This seemed to be on the basis of staff 'selecting them out' of the other school options.

The main issues with which the group became involved were twofold:

Housing repairs

For years the houses in the area had been allowed to degenerate physically. Because much of the area was scheduled for clearance, basic repair work seemed to have ground to a halt. The tenants' association launched a drive to let people know of their housing rights and the way in which tenants could speed up the process through what was known as 'section ninety-nine Complaints Procedure'. The pupils became involved, first of all in learning about housing rights, repairs procedures, and the section ninety-nine complaints forms themselves. They then joined in a systematic coverage of all local streets, explaining the complaints procedure and returning with names and addresses of the various residents who actually wanted to do something about their housing conditions. The tenants' association (in conjunction with the pupils) then sent the completed forms off to the Environmental Health Department and followed each complaint through until it had been dealt with. At a practical level this gave the pupils first-hand experience of housing situations they were likely to encounter for themselves within a few years. It also gave them the opportunity to look at how and why the Council dealt with such situations, and the greater responsiveness which was produced once tenants banded together. From the tenants' association standpoint, the involvement of this group helped to add considerable momentum to the housing work. In addition a number of members of the group began to feed information to their own parents and were soon taking home housing complaint forms for their own family use.

Play facilities

The area totally lacked play facilities and the tenants' association was pressing for the establishment of an adventure playground in the area. The children identified very strongly with this campaign. They were only too well aware, from their own experiences, of how far a lack of creative play facilities promoted petty crime and general delinquent behaviour, as a form of entertainment if nothing else. The campaign involved a great deal of survey work, collecting petitions, lobbying for support and drafting proposals (and plans) for the adventure playground. At one stage there was also a full scale demonstration outside the Council House. It was taken for granted (by the community worker and teacher involved) that the group would be there. They also sat through one of the Council meetings which briefly discussed and hastily rejected these proposals. That the adventure playground did not 'take off' until a year after the group finished, is in no way an indictment of the group. Rather it is simply part of the reality in which action strategies have to exist and be fought over.

All this may seem nice and cosy. However, the project has to be set in its own political context. Since the general theme might have been 'Education for Democracy', the group itself was run as democratically as possible. Rules and regulations were worked out in the group. Needless to say they differed from school regulations. Everyone was encouraged to challenge statements they disagreed with, and to be prepared to be challenged on statements of their own. They were expected to take an active part in shaping the development of the work. The outcome was that the activities were noted not only by the local Council, but also within the school. Some teachers welcomed the growth of critical faculties in the pupils; most didn't! Pressure began to be put on the headmaster to put his house in order.

69

A visiting HMI added to this pressure following a session in which the group frankly discussed truancy, their activities whilst 'nicking off', and the reasons why some of them sneaked back into school to get to some lessons or alternately sneaked out just to miss others. What worried the HMI was that the session was not put into the context of saying the kids *ought* to go to school. To leave that open for them to debate (let alone decide upon) seemed altogether beyond the pale. This was probably the straw which broke the camel's back. The headmaster recalled the group. Smoking, swearing, making their own coffee were all prohibited. The group were not supposed to leave the school grounds except in a 'crocodile' line. The bubble had burst. The pupils lost interest and so did the two staff. What the kids had learnt could not be taken away from them but the final lesson became all the more painfully obvious. 'Conscientization' might be fine in the Third World, but in this country the realities of power and vested interest ensure that, at least within the school system, social enquiry gets no nearer than antiseptic voyeurism.

Problems

1 The more effectively the group functioned the more uncomfortable became its relationship with the school and the local authority.

2 What began as a convenient way of dealing with difficult pupils came to be used as a way of controlling their behaviour in other aspects of school life. Although all the pupils were accomplished truants they never 'nicked off' from this project. Sometimes it was the only thing they came in for each week. Paradoxically, as the project's undesirability grew, so it became more useful as a control mechanism for the school. Initially it was a dumping ground, then as the pupils identified with it, it became a privilege.

3 The school, the Education Authority, the police, the Education Welfare Office were clearly discomfited not only by being invited to join in genuinely 'open' discussions on truancy and the like, but also that such discussions were allowed to take place without an element of pressuring the children to accept official wisdom.

4 To the extent that these kids responded to the project life, the rest of the school system was probably that much harder for them to identify with.

5 The kids had clearly got nothing from the formal education which equipped them to confront the realities of living. The outburst from one lad during the first year made this abundantly clear. In a heated debate the lad turned on the worker and shouted,

> 'It's alright for you to say think of why this or that happens. You forget that we never have to bloody think. All we have to do is keep quiet and write down what we're told.'

The accuracy or otherwise of this statement is less significant than the fact that it represented a view of themselves (in the context of the school) which was commonly held throughout the group. Education had helped them to identify themselves as useless.

The Community Planning Project

In the Spring of 1977 the new Conservative District Council called a halt to current house building. Everything was to be re-assessed, including land allocated for new development. The Conservatives decided to build no more council houses. All development land (including Raleigh Street) was put up for offer. A series of hastily convened meetings in the area resulted in a proposal being submitted to the Council that the residents would handle the redevelopment of the area themselves. The proposal went in under the name of All Saints Residents' Association (ASRA), the recently formed umbrella organization for residents in the area.

ASRA's proposals were rooted in a clear recognition of their strength and weakness. Their weakness lay in the fact that they had never built, managed or financed a project of this size. Their strength was that they were able to pull together resources around their firm belief that the residents of the area were the best people to decide on the sort of housing which should be built, its layout, its allocation of open space, its internal design and its traffic pattern.

ASRA's proposals were submitted with the backing of,

1 a local housing association—which, as ASRA's agents, would deal with the financial and administrative work

2 a firm of solicitors

3 the University School of Planning—who would act as consultants to residents and help them to produce a viable set of plans for the area.

The total project never materialized. The land was sold to a national housing association and that, thought the Council, was that. The residents however continued their plans to work with the University to produce their own proposals for the area as a basis for negotiation. The Council were not amused. Participation was supposed to wait until the fundamental decisions had all been made. 'It's unethical' was the cry 'to confront the housing association's architect with other architects and planners working on the same scheme.'

The professor of the Department ignored this and got on with the exercise. During the summer he and the residents' association did a lot of ground work to prepare for a start as soon as the University year began. Some students returned early to add their help. In September 'planning'

71

began in earnest. For three months the whole of one of the department's option courses was devoted to working in Raleigh Street. The students were given a base in the area and kept the base open every day for people to call in with their ideas. A huge scale model of the area was rapidly constructed. In addition there were a large number of flats, house types, shops, community facilities and maisonettes which were available for people to allocate, wherever they wished, within the cleared central part of the area. Individual preferences were identified in this way, but they were assembled by means of a weekly planning session open to everyone. At these sessions people were divided into groups and each group had to argue out a set of proposals to put forward for the area. Then the various groups came together to argue over the different proposals which had emerged. Whole families were involved in this exercise. Needless to say some proposals were mutually exclusive on a site which at most could accommodate 200 houses. Others, like the airport which one lad wanted, couldn't possibily have been fitted in, even if the rest of the world had agreed with it.

During the three months a great many ideas were generated, amended, incorporated or rejected. The layout was continuously altered (sometimes as a result of visits to other estates); so was the housing mix. Finally, a plan emerged which was startlingly conventional. People wanted houses in terraces; big windows rather than pokey ones; their own gardens rather than public open space; houses made of brick; ample accommodation for larger families; limits on through traffic; a residents only parking scheme; and gas or coal heating.

The significance of the proposals was twofold. They represented the first bid to be put on the table and this was a very important bargaining position. Secondly, and more importantly, they were the residents' own plans. The significance of this sense of belonging and identification cannot be overestimated. Virtually all of the principal aspects of these plans have now been accepted by the housing association concerned, and the residents are now recognized as one of the legitimate, negotiating interests in the development of the area.

Problems

1 *The process*

The dialectic between the students and the residents—was not one which was understood particularly well by either group. The students were valued because they had planning skills which could turn ideas into models or workable drawings. They were also valued because they, in turn, valued and listened to the ideas of the residents. Being seen to be 'of worth' by 'professionals' is not an everyday occurrence in Raleigh Street. However, the students were suspect because they were not always good at coming out into the open with ideas they had. The belief that the system is there to screw you is not one which is easily abandoned, even where the prospects of playing and winning are extremely good. In their turn the students often found it frustrating that residents did not readily grasp common place planning themes; did not focus their thinking too clearly and precisely; and did not get more people involved in the exercise.

Perhaps the most significant problem in the process was the lack of understanding of the respective rate at which the students and residents moved. The students never really understood how much it was taking out of people to run along at such a pace on an issue which, although important, had previously been seen as being right out of people's depth. In their turn the residents never fully appreciated the ideological commitment to 'making participation work' which many of the students had, and the inevitable tension and frustration which this generated.

2 *With the Council*

Essentially the local Council does not believe in participation. Most of the officers are happy with participation once plans have been drawn up. Participation is seen as being concerned with the colour of the icing, not the substance of the cake. The present Council would rather see residents participate somewhere else. This culminated in a verbal directive from the leader of the Council to the effect that no employee of the Council was to have anything to do with the residents' planning exercises. (The Council had been invited to join in as experts.) Three members were interested enough to brave this veto, although they insisted on doing so incognito.

3 *The Housing Association*

Even though the association accepted most of the proposals they were atrocious in their part of the participation process. Residents wanted them involved from the start but the association either ignored letters or fobbed off residents with replies like 'we really must arrange to meet soon'. To put the issue in context, the association probably accepted proposals because it stood to gain a lot from doing so. The proposals would mean that more houses would be built on the site.

The association therefore got more money from central government for this project. Financially they will probably benefit to the tune of an extra £1 million. They also cashed in on a lot of good radio and TV publicity. Significantly the main issue they refused to support was the retention and conversion of a factory in the area which was wanted as a community centre. This would have taken a small part of the land away from them, and community centres are not things for which central government pays[4].

Conclusions

The conclusions that can be drawn from the description of the work under-taken with the three groups are specific to each, but we feel it is possible

73

to draw some general conclusions about the relationship of community education and community action.

With the students
The specific conclusions we have drawn are first to do with the students. The process of education they undergo on their course, with its emphasis upon individual success and the examination and regurgitation of other people's writings, ill equips them for a community education process in which they have to collect, assemble and interpret data as an aid to a community group.

If such work is undertaken with students then minimum conditions for doing it need to be obtained from the educational institution. In discussions of this paper, it was made very clear, by group members, that the task set for students was unreasonable, given the time scale of twelve weeks and four hours a week. It was suggested that the *whole* of a term should be devoted to it, and that much closer contact and feedback between students and residents was required. This would also have helped increase the level of student commitment.

What Freire describes as 'dialogics' can only really work when those involved are critically examining their own 'reality' as defined by them. In discussion it was suggested that a student investigation into their particular housing problems and the way their pressure for housing affected Raleigh Street tenants would have been more appropriate than to ask them to do work on issues defined by someone else.

We find this conclusion hard to swallow. In our view, if the conditions for undertaking the work are carefully thought out then such a partnership between students and tenants can be fruitful and beneficial to both. From it students can better comprehend the nature of the pressures on residents (which they themselves claimed and which we would argue *a priori* makes them potentially more useful as teachers in areas like Raleigh Street). They also experience an educational process which stresses collective action and a direct relationship between acquiring knowledge and using it to inform collective action, albeit action by the tenants rather than by themselves.

Our firm belief that, whatever the difficulties involved, the students' work should involve interaction with the residents on issues which were important to the residents, is perhaps best summed up by Freire himself[5]:

> Critical and liberating dialogue, which presupposes action, must be carried on with the oppressed at whatever stage their struggle for liberation has reached.

With the Comprehensive School Pupils
The most obvious conclusion is that the schooling process, experienced by the youngsters worked with, did not equip them with either the *skills*, nor indeed the *confidence* in their own ability, to run things that were essential to the effectiveness of the work.

Having said that, it is clear that they can acquire both skills and confidence in a comparatively brief period—even when those selected out by the school to engage in the work are the school's failures and drop-outs. Indeed it might be interesting to speculate whether those who have been labelled as failures are not more able to engage in this kind of educational process than children more accepting of the schooling process.

The major obstacle to any advance in this way of working is the attitude and the fine-talking requirements of the school authority. The project started with a sympathetic Head who was subsequently subjected to heavy pressure from the authority in the shape of the HMI and from members of his own staff—and he not surprisingly gave in to it.

Inevitably one is forced to ask whether schools really have any intention or desire to produce critical, liberated people.

With the Residents of Raleigh Street

We would argue that it was with this group that the educational process undertaken was most successful and of most value to those engaged in it. There was a direct relationship between their collective need to influence the decisions about redeveloping their area and the process they undertook in the planning exercise which gave shape and direction to their collective action.

Moreover, the partnership with the trainee professionals from the University Planning Department was valuable for both parties. The students came to a better understanding of what participation meant to local residents, whilst residents were able to build up their own image of themselves because their ideas were treated seriously and with respect.

The reaction of the Council and housing association to residents' efforts were disappointing but hardly surprising. In one sense it brings home very clearly that the process of 'conscientization' is hardly one that those in authority are likely to be enthusiastic about. Its value is for the oppressed themselves and therefore there is little point in worrying overmuch about its possible impact on councils or other bodies when you, as educators, or community workers, engage in it. What came across clearly was that 'conscientization' is not about 'tokenism' and therefore is unlikely to be welcomed by the powers that be. Again to quote Freire[6]:

> to the oppressor consciousness, the humanization of the 'others', of the people, appears as subversion, not as the pursuit of full humanity . . . To be workers in this situation and to be unprepared for it, is both naive and irresponsible.

General Conclusions

One of the most interesting outcomes of the work undertaken with all three groups (students, pupils and residents) was the recognition by participants of the limited nature of the 'success' achieved and the implications of that recognition.

Residents were quick to perceive that the apparent success in having their proposals accepted by the housing association owed much more to the benefit the latter derived from the proposals than to any commitment to the process by which the proposals were arrived at. One of the greatest criticisms of community work has been that it has been initiated by poverty programmes based on the social pathology model which attributes the continuance of poverty to the inadequacies of people in neighbourhoods. The argument put forward powerfully in the CDP document 'Gilding the Ghetto' is that community work which concentrates on the self-help process implicitly supports this analysis rather than pin-pointing the real causes of poverty. In contrast, it would be our contention that in this process of trying to change the situation they find themselves in, residents come to a deeper understanding of the factors which affect their lives and realize much more clearly the need for coordinated efforts with other organized groups to achieve any significant shift of resources towards themselves. The language used in the process indicates the shift in awareness. Initially the concern is with 'information' for use in preparing plans. Later it is a concern with the 'resources' of capital and labour and their 'control' and 'management'.

In the case of students and pupils the conclusions drawn were more limited—perhaps because the issues pursued were not as 'real' to them. The students, at best, ended—in the majority of cases—by perceiving that the agencies who were trying to help (e.g. Council Housing Department, Church, Education Department), could in fact act as 'deprivers' themselves because of the policies being pursued. Some of the students, at least, stopped 'blaming the victim' for the deprivation in Raleigh Street.

For the pupils the major conclusion drawn was that their schooling had not equipped them to undertake the work involved, even when they themselves were interested in it. For most of them this realization was too late to be of much use.

What made it harder for both students and pupils was the realization that the process they were involved in set them at odds with the schooling that they were undergoing. The criticism of the work undertaken with them was that it raised doubts and uncertainties about the nature of the education they received without offering ways of changing this.

It is our final contention that the value of linking educational work to community need is indisputable. Despite the difficulties involved in overcoming the restrictions imposed by educational institutions we believe that any situation that offers the prospect of setting in motion a dialogical process which involves the oppressed in examining their oppression, and working out ways in which this reality can be altered, is worth taking on.

Notes

[1] *The County Area Deprivation Study.* (1974) Nottinghamshire County Council.

[2] ALINSKY, S. (1971) *Rules for Radicals*. Vintage Press.

[3] We found DAVID TRIESMEN's article in *Reconstructing Social Psychology* ARMISTEAD, N. (Ed.) (1974) Penguin Educational, invaluable on the radical interpretation of data.

[4] This is no longer accurate since the Inner Areas Programme for 1978–79 does make provision for Centres. ASRA have applied.

[5] FREIRE, P. (1972) *Pedagogy of the Oppressed* Penguin p. 41.

[6] *Ibid.* p. 35.

Sidney Stringer School and Community College

Arfon Jones

When Sidney Stringer first started I felt confident in relegating the role of the school on community development, feeling that it had little influence, or that if it did have a role then it alienated sections of the young or became an instrument of the state. After six years, with less confidence admittedly, I would emphasise the importance of the school as a major instrument of community development and as an instrument for social change.

Background

Sidney Stringer School and Community College is situated in a densely populated area of Coventry with many new high rise flats or old Victorian terrace houses. It had been the focus for a considerable amount of redevelopment for over twenty years. In 1969 it was deemed a suitable area for a Community Development Project. The catchment area reflected roughly the school's population which is approximately fifty-one per cent Asian, forty per cent English and European, seven per cent West Indian and two per cent 'others'. Initially it was conceived as a dual purpose institution, but it was agreed that it would be under the direction of a single head who would control an integrated staff.

Aims of the Enterprise

1 To raise the level of consciousness of the people who live in the area.

2 An enterprise seen by residents as theirs; which has their interest at heart; in which they feel welcome and secure.

3 It was to be a community centre managed by the residents for their own benefit with as little interference from the professional as possible.

The questions that were not asked and therefore not answered were:

Who controls the enterprise?

Who makes the decisions?

and these have remained fundamental to the development of participation and democratic decision-making at Sidney Stringer.

The School

The school was created from the amalgamation of two secondary modern schools. The major elements at Sidney Stringer were a commitment to mixed-ability teaching, to an intensive home-school links programme, to team—teaching; supported by an approach to the development of personal relationships which abolished corporal punishment and school uniform.

CSE Mode 3 rather than 'O' level was emphasized, though the last three years have seen the emphasis change. As part of its common core in years four to five, students had to undertake a compulsory two-year course in Social Studies, which was to equip them to understand and analyze their environment, and in particular that of their community. Contributions to the curriculum would come from adults living in the area. In its clearest form Community Service was seen as paternalistic and regeneration would come from the students' new understanding and insight into the social structures and relationships, the flesh and bones of the community. Among certain staff there was the belief that this might lead the institution to take a critical stance in relation to the local authority and that this would be shown in the curriculum.

The first two years were difficult. There was racial violence, truancy, and the inevitable and natural parental reaction. Perhaps wherever two inner city schools are amalgamated there will be major problems. I feel that the attempt to establish new techniques and norms exacerbated the problem. After two years, mainly because of these new techniques, the school slowly became a success story on all indices, where children are educated in an atmosphere described by all as warm and happy and hard working.

This success would not have been achieved if parental opinion had been effective. It would not have been achieved if power and control had been passed to a staff body. In the first eighteen months the majority of staff and parents would have voted for a return to established and traditional forms of education with an emphasis on strong discipline equated with corporal punishment. There would have been decisions which would have divided school from community use of premises. Because power had been invested in a small number of senior staff they were able to maintain allegience to the established principles of community education combined with new educational strategies. Traditional structures, at least in my opinion, would have exaggerated racial tensions and produced an atmosphere counterproductive to the involvement and participation of those members of the community least likely to take up activities.

The following are examples of three possible guides in developing a participatory strategy with members of the community unwilling or unable to take up activities.

A Mothers' Group

Most community colleges have a mothers' group. The Sidney Stringer group had certain differences. It was all white and was brought to Sidney Stringer by the local Social Services Department. A Community Worker who was also a qualified teacher of Home Economics was attached to the group. They were given a space in the Project Area where teaching in aspects of child care, in needlework and fashion to children of statutory school age, took place.

A small creche was established for the pre-school children, looked after initially by a rota of mothers and pupils in child care CSE courses. The mothers drank coffee and gossiped while gradually and with increasing confidence eavesdropped on lessons that went on simultaneously. The community worker, who by this time had gained their trust, then took certain lessons in child care, and the teacher sat among the mothers. The next step was to ask the mothers to exhibit some points of child rearing such as nappy changing to the pupils. Gradually, discussion, informal and unstructured, started to take place which evolved to such a time as when the community worker with the teaching staff and outside help could start a formal structured adult education course in child rearing.

Once mothers had confidence and security in education the next stage was to disseminate their knowledge and new perceptions to other mums living in their neighbourhood. Mums, some of whom had rejected school, had experienced with confidence an adult education class, where theory and practice, where discussion and debate had been natural and acceptable aspects.

Some of the fifteen and sixteen year old girls would also have been a part of this group. Their future would be similar in some instances to the reality of the lives of the mothers. When they become mothers, perhaps at seventeen or eighteen, they too might face life in a high rise flat. It would not be sufficient to know that a play group existed at Stringer. It would be essential that the girl knew a welcome awaited her, that her response to school was positive and that she felt it to be a warm and caring atmosphere: that people she knew as teachers whom she knew had cared for her still existed, and did not evoke hostile memories or threatened her hard earned and won adult status. There would be no possible way that such a girl would involve herself if she had spent most of her adolescence in the D stream, forced to wear uniform, and made to feel a failure. This is the reality of the total community concept.

And what better person than this eighteen year old mother to talk to those girls now fifteen who remembered her as a pupil when they were twelve, about the realities of pregnancy and child rearing.

This is a more relevant form of adult education than the classes we put on. More importantly, it raises questions about the more general nature of community development with its emphasis on resident groups and leadership.

81

Tensions in Development

House Head

The parent is a key figure for any school. His first and obvious concern is his child; but he is also an adult facing the same problems, with the same needs as other members of the community. He is interested in leisure in his own right.

In our very early days we insisted that the House Head, who was responsible for the academic and social development of 120 pupils for five years from the year they arrived until the year they left school, was charged with making at least one annual contact at the home of the child.

Despite initial difficulties and fears by House Heads worried about visits to homes, this became an established practice. There are obvious beneficial results in children's motivation. However the crucial result was the involvement of the House Head in the family. At best (and we stressed that the visits should be positive; that the House Head should visit not because Johnny was in trouble but because he was doing well) the House Head became immersed in the family. Once a relationship has been developed the House Head would ask the parent to attend important meetings, even those to discuss the curriculum. In some instances the families' problems would be discussed.

The House Head acted as a lever to any excess flights of curriculum fancy by his more ambitious colleagues, and was able to keep taking the tempo of community feeling, not only about the feelings of parents but that of adults as well, and this he could feed back into the organization of the college.

He could involve parents because his role was easily recognized and trusted. The 'pure' community worker has great difficulty, until he too disguises himself as a teacher, or someone concerned with adult education.

At its most extreme, or at best, the teacher's role widens and he can become teacher, social worker, friend and community action politician, though this is extremely demanding and few can manage more than two functions. But at the very least, the member of staff's knowledge and experience of the community gives greater depth to his analysis and understanding of the needs of his pupils, to the relevance of the curriculum, and to attempts to communicate the value of education to parents and residents.

He also widens his outlook to see himself as part of a multi-professional team; a team composed of social workers, community workers, teachers from junior and infant schools, as well as his own colleagues with different functions in his institution.

16+ Centre

It has always appeared wasteful that after close contact with parents and youngsters, at the age of sixteen, years of work should be forgotten. The fact of unemployment intensifies the relationship, and focusses anew on the content of the youth programme. Too often it is an activity based programme, with the youth worker delegated to that of supervisor. A method of involving the positive experience of his school life: the school's detailed experience of his family and his weaknesses and strengths, should be evolved, to co-ordinate a post-sixteen experience; relevant to the youngster and in particular to his employment needs. It might even make us ask questions about the pre-sixteen curriculum.

Accordingly a 16+ Centre has been established at Sidney Stringer which will be part of the Sixth Form and while we haven't any solutions as yet, I feel we are beginning to ask the right questions.

School and Community Association

However, the above are aspects of participations, and as yet avoid the problem of decision-making. The major impact of the last four years has been the establishment of a school and community association, and a Board of Governors.

A Sidney Stringer School and Community Association with its own constitution, developed in consultation with the LEA, was set up. In essence it was open to all people who lived in the catchment area, and was an attempt to widen responsibility for decision-making. The basis of the Association was the Council which debated and voted upon major issues. It in turn set up sub-committees composed of parents, users, students and staff examining in detail various aspects of the institution; Education-School sub committee, Resources and Finance, Youth, Leisure and Sports. These sub-committees were financed on the basis of application from the monies received by the Council. The intention was that each sub-committee would play a major part in policy initiation and also in helping to administer various activities. While the Head was ex-officio on each committee the relationship between his powers as laid out in the instrument and articles of government and that of the Association was never made clear.

The direct link between the Association and the Board of Governors was established by election of individuals from specified categories of membership of the Association. It was felt that a large number of individuals elected by the Association was to be able to safeguard its interests and allocate funds to its development. Difficulties arose between those who saw themselves as accountable representatives of the Association and others who saw themselves as Governors with a wider brief than the Association. others saw the Association, not as the integral basis of the institution, but rather as a useful subsidiary, analogous to a Parent Teacher Association.

It would seem that a two-tier system of democratic decision-making in the government of the college was being set up. At all levels there was a two-tier system of accountability. In the case of staff representatives, from staff to Council staff representatives to staff Board of Governors.

There were some problems. The Local Authority in its genuine attempt to set up a democratic structure perceived the Sidney Stringer Centre as fulfilling the needs of the area of benefit and felt it necessary to give power to the community. But what was clear from the previous liberal attempts of CDP's (Community Development Programmes) to devolve power was that one was passing power, not to the participating masses but to those who were clearly adroit at using, for instance, committee work and constitutionalism. In the often humdrum details of committee work, it was a particular type of person who maintained sufficient enthusiasm to develop control. The majority of people in the catchment area were unused to the ethos of committee work or were bored or made insecure by the genuine manipulation of procedures. Community staff may have found themselves in the position of having brought carefully nurtured members to committees only to see their proteges' insecurity heightened or their own close relationship demeaned by the genuine but complex formal structure of decision-making. A person who enjoys committee work even for the greater good is not typical of the majority especially in an inner city area. Sidney Stringer Council became dominated by staff and its racial balance did not adequately reflect its catchment area. Attempts to increase members and participation failed because the structure, albeit democratic, inhibited involvement. What appears to happen is that individuals gain control by the support of other small groups and maintain that support through the use of power.

A kind of working-class bureaucracy is established, whose major impetus follows closely certain aspects of Weber's analysis; not so much in the disciplined subordination to a hierarchy of command, but rather in presenting a barrier in which even the willing local citizen has difficulty in participating, and in perpetuating its own existence. And when the committee has also the power to give out cash grants, the action of the local authority in transferring parts of its financial control to the local community is not democracy but the passing of power to a smaller group who desire to do good from the limited perception of a detailed knowledge of a small segment of a community or neighbourhood. And this perception, though not thankfully at Stringer, could be racist, prejudiced or ideologically motivated.

Very little education in democracy takes place since the elements of control and power are already well understood. Liberals and radicals who advocate the power of association and neighbourhood groups must be clearly aware that they are not handing over power to the people but to small networks of hardworking, persevering individuals whose actions and involvement in constitutional and democratic frameworks are often a major barrier to participation by larger groups of individuals. There is a specific danger clearly outlined by D.P. Moynihan in his criticism of the American poverty programme which the Stringer experience could not, to date, refute.

To guide groups into participation, in an attempt based on a tenuous theory about the alienation of the poor and the evils of powerlessness, and attempt to produce widespread democratic control and participation, is really to pass power to yet another group and perhaps deny those in most need, from the benefits of an enterprise set up to satisfy those needs.

84

Role of the Professional

When is a teacher not a teacher? At Sidney Stringer a member of staff can join the Community Association. There he is free to speak as the dictates of his conscience allows, even though, in some instances, this may contradict the policy of the institution. He speaks to the Community Association as a member of that Association, but to all lay people he is perceived as a teacher and a member of staff. To ignore the formal and informal power of the professional is to falsify the analysis. Whatever democratic structures surround him, ultimately, he is paid to interfere/intervene in people's lives. In motivating a child from a non-academic home into academic success he influences that family: as happens when the black child is orientated into British culture. Only an exceptional layman can compete with his expertise.

At Stringer we have found that meaningful participation is closely related to the professional worker, who in this context acquires immense responsibility analogous to the process of teaching where guidance is a central concept. We have found that the participation of adults too often rejected by the educational system as being uninterested, is closely related to the ethos and values of the school and their school experience.

We have found that democratic structures help to alienate the very people to whom liberals and radical authorities have attempted to transfer power. In some instances, given guidance by professional workers, many groups normally classified as non-participants, may raise their consciousness and perhaps demand a say in running an institution.

Community Colleges have been asked to take a leap in the dark. I think we are willing to do so. I am anxious that when we land, it is on a bed, with a partner, not just willing, but in most need.

3

COMMUNITY EDUCATION: THE PRACTICE

Introduction

Issues become more tangible and clearly defined when those responsible for centres of community education discuss their own approaches. Theory and skills have not yet separated in community education; the doers are also thinkers and there can be no doubt that they have strong convictions. In this section it is suggested that traditional roles must change, that learning to learn is a life-skill which tomorrow's adults must have and that control, management, and government are issues which cannot be avoided in community schools.

John Watts distinguishes between change, which can be external and appear inevitable and innovation which is exercised by choice. He argues that in the face of social mobility; materialism; media effects; the questioning of authority and the explosion of knowledge, schools either 'innovate or crumble'. Such innovation places increased demands upon the teacher, who ceases to be a moraliser, becoming instead a guide and mentor in the problem-solving process. The demands upon the teacher are therefore to change the style of relationships, to realize that the classroom is far from being the only arena of action and to learn to use, with others, the power being shed by a headteacher who rejects the traditional distribution of power. This leads to the need for more organic, open structures of government in schools and colleges and more vital community control.

For Ron Mitson the idea of resource symbolizes a much needed change in values. By illustrating his theme with the details of a pupil pack he is able to emphasize the gains in independence. His view might even be summarized as 'our over arching concern in community education must be to help our students to become adults'. Without this commitment to their 'becoming'—and anticipating what they, as adults, can expect—then change is something only discussed and achieved by switching labels. The issue which Mitson quarries out in his approach is that macro-changes will be ineffective without a multitude of micro-changes by the teacher in the classroom.

Stewart Wilson's paper takes a series of focii and does so with a steady thunder of home truths. Challenging questions are piled upon each other. The school is not a separate oasis, it has the responsibility to engage. The main task is to remove artificial barriers. This is innovation in itself. He drives home his main point, that school and community are actually inseparable, as part of a discussion concerning barriers and principles. One such principle is to move away from the titles 'Schools' and 'Colleges'.

Sheffield has a history of making its own moves in education. Such is the case with the Rowlinson Campus where, as Sylvia Coupe shows, if an effort is made to understand why adults drop out of courses all kinds of innovations are suggested. Her account carefully shows how 'mind stretching' courses have meant sharing the programme of work with students and how 'return to learning' courses first developed through counselling and 'free samples'. Then came the demand to go further and a link with the Open University was forged which works according to Rowlinson's rules rather than those of the University.

Stewart Wilson has already included the eleventh session in his principles and now examines the topic in more detail. The involvement of children of all ages, families and adults leads to the idea that classes in community education are mixed in many senses of the word. These classes can also give a home to an existing group or help one to form. Adults will know best what they want, the question is whether or not they are joined in a shared effort to achieve it.

Lovett opens with two related propositions, Northern Ireland is not hugely different from England in that adult education has become a middle-class preserve and 'adult education has been most effective in catering for the needs of the working-class when it has seen itself as part of a larger social movement amongst that section of the population'. Thus, groups already exist who have needs and are doing something about it. A two-way flow opens up between these 'activists' and those who control the resources they need. This is the beginning of a process rather than an end in itself and leads to conferences, study groups, courses and the securing of more resource commitments from other bodies. The Institute of Continuing Education in Derry is a substantial effort to promote 'learning by doing' and leads to resource centres within working-class communities rather than sustaining a dependence upon the University's resources. The University is also in a position to offer a certificate course with strong local links and on which some students can be part-time tutors. Action, in the sense of stating and getting what is needed, is therefore part of the process rather than something which the adult-students do in other guises.

The Community College: Continuous Change

John Watts

May I for the sake of this argument suggest that 'change' is something that happens to us, and that 'innovation' is something that we choose to bring about. (Of course, by this definition, one man's innovation is another man's change!) It seems axiomatic that change is inevitable and stasis is an illusion. The metabolism of our bodies ensures a steady change of its constituent parts even whilst we are aware of our personal continuity. So with institutions, even where tradition preserves an identity, change and decay are inescapable. Attempts to repeat old practice in the belief that the past is being maintained are in vain. *Si duo idem faciunt, no est idem.* If two people do the same thing, it is not the same thing. The conditions never recur exactly. The conservative can at best retard the rate of change.

And of course it is *rate* of change that most affects us. Human kind has survived any number of changes because there has always been time to adjust. The peculiar feature of our own time is that the rate of change has accelerated to the point where, like Alice and the Red Queen, we have to run hard just to stay where we are. In Alvin Toffler's catch-phrase, 'The Future is Now'.

There is little need to run the risks of speculative futurology in asking what changes we need to accommodate in education. The writing on the wall describes what is already with us, and survival with sanity, into the next century needs us here and now to take account of the changes that have already occurred, however much we have tried to shut them outside the school gate. My own conviction is that unless we innovate, hard-headedly, so as to come to terms with these changes, already irreversable except by catastrophe, they will crack open our schools to the point of collapse. The currently trendy cry of Back to the Good Old Days is possibly the most subversive voice in our present predicament. We must innovate or crumble, and we must innovate not so as to produce a permanent new solution, but in the hopes of creating mutable systems, themselves open to continuous modification, ever-sensitive to new needs.

What are the changes that already strain our cultural and moral norms, and that any system of education must acknowledge and adapt to? There are five that I wish to identify briefly. Their manifestations, if not self-evident, are more fully recorded elsewhere and I do not want to pursue them at length but rather to point out the implications they seem to me to have for our education system, particularly for secondary and post-secondary education.

89

First, people in general are more mobile than ever before. They just get around so much, over large distances, by motor-bike, car, plane, 'hitching'. This is true even if they return home to the same place. But they also change home and place of work more freely. Thus they change their social contacts, including their marriage partners, more frequently.

Movement has left people more informed. It is easy to scoff at the English family abroad demanding their fish and chips, but even at a superficial level a knowledge of other places, people and habits has been picked up. Even without travel, knowledge has come to us through television. All those exciting objects that teachers used to import to the classroom as stimulating visual aids have all been seen repeatedly by our children.

Amongst that catalogue of now familiar objects, once remote and mysterious, is the whole array of potential material possessions. The whole Aladin's cave of our consumer society has been thrown open with the cry of 'Treat yourself to this—you deserve it'. By implication, it is suggested, no-one has the right to keep it from you. Thus in our time, as teachers, parents, fellow members of any community, we have to contend simultaneously with this vast increase of material goods and a lowering of respect for other people's property.

The fourth phenomenon to pick on is the discredit of authority. It is not uncommon to hear this attributed to the softening effort of progressive ideas at home and in school. The weakness of this argument lies in the lack of evidence of any widespread adoption of progressive methods and permissiveness in schools, the case being rather that much the same attitudes are shown by teachers in schools as were shown fifty years ago. The widespread questioning of orders issued by Them, particularly the older Them, is more likely to have stemmed from the First Battle of the Somme. Since the First World War, the rank and file have wanted to know 'the reason why'. (Even though men and women marched again in 1939, it was not again in blind patriotism, but with a belief, however mistaken, in a reasonable cause.) But whether my diagnosis of origin is right or wrong, whether we like it or not, the days when teachers could expect to hold their pupils in awe by their granted authority are over. If they were not over before, they certainly have been since the last two raisings of the school-leaving age. I shall take up the implications a little further on.

Last in my brief selection of changes that radically affect us in education, is the dramatic explosion of knowledge. Parallel to the popular familiarity with a range of diverse experience, goes this enormous increase in substantiated information on every branch of enquiry and a similarly spectacular increase in the subdivisions of knowledge. New subjects, let alone new research findings, burgeon on every hand. Out of all those constellations of knowledge, which bright stars shall we select as the ones most likely to be relevant enough to guide our students into their later careers? How can we possibly know in the face of the accelerative thrust of change?

All these are symptoms of what Karl Popper long ago identified as an increasingly Abstract Society. Its strains are similarly identifiable. We have already come to live, in our vallium-soaked society, alongside mental breakdown of epidemic proportions. Education will not change the pressures. It is an exploded myth that education will save society, or change it at all directly. What it can do, if the educators cease trying to be Messiahs or Napoleons, is help people to lead more, rather than less, stable and satisfying lives in the face of these pressures. But we must innovate, and on a wide scale, if we are to be of any use. For the most part our scheme of education is still designed as if for a static society, dependent upon teachers for knowledge, dependent upon teachers for their morality and acquiescent to authoritarianism. This is not congruent with the world around us. What innovations in our school system are incumbent upon us if we are to meet these social changes that have already overtaken us? How far have we met the challenge and what response has it elicited from the users?

Let me work backwards over my short list of changes by claiming first that the enormous growth of knowledge in our time has finally knocked on the head the notion of anyone learning all that needs to be known. This is not to deny the need for a basic body of essential knowledge, including 'times tables' and how to read. But if this has not been mastered by mid-secondary age, certainly by the age of fourteen, the school-leaving age of my own generation, then school has missed the chance. Beyond those basics however, selection of knowledge for much more than examination requirements runs against huge odds in the relevence stakes. The whole emphasis shifts instead onto quite other learning skills.

Instead of learning to memorize information selected by the teacher to answer questions also selected by the teacher, today's student, of any age, needs to learn among other skills, surely the following:

1 The identification of a problem i.e., finding out what needs to be known and done in an area where an impasse has occurred.

2 Devising strategies for solving a problem.

3 Retrieving information necessary to any strategy. This may involve the use of a whole range of resources, printed, visual, or most frequently, other people.

4 Classifying and collating information so as to form hypotheses.

5 Testing and modifying hypotheses until a working solution is found.

6 Getting things done so that the strategy, planned in this way, is put into action.

Now all this may appear obvious, and certainly it has all been said before, but it is a far cry from doing the school tasks that teacher has set. And yet it seems a necessary requirement of a generation of school-leavers who will need to be less dependent than ever before on precedent, tradition and dogma.

To lay down such new requirements of the student does not imply just another set of instructions to be carried out for the teacher. It is consistent with an approach by the student that questions what is asked of him. The set of skills that I have just outlined, and the duty of the teacher to know how to impart them, follow from the very question 'Why are you telling us this?' The starting point is the conditional If. 'If you perceive this as a problem to which you desire a solution, then . . . ' The teacher has authority, in that he should know how to develop the necessary skills and how to encourage and monitor progress in their acquisition. He must also create and indeed insist upon the conditions that will make such learning possible. But this authority will be rationally defensible and totally different from authoritarianism, the wielding of conferred power without the acceptance of its ends by those subjected to it. The teacher can no longer say, 'This is important for you because I say so'. The kind of obligation he imposes is of the order, 'If you accept that this is important for you, then you must do as follows'.

There are moral implications here, just as there is a moral dilemma for the teacher when faced with plural values in the world from which his students come. He may well know where he stands over the protection of property within the premises, but in many other areas of morality where heads pontificating in morning assembly were wont to expatiate, he would be better now to remain silent. There just is no clear pattern of social morality to which all our community subscribes. The teacher who inveighs against divorce or single-parent families or sex outside marriage for instance, is inevitably going to conflict with many of his parents, perhaps as many as if he preached the very opposite. He would be wiser to reconsider the traditional role of teacher as moralizer.

On the other hand, the teacher cannot withdraw from social involvement and its moral implications to become merely a facilitator, an intellectual technician. Far from it. The social and moral changes that I identified suggest an increase among our students in knowledgeableness accompanied by a thinning of relationships. This holds true for people of all ages, but particularly the adolescent right at the time when he or she needs to establish a firm sense of identity. This need for personal interaction is at the very heart of learning for this age-group. A fact is not a fact until it engages and modifies the whole person of the learner. The emergence of any clearer view of oneself in relation to the surrounding world depends upon a complex series of interactions. For the teacher to be effective in this development, he needs to create a genuine reciprocity of interest and ambition with his students. He needs also to be mature enough to have ideas bounced off him by youngsters trying out the strength of their arguments and identities.

The demand upon the teacher is colossal. Some might say it is an unreasonable demand. Yet I would maintain that unless drastic changes take place in attitudes, and the roles that stem from them, the teacher and school will become increasingly irrelevant, useless except as a pro-tem warder and watchdog, merely containing the unemployable masses until put to work or putting them through exams that pretend to qualify them for jobs, even if there are not many jobs available. The new demands upon the teacher include these:

1 to become more rational, less authoritarian;

2 to become more of a learner, less of a dispenser of knowledge;

3 to become more accessible, less hedged by rituals of professionalism and status;

4 to become more collaborative, less insulated and independent with regard to colleagues, students and the surrounding community;

5 to become more aware of the whole potential curriculum and less of a subject chauvinist;

6 to become more resourceful in facilitating learning, less bookish, more aware of the resources within school and the local community;

7 to fuse the concepts of 'academic' and 'pastoral' in his work;

8 to become more concerned with education as a lifelong occupation, less with examinations as the definers of the task;

9 to abandon the desire to dominate and to replace coercion by contract;

10 to operate with mutable structures, become less dependent on fixed schemes of organization.

The implications for teacher-education are enormous. It is not even enough to rethink initial training radically: continuous change must be matched by continous in-service education for teachers, an area in which the ten objectives just listed have not yet received serious attention.

In summary, what is asked for as a matter of urgency, if those ten objectives are to be realized, is a fresh contract between teacher and student, and a fresh contract between teacher and the community, which at present has too many conflicting and unreasoned expectations of schools and teachers. It is not enough to pay lip-service to the aims I have listed for the teacher. If they are translated into practical strategies, the process is going to be painful and the innovation not for the half-hearted. What sort of innovations, already undertaken here and there, at home or abroad, illustrate the application of these ideas in practice, and what problems do they give rise to? I want to consider two particular areas of innovation.

Perhaps the most significant innovations are those that have involved the fourteen to sixteen age range. Here we have school students in compulsory attendance for the first time in history, at an age when their forefathers, often at risk to their lives, received at least a modicum of adult status and a sense of usefulness, of being needed within the functioning of society, let alone wages for their pains. What is so astonishing, indeed scandalous, is that for the most part this whole stratum of society has been ascribed this changed status, in their own eyes all too often an enforced and humiliating prolongation of childhood if not a form of imprisonment, as if it were the simplest and most natural thing in the world. Just keep them at school two years longer. The commonly held image of the schoolchild has hardly altered: only surprise and righteous indignation has frequently been expressed that the schoolchild has grown larger and more unruly. The possibility that by this age, adolescents might reasonably resent being herded together, instructed by teachers they haven't asked to work with, on subjects they have expressed no interest in, at times and places not of their choosing, all without pay, seems to have escaped most otherwise quite just-minded adults.

The centre point for innovation in such circumstances would seem to be the working agreement made between teacher and student. (There always has been *some* sort of working agreement, if only of the order 'Do as I say or I'll beat you' and 'I'll do as you say if you don't beat me'.) It has been found possible for the agreement to be one of student choice within the range of options made possible by the teacher, governed by a process of negotiation. The two, choice and negotiation, must go together, and competence in each needs to be learnt, not being an inherited characteristic as far as I can tell.

We are fairly accustomed to the term 'options' in school these days, but they almost invariably represent a very limited innovation—the choice between a number of fixed combinations of timetabled studies, probably as an extension of a compulsory curriculum core. What is much more rare is an organizing of curriculum so that individual combinations may be made by each student, as it were compiling his own portfolio. Because there will always be limits to what is available and because there will always be more resources for learning available than the student, unadvised, will be aware of, the choice must be negotiated between student and staff. To be thoroughly effective, the operations need to be continuous so that new circumstances, new problems, lead as a matter of course to renegotiation. Thus each student will have a personal timetable which is a contract with staff, what they have agreed to, each with obligations to make it work, but in the knowledge that the contract is renegotiable.

94

Such a contract will have taken account of the student's expressed wishes over what to study, with which teachers, in company with which fellow-students, where and when. In the process, the student will learn the necessity of compromise, the acceptance of constraints, but as understandable limitations, not random impositions of an abstract bureaucracy.

The result is one of qualitative change in the relationship of staff and students, though it only comes about if and when students prove for themselves that it is all for real, that the teacher hasn't got a cane up his sleeve. It will only come about if the teachers have made positive moves to render themselves obviously open to this continuous negotiating. It is no use their wrapping themselves in their academic robes and shutting themselves in their staffrooms, displaying themselves on a raised platform by way of introducing each day's proceedings. They have got to look more like normal people in other walks of life familiar to the student, and to mingle with the students by sharing their working facilities. One thoroughgoing move in the direction of achieving this aim would be for instance, for a staff to abolish its common room and exclusive toilet facilities.

Perhaps as I spell out the description of such a departure, the obstacles to it become obvious; even without the more alarming elements of this account. Even if the senior staff retain their executive loo and queue for coffee at their own counter, other steps towards a shared membership of the college by staff and students will raise the hackles of professional tradition. Murmurs of 'familiarity', 'disrespect', 'control', 'responsibility', will arise, not only from the teachers, though, but from anxious parents, politicians and employers. All of those who watch from the wings will have their expectation of what a school is, based on what they remember from childhood and, unlike their images of say dentistry or accountancy, anything from quarter to half a century out of date. Terrible consequences will be forecast by extrapolation from a shared conviction that adolescence is a psychopathic disorder, and every slightest evidence that would support the predictions being realized will be seized upon and reported in the press and the council chamber.

An ill-prepared innovation of this kind could well be abortive in the face of concerted opposition. And of course within a public system of education where we are democratically accountable to the community, the possibility of external constraint must be accepted. An innovation that *was* harmful to students would need to be stopped. The moral for the innovators is that they should prepare their ground thoroughly. They need to have thought out the implications of their proposals, not just in general terms (e.g. 'to improve good relationships between staff and students') that no-one will argue with, but in specific detail (e.g. 'this could probably lead to staff and students being on first-name terms with each other'); which many undoubtedly *will* argue with.

They need then to talk these through with those upon whose support they depend, officers, governors, and above all, parents, so that a partnership is formed committed to carrying the innovation through. The whole art of the innovator is in knowing how far he can run ahead of his community supporters without risking loss of their confidence and support. If he doesn't stay ahead and make the running, nothing will happen: if he goes too far into the lead however, he will become hare to their hounds. The legend of Actaeon might provide a parable for the incautious innovator. He was bedazzled with a vision of the naked goddess bathing—raw inspiration. He went too close and was punished by being turned into a stag which his own hounds then killed.

If I turn to the second of my two selected areas of innovation, I want to consider aspects of individualized programmes of study in school, resource-based learning and consequent community involvement. These represent, in my experience, the unfolding of one innovatory sequence. The starting point is once again the learning need of the individual student. If the teacher shifts his position so that he is no longer the imparter of a pre-selected body of knowledge but has become the helper and guide to the student in the identification and solving of problems, then, as I have suggested, he needs to become expert in exploiting the whole gamut of available resources. He has also to be prepared for the unexpected: he is no longer the sole poser of problems: the student will come up with his own.

Where attempts have been made to base a school's study on individualized access to resources, the task before the teachers has been immense. Establishing a resource centre is now possible with the help of other pioneers' experience. This whole area has been talked and written about in ways that save me the space here. What has *not* been adequately investigated is the way in which such an approach to learning can revolutionize a whole school. A thoroughgoing scheme of individualized and flexible group study virtually erases 'the class', as we have known it, and will also blur the defining boundary between a school and its surrounding community.

Take the first point—the erasing of 'the class'. School has always been a concept based on 'the classroom'. School has been a multiple classroom. Most school architecture, even most large, purpose-built comprehensive schools, has essentially produced sets of classrooms, in clusters, in chains, in piles, but, give or take a few flexible halls and studios, it has been the class, after cell-division. Thus a whole-hearted reform of study towards individualized, resource-based programmes is a threat to the natural order of schooling. That is why most innovation in this direction has been half-hearted and a basic architecture of varied spaces arranged around a resource-centre, and encouraging easy modification of spatial arrangements, is still rare. Leicestershire's employment of Farmer and Dark made it possible at Countesthorpe, and there in the early seventies we had to learn rapidly how to use the design to demonstrable advantage, or go under.

However, the disappearance of the recognizable classroom only makes sense if accompanied by a total redirection of the student to his resources for learning. Granted that the teacher will remain the single most important first resource, he or she has to master the whole range of accessible learning points to which the student may be directed. Not only does this mean familiarity with what is available within the school among books, other people, films, tapes, microfiches or whatever, but increasingly as the internal limitations are realized, familiarity with what are the learning points within the local community. The teaching staff needs to know collectively, and in a co-ordinated way, where co-operation can be found in local industry and trade, libraries, archives, registries, where the living record exists in buildings, town layout, coastlines, land utilization, and who are the people with special knowledge that they are prepared to share. The staff must have become outgoing, themselves skilled in social negotiation. Here is yet another area as yet neglected in teacher education.

Logically, the process of community involvement becomes reciprocal. A transaction occurs by which the school student exploits the resources for learning in the community and the community, unless deliberately shut out, begins to exploit the resources within the school. Men may look for ways of using the workshop, young couples book the badminton courts during the twilight periods, mothers organize a creche so that they may use the sewing machines or the library during the day. The walls no longer have broken bottles on top of them: in fact the walls are down.

Although logical, the reciprocal penetration of school by community is not inevitable. There needs to be an act of will expressed by the local authority, the principal and staff. This has happened in isolated cases earlier this century, as when Terry O'Neill opened the doors of his village school in Lancashire between the wars. It has now happened on a wider scale in Community Colleges. And where it hasn't happened, the people need to be led round the walls until some Joshua orders the trumpets to be blown. O'Neill proves that the starting point is not in purpose-built innovative complexes but within the hearts and heads of ordinary people. Now once we have experienced this, the Jericho effect, things are never going to remain the same. A lot has been said recently about control of the curriculum. Most of it has implied that the curriculum can and should be predicted, either by politicians, educational bureaucrats, industrialists, teachers, or a consortium of all four. It has largely overlooked the commonsense point that however authorities may prescribe syllabuses and examinations, what is *learnt* is determined by the learner. The curriculum is nothing if not the sum of learning possibilities within a school, college or system. Unless the institution is a useless sham, the learning outcomes will depend not just on teachers' competence but on students' ambition and interest. We may prescribe what ought to be taught, but we cannot prescribe what the learner will learn. From this we may first take great heart: there is little chance of centrally directed curriculum being effective, however much of a nuisance it might be. But more especially, given the advent of wide-scale community schooling, the curriculum will remain alive, constantly evolving, because democratically based. Here is the real possibility of a continuously changing curriculum, sensitive to and matching the continuous change in the society that it is serving.

It remains to explore the possibilities and practicalities of organizational structure that may accommodate continuous change in its curriculum. It has been well demonstrated that the more hierarchical an institution, the more impervious it is to change, except by the installation of a new innovatory head. It is relatively easy to communicate from the top downwards, relatively difficult, sometimes impossible to communicate from the grass roots upwards. It is quite insufficient in those circumstances for the principal to be a nice guy who makes himself accessible. It may make the situation pleasanter for those working with him, but it won't change anything. And for a school that has tangled with its surrounding community, an impervious institution, even with a charismatic principal, is heading for irreconcilable conflict and disillusion. Charisma fades, and everything else is much as it was before.

The problem is therefore one of how to create structures that permit innovation to have its starting point not just near the top, but wherever the creative idea may spark. (By what perverse judgement does any chief administrator believe that he has more or sounder new ideas than others, particularly those younger or more recently arrived with a fresh eye?) A system needs, obviously, to be safeguarded against crack-brained or ill-thought out innovations. Fresh insights need to be worked on, experience and specialized knowledge brought to bear upon them until the eventual implementation has adequate support and commitment from those involved, by which time the originator's idea may have been quite transformed. This transformation of the first author's idea is important and in no way contradicts my thesis: the fresh idea will have been fertilized, where in so many schools it languishes and dies of despair.

The structure that will be open to the fertilized idea is one modelled on some pattern of federated and mutable groupings, responsible to each other, and ultimately to the collective institution. Many variants are possible though few have been realized—very few indeed in schools. This is not entirely surprising since it calls for the principal to shed a major degree of the internal power still traditionally vested in him, while still being contracted to carry the same degree of external responsibility, accountable to governors and local authority. He needs to be there to advise, influence, giving continuity and co-ordination, without directing. He needs to be informed about all that is developing, but humble enough to accept that it is not his baby. No local authority has yet, to my knowledge, contracted a principal in stated recognition of his power being shared within the college. They need, and particularly at the present time of tendencies towards political control, to have someone's head on the block, and not someone's at Shire Hall. It may seem rash to put one's head on the block without retaining control of one's organization. Yet this is what chairmen and directors do. Why not principals?

And yet such power shedding must come about if innovation is to keep pace with social change in the way I suggested earlier. No greater hope for this exists than in the community college. The Taylor Report gave a nudge in the right direction by urging a shift of power towards the community of users of a school. But it does not go nearly far enough. There still remains that Governing Body, meeting infrequently, still offering too many of its places to worthies with little conception of what the college is striving to do and with little commitment to anything much more than a cosy repetition of the past, when what is required is a government of the college by those whose interests are most deeply vested in it, namely the users.

Now if those users include not only those employed there, but the students, increasingly mature as statutory leaving ages are raised, extended to learners of all ages who have identified their needs and educational ambitions on a lifelong scale, then there is distinct possibility of the creation of an organic college, community-based, sensitive to the ebb and flow of varying activities, open to constant grouping and regrouping, never finalized and accepting a continuous change as the normal course of events.

One form of open structure, capable of steady evolution, would be a structure that balanced control between a broad-based community council, a professional executive and some ultimate general assembly of users. The first body would involve parents, staff, students, community members free of remoter politicians and other deadwood that are to be found in normal governing bodies, and it would meet more frequently than Governors do, say monthly. The professional executive would work in close contact with officers of this community council, and operate through such sub-committees and working parties as necessary. This executive would replace the principal as we now know him. The final appeal body and upholder of policy would be the general assembly, called as needed or anyway once a term. This would consist of all users, parents, students, class and club members, teachers, in such numbers as cared to attend. Its constitution would require agreement by consensus in which no one group of membership could impose its will on the others. I offer this not as a final answer but as a discussion model, a contribution to the urgent search for new paradigms. There is sufficient chance of such an apparatus working for it to merit consideration by a local authority. We hear a lot about trusting the community to help itself. Perhaps one day we may see sufficient power being handed to a local community to run its own college in some such way as I have outlined. It might in the long run be a way that will enable people to find that change is not just something unpleasant that can happen to them but something they can control so as to choose to bring it about to their own advantage.

The Practice

Bibliography

HOLMES, G. (1952) *The Idiot Teacher*. Faber. Re-issued by Spokesman Press 1977.
MASON, S.C. (Ed.) (1970) *In Our Experience*. Longman.
PETERS R.S. (Ed.) (1976) *The Role of the Head*. Routledge.
POPPER, K. (1945) *The Open Society and its Enemies*. Routledge.
TOFFLER, A. (1970) *Future Shock*. Random House.
WATTS, J.F. (Ed.) (1977) *The Countesthorpe Experience*. Allen & Unwin.
WATTS, J.F. (1980) *Towards an Open School*. Longman.

Resources for Learning in Community Education

Ron Mitson

Resources play a crucial part in any community's morale and its development towards becoming self-supporting and achieving maturity. The access to and control of resources is of great significance. The community that is deprived of access to, and eventually some control of, resources will lack any incentive or motivation towards achieving a hoped for maturity. It will either stagnate in apathy—or its self-motivation, as opposed to the whips and carrots of external influences, will challenge the right of access to and control over the resources, or go towards a divergent culture that can be supported by whatever range of resources it does have some access to and control over. This applies as much to our community of pupils in school as it does to the more adult community they will later join.

The widely-held view society has of school is that it is a place where one should work to become educated, and that education includes access to important ideas, concepts and skills. Unless the teacher offers access to these, whatever else he may believe education includes, he will not convince those who come, steeped in that widely-held view, that he is providing what they need.

Community schools and colleges cannot escape from the fact that their major function must still be the education of their students, although that education must be coherent with, and compatible with, their overall philosophy, aims, and involvements with community.

For that reason, I shall make no more than a passing reference to the local community as a resource for learning, to volunteer parents, or to the use of people in the community as resources. In developing Codsall Comprehensive School as a community school in 1971 we suggested that the local community might include people with interests and enthusiasms that they would like to share with other people. We offered, if they came forward and were willing to involve our pupils as well as adult members of the community, to help in advertising and forming the groups, and to provide facilities as cheaply as possible. By the end of a year we had established ten joint adult/pupil groups, nine of which were run by members of the community, not teachers. There must now be many schools throughout the country able to offer such examples of people used as learning resources, shared between school and community.

Nor shall I deal particularly with curricular aspects such as community service, learning about how society is governed and provides services, and may be served or modified, or about the varieties of social institutions, such as trade unions, and their implications. These are now regarded more as elements of a general education and many schools include them as part of curriculum. Perhaps we fail sometimes to remind ourselves that every school is, must be, a community school to a greater or lesser, or better or worse, degree.

The validity of any school's regard for itself as a community school must depend on the relevance and quality of the community resources that it makes use of and the aspects of curriculum that it values. My main concern about resources for learning here relates to our use of them in creating the learning environment. In dealing with this more fundamental issue, I enter the arena of what is commonly known as 'hidden curriculum'. This applies to anything the pupil is learning by implication from the situation he finds himself placed in or from the learning environment that has been created for him. It may not be the explicit or implicit message that the teacher or the school intends the pupil to receive, and can be illustrated by the pupil's reaction: 'How can I hear what you say, when what you are is thundering in my ears?' Needless to say, what we are is often demonstrated by what we do and the systems and situations that we create.

Community implies a group of people sharing together, despite many individual differences, in a common major purpose. Many of us have envisaged a change of relationships between teacher and pupil in community schools, so that both become partners in the enterprise of learning. The reality is much more difficult to achieve. So many teachers come straight out of training imbued with the ideals of respecting pupils—wanting to treat them at the level of equality in human relationships, and be nice and polite to them, and say 'please', assuming that they will respond in like manner—and are astonished at what really happens.

The teacher may even believe in the educational value of handing over some aspects of control, and offering pupils the opportunities to express opinions, and form councils, and vote. All this, however, will be in relation to peripheral things: how the school fund should be spent, for instance, or what should be sold in the tuck shop, and will have little relevance to what the majority of pupils will inevitably believe that school should be all about—the work of learning what society feels that they need to know. The teacher remains in the dominant control position of doling this out as and when he thinks fit or is able to do so. To pass control over to his pupils would mean giving them access to and control over the use of learning resources. As long as the teacher remains the only resource in the sense that he must be involved himself or be the sole interpreting intermediary between the student and the use of all other resources, that remains impossible. The pupil's access to and control of the use of the important resources remains therefore severely limited.

The truth is that the working environment creates the relationship. If the normal stance in teaching is the authoritive one, communicating to the passive recipient, who is part of a captive audience already, that which it has been decided he must know, then that is the fundamental relationship, the one that matters. The injection of a pleasant smile and politeness into such a posture will not change, and indeed never has changed, it radically from the 'them and us' to the 'we' relationship.

In a sense, the national move towards comprehensive education and concomitant mixed ability was a major move in hidden curriculum. You cannot say convincingly 'All have equal opportunity and their contributions are equally valued and respected' in a society with imposed segregation or a school with imposed selection. The problem is that we often claim to have mixed ability classes, but many work no more effectively in offering equal opportunity than streamed classes previously did. The pupils have been mixed but the teaching approach has barely changed.

Too many teachers still act as the single central resource, projecting the message at their speed, regardless of whether it is too fast for some and too slow for others. Those who attempt to group at different levels of ability within the mixed ability class but leave so much depending upon themselves as the main central resource, find it impossible to start and support all the different groups without leaving some spending far too much time waiting for the teacher.

Again the reality is often that the teacher is available only at certain set times, can communicate at those times in a way and at a speed satisfactory to only some, not all, of those whose time it is, and can give further individual help at that time to only a small number of those who may need it.

It is often when the teacher finds himself attempting to avoid such difficulties that the structured individualized programmes for thirty or so different pupils that appears to be the logical alternative proves too difficult and time-consuming to create. The agreed compromise is often a series of individualized verbally negotiated programmes so difficult to monitor and so lacking in structure that mixed ability offers the pupils the worst of all deals and is given the worst of all names in 'progressive' education. It is interesting, nevertheless, that in Dr Neville Bennett's researches on the effectiveness of traditional and progressive education in the Lancaster area, the example of structured progressive education came out very well indeed.

At the Abraham Moss Centre, we are attempting to provide this structure by concentration on the early development in all pupils of the skills of learning and using resources so that they are gradually weaned of over-dependence on the teacher and become able to organize the development of their own learning. Alvin Toffler in *Future Shock* said:

Psychologist Herbert Gerjuoy of the Human Resources Research Organisation phrases it simply: The new education must teach the individual how to classify and reclassify information, how to evaluate its veracity, how to change categories when necessary, how to move from the concrete to the abstract and back, how to look at problems from a new direction—how to teach himself. Tomorrow's illiterate will not be the man who can't read—he will be the man who has not learned how to learn.

and in the report of the Committee on Continuing Education, Open University 1976. It states:

The priority should be the provision of preparation for independent study wherever it may lead. Preparatory courses which equip students with basic educational skills therefore seem to the Committee to be obvious subjects for collaboration with other institutions.

Such a move away from over-dependence on the teacher can be successful only if the teacher arranges the introduction towards resources, or guides to resources, structured in such a way that they can be used either:

1 by the teacher with his pupils if he feels it necessary. The intention is by no means to exclude direct contact between teacher and pupils either in the form of expository teaching, when inspiration or illumination is necessary, or in the form of seminar groups or one to one relationships, when the interplay of minds or feelings, or encouragement, or other human inter-relationships may be thought valuable. In fact, the eventual position would allow the teacher the flexibility for more of this in a working environment less stressful in nature, because his involvement with one pupil or group of pupils would not bar the rest from access to the information, etc, on which the whole course was based; or

2 by the student on his own at any time that he chooses, working at his own pace.

For those who find reading extremely difficult, supportive material can be provided on the richosyncrofax, on tapes, and on tape-linked resources; and more teacher-time should be available for their benefit as the brighter pupils can be more self-supportive within such a well-structured situation.

At this stage we distinguish between independence in learning and individualized learning, and are concerned with the former as a priority. If we attempted to concern ourselves too much with the latter, the step-by-step structure that helps our pupils gradually to learn what it means to organize the development of their own learning would be impossible to create for each individual within his own separate programme.

This approach to learning could also be the beginning of a changing relationship between the pupil and the teacher, as the learning role of the one is not so completely dependent upon the role of the other, and elements of a partnership are involved.

From the third year onwards we are attempting to take one step further, although this is proving extremely difficult. We hope to create the year's self-contained courses in particular subjects which at the beginning of the year indicate to the pupil:

1   the information he has to make his by the end of the year;

2   the ideas he has to understand, and use in his thinking, and relate to that information;

3   the skills he has to practise and become proficient in, linked to a range of skill-building packs, so that, when the student has to lead or join in a discussion group, carry out an interview, or provide a statistical analysis, he will be able as an individual to improve his competence in this activity by consulting the appropriate skill-building unit at this level;

4   an indication of a series of areas of further reading and study and research related to the development of the course.

All this is intended to be arranged around a series of sessions with the teacher throughout the year; otherwise the teacher acting in the capacity of tutor, making regular checks on the progress of each student and helping out where problems arise.

An example of one of our work programmes can be seen in figure 5 and an example of a more advanced structured course unit can be seen in figure 6

It is only by exploring such possibilities as this that we may begin to establish an appropriate working environment and relationships. We cannot tell our pupils that because they are fifteen or sixteen years old we expect them to show a more adult and responsible approach to their work, and at the same time leave them in the completely dependent situation where they have no idea what work they are expected to do next, hour-by-hour, until the teacher walks in at the door of the classroom and says: 'Now today we are going to do "so-and-so"'.

This comparatively childlike dependence may be accepted without complaint by those who have an academic motivation and see an academic reward at the end. However, now that the statutory leaving age has been increased gradually from fourteen to sixteen years for the whole cohort, we have to recognize that many young people, who can already appreciate their budding adulthood, will not necessarily derive much incentive from the 'interest' or 'relevance' of much of their work, and indeed it would be a mistake to educate them to hold the view that all work must, by definition, be interesting. They will gain far more incentive and motivation from being placed in a position where they are able to adopt a comparatively adult approach to their work, and have some control over their own destinies in being able to an increasing extent to organize the development of their

Figure 5

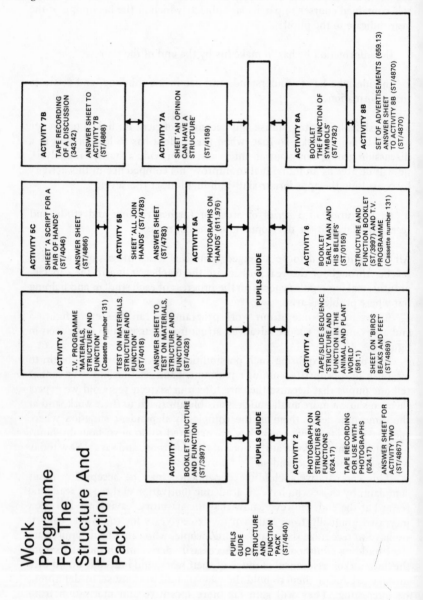

Work
Programme
For The
Structure And
Function
Pack

PUPILS GUIDE TO STRUCTURE AND FUNCTION 'PACK' (ST/4540)

PUPILS GUIDE

ACTIVITY 1
BOOKLET STRUCTURE AND FUNCTION (ST/3997)

ACTIVITY 2
PHOTOGRAPH ON STRUCTURES AND FUNCTIONS (624.17)
TAPE RECORDING FOR USE WITH PHOTOGRAPHS (624.17)
ANSWER SHEET FOR ACTIVITY TWO (ST/4867)

ACTIVITY 3
T.V. PROGRAMME 'MATERIALS, STRUCTURE AND FUNCTION' (Cassette number 131)
TEST ON MATERIALS, STRUCTURE AND FUNCTION (ST/4018)
'ANSWER SHEET TO TEST ON MATERIALS, STRUCTURE AND FUNCTION' (ST/4028)

ACTIVITY 4
TAPE/SLIDE SEQUENCE 'STRUCTURE AND FUNCTION IN THE ANIMAL AND PLANT WORLD' (591.1)
SHEET ON 'BIRDS BEAKS AND FEET' (ST/4869)

ACTIVITY 5C
SHEET 'A SCRIPT FOR A PAIR OF HANDS' (ST/4046)
ANSWER SHEET (ST/4866)

ACTIVITY 5B
SHEET 'ALL JOIN HANDS' (ST/4783)
ANSWER SHEET (ST/4783)

ACTIVITY 5A
PHOTOGRAPHS ON 'HANDS' (611.976)

ACTIVITY 6
BOOKLET 'EARLY MAN AND HIS BELIEFS' (ST/0159)
STRUCTURE AND FUNCTION BOOKLET (ST/3997) AND T.V. PROGRAMME (Cassette number 131)

ACTIVITY 7B
TAPE RECORDING OF A DISCUSSION (343.42)
ANSWER SHEET TO ACTIVITY 7B (ST/4868)

ACTIVITY 7A
SHEET 'AN OPINION CAN HAVE A STRUCTURE' (ST/4159)

ACTIVITY 8A
BOOKLET 'THE FUNCTION OF SYMBOLS' (ST/4782)

ACTIVITY 8B
SET OF ADVERTISEMENTS (659.13)
ANSWER SHEET TO ACTIVITY 8B (ST/4870)

PUPILS GUIDE

Figure 6

An example of a more advanced structured course unit:

STRUCTURED GUIDE
(at two reading levels: average and easier)

Teacher's note: indicating aim of unit, target group and intended use.

Pupil's note: simple indication of how to use it.

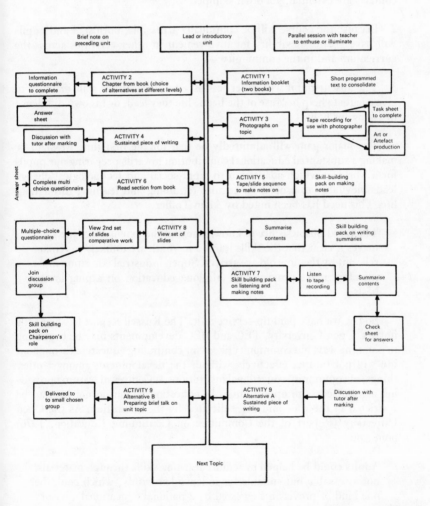

own learning. Conversely, any adult placed in the position that we still place the majority of our fifteen and sixteen year olds in, of remaining dependent on being told almost hour by hour what to do next, would be completely demoralized and lose any incentive to work.

There will be additional gains in adopting such an approach to learning:

1   Because the basic information and ideas are accessible to pupils without the teacher having to spend so much time explaining and rehearsing them, the teacher will have much more time and energy to spend on the aspects of courses and of community education where human relationships and contacts are essential, yet often skimped.

2   Because the course will be continually accessible, both staff and pupils will have greater flexibility for involvement in other activities across the curriculum and in the community.

3   The absent pupil will suffer less as a result of either staff inability to give adequate help because of the hectic life they lead, or his own diffidence in asking for help.

The major gain will admittedly be that for the first time we shall be making a substantial educational contribution towards preparing our pupils for a world in which adaptation to rapid social and technological change leads inevitably to a need for regular retraining and learning throughout life. This need has been noted by Alvin Toffler:

> The rapid obsolescence of knowledge and the extension of life span makes it clear that the skills learned in youth are unlikely to remain relevant by the time old age arrives. Super-industrial education must therefore make provision for life-long education on a plug-in-out basis.

So far, we have paid lip-service to it. The Russell Report has had little impact. Open University, TEC and BEC developments may be beginning to point the way, but community needs for continuing education throughout life will not be met effectively without the development, amongst other things, of community educational institutions as Centres of learning providing a wide access to opportunities in education which do not have to be restricted to the time and place dictated by the institution. As the Open University (Report of the Committee on Continuing Education, 1976) points out:

> Adults could be helped to acquire learning skills through materials, not assessable but suitable for independent study, which could be one kind of provision suggested by a national educational advisory

service. Such materials could be made available in a package which not only identified the student's shortcomings, but also helped to correct them by providing appropriate remedial activities, and this could co-exist beside a range of preparatory courses currently provided by the National Extension College and local colleges of further education throughout the country.

The Abraham Moss Centre is possibly most favourably placed to become such a centre of learning, meeting the needs of different groups in different ways. We are already aiming to help our pupils in school to know how to organize the development of their own learning and, given that some students, because of their ability or because of the type of course they are following, will always need more teacher help than others, it seems eminently sensible to organize the education we offer to people in the area on a discriminatory basis in terms of teacher contact.

In practice, this would mean, amongst other things, that we would:

1 provide regular and close contact with the teacher for those students who need it most, whether because their basic skills in terms of literacy or numeracy will not allow them autonomy, or because they need the teacher's constant help and guidance in laboratory work, technical work, craft and other creative arts.

2 provide packaged or plug-in courses for those students who are capable of working at home for part of the time, and in those subjects or areas of subjects where that is possible—so that a course might vary from eighty per cent centre-study with the teacher, and twenty per cent home-directed study, to twenty per cent tutored study with the teacher and eighty per cent home-directed study.

3 make facilities and accommodation available to groups in the community who wish to make use of them on a self-supporting basis and to groups who wish to make use of them on the basis of occasional teacher help and advice. The group which meets year after year because it enjoys the social occasion of, let us say, a dressmaking class should not be discouraged from doing so. The need to meet is there. It may not however warrant the time of a full-time teacher when there are other groups whose greater needs we may not be able to meet because of the lack of a teacher.

4 be able to expand our teaching force and our influence beyond the finite limits of the walls of the centre, and meet the needs of people throughout the area more flexibly and effectively.

Obviously, we have a long way to go before we reach such a goal, and much thought and planning needs to go into its achievement during the next few years. Our over-arching concern in community education must be to help our students to become adults able to take advantage of such opportunities and able to some extent to develop the autonomy of their own curriculum. In the report of the Committee on Continuing Education (Open University, 1976) it is suggested that:

> Changes in technology have exerted powerful shaping forces on society but have led paradoxically to an increasing emphasis on the need for individual independence and opportunity.

They will not learn this independence of the teacher and ability to organize the development of their own learning merely by the telling. Unless we structure their learning in such a way that they gain the experience and our explicit aims are reinforced by the implicit messages of the hidden curriculum, they may remain dependent because we keep them so in practice.

The Open University's view that sixteen to nineteen year olds, for instance, do not have the maturity, and therefore do not exhibit the ability, to cope with independence in learning, and therefore opportunities should not be extended to them is naive in not taking into account the fact that so far the sixteen to nineteen year old groups' earlier experiences in our education system have not been designed to wean them gradually of dependence on the teacher. Eleven year olds are capable of some independence in learning, and thirteen to fourteen year olds of even more, given the opportunity through well structured experience to learn to cope. In such a developing situation, of course, literacy must have a high priority in the teacher's, and will have a high priority in the pupil's mind.

The teacher must therefore accept his status as the most important resource, but be willing to create alternatives to himself. Indeed, in many cases he may structure resource guides and resources so that they are dual-purpose, and so that the teacher may use them in his teaching, or, because they incorporate instructions and guides that will interpret them and their possible uses directly to the student if the teacher is not available, the student may use them alone in following the course of his study. To this extent, the teacher's status will increase, because he will add to his still-needed expository and human relationship skills, those of the creator and manager of effective learning environments and opportunities. Freed from having pupils dependent upon him for the transmission of the essential information, he will be able to maintain closer contact with, and more flexible relationships with, individuals and groups. Positive discrimination in the classroom and school will become more feasible, and move more towards those who need most help with learning. In community education terms, positive discrimination in staffing to help small 'A' level groups survive in diminishing sixth forms is a misapplication of resources that could be better used elsewhere. If small sixth form groups are to survive, they should do so by greater reliance on the students' ability to organize their own learning.

Creating such learning opportunities makes increasing demands on the teacher's time outside the classroom. To some extent, this may be alleviated by collaboration with colleagues. When resources have to be created or adapted to meet the particular needs that the teaching staff of a school are conscious of, a group of staff working together in planning the courses, in benefiting each other by the cross-fertilization of ideas, in pooling suggestions for materials and in the joint reappraisal of materials after use, offer valuable opportunities for professional support and growth to one another. If they share the production of resources they decrease the amount of work that might fall on one member of staff.

It is by no means necessary to create the full range of resources in order to provide such learning opportunities. A well-structured guide can direct the student towards a variety of resources at different levels of difficulty, the vast majority, if not all, of which may have been bought commercially and either annotated or supplemented for the purpose or used unmodified.

Above all, in this connection, the time may have come for us to examine as a profession the stress we place on ourselves by claiming what is in any case a virtually impossible autonomy for the individual teacher. Many teachers impress only themselves with claims of autonomy when tied to the same text book or course book that thousands of others use. Any teacher really exercising that vaunted autonomy and insisting on producing everything for his own course must absorb an enormous amount of his own time and energy on this task and may still not produce material of equal merit to published resources. The lack of resources published in such a way that the teacher might use them or students might use them independently could be largely overcome if there were some commercial or wider professional move towards producing ranges of such materials. Lending themselves to self-directed study, with guides leading to the central core of resources and banks of options, such banks of material might cover the informational aspects of the whole of a regional and national examination board syllabus at 'O' or 'A' level, for instance. In the report of the Committee on Continuing Education (Open University 1976) it states:

> The re-shaping of tomorrow requires considerable commitment to and expenditure on the education of adults today. In this context the extended provision of adult education can only be achieved if it is made with utmost cost-effectiveness. To this end it will need to utilise to the full the savings which accrue when learning resources have standard elements which can be widely used, and which encourage independent learning.

The teacher would then be able to adapt or modify to suit his own purposes without an unwarrantable expenditure of time and energy, and the student would have both a learning experience that would help him develop independence in learning, and a fall-back situation if he preferred or had to rely on his own resources.

The Practice

Professionally, all this would require, amongst other things:

1 Some agreement at local, regional or national level about the basic core elements of information, ideas, skills and concepts to be included in certain courses. Some of these agreements might be based on Examination Board, TEC and BEC syllabii.

2 Collaborative arrangements at local, regional or national level to produce, keep under review, and update the range of resources, or guides towards resources, that would act either as the pupil's base for independent study, or the base which the teacher might use to elaborate a range of strategies for teacher/pupil involvement in learning. 'The development of centrally produced materials to be used as resources should be encouraged, as should the stimulation of resource production locally.' (Open University, Report of the Committee on Continuing Education, December 1976.) In each case the range of resources would be at different levels of understanding and vary in type, structure and approach, depending upon the subject and its needs.

Nevertheless, if we are to function effectively at a professional level, sharing all the planning, and developing work, and reappraising, we need regular times during the working year when teachers come together to do this not merely because of their goodwill but because it is a required part of their professional involvement. Teachers try to fit in to the hectic corners of a harrassed teaching day too much that could be more effectively done at times when they are not conscious of their immediate responsibility for pupils also.

Creating such a learning environment will not be effective unless:

1 Resources, including expensive audio-visual resources, and equipment are centralized as much as possible so that they may be shared by as many different people as possible and be used to fulfil as many different purposes as possible. The Art Department may use slides of the miscroscopic world bought by the Science Department, to stimulate its students to creative art about the microscopic world.

They should be accessible to the community also. The student who wishes to review some work, for instance, may have as much need of access to an audio-visual aid as the member of staff who may initially have used it with him. At the Abraham Moss Centre, access is shared through the public library so that school and college use all the public resources and the community may use resources originally bought for school and college use. 'The Committee therefore recommends that the Council of the Open University should strongly support the integrated development and use of the library services, both public and in educational institutions such as universities, polytechnics and colleges, as part of a general improvement of this national resource in continuing education.' (Open University, Report of the Committee on Continuing Education, December 1976.) Students who have used audio-visual aids are not released into an adult world where these are no longer available.

2   Support services for those involved in creating such learning guides and opportunities and adapting and modifying materials should include an effective storage and retrieval system, to help staff, students and members of the community find the resources they need with ease, and good secretarial and technician help and reprographic facilities to ensure that any home-produced materials do not appear third-rate in comparison with commercially-produced ones.

3   In-service training at 'shop-floor' level. The major part of this comes naturally in the cross-fertilization of ideas and in the drawing on and learning from colleagues' strengths that takes place in planning and working as a member of a team rather than in isolation.

Many of the changes involved in teaching approach are radical and, as most of us have been conditioned for fifteen years as pupils ourselves to view directing the class from the front at a single pace as teaching, we need help in adapting to new methods. Exposure to new theory and ideas is not enough help. Teachers will not lightly desert that which they know and are, to whatever degree, successful in, for the insecurity of a new approach of which they have comparatively little experience. The more successful they are, the more they will prefer to stay with the methods that they have proved themselves capable of operating. Only the opportunity for them to discover that they can achieve adequacy in the new methods by having a go at them in practice, as it were, will help them feel secure enough to introduce the new methods into the classroom. For that reason, we try to take three or four of our staff off timetable for as much as a week at a time to give them the opportunity, working with those who have already been successful, to explore the new methods at the level of experience, discovering how to structure materials to fit the new approach and learning many things about the new classroom situation. Staff can only be released from timetable in this way because colleagues have been willing to accept the reciprocal professional benefits that accrue to all if being willing to cover for colleagues means eventually being released because they will accept the need to cover for you for the same purpose also.

Inevitably, this must be linked with opportunities for in-service training outside the institution. The teacher has as much need as any other member of the community to adapt to the increasing pace of change in the world. The real impact of computer chip-based technology on education, and particularly home-learning, has yet to be felt. Alvin Toffler's vision in *Future Shock* anticipates that:

Advanced technology will, in the future, make much of this unnecessary. A good deal of education will take place in the student's
own room at home or in a dorm, at hours of his own choosing. With
vast libraries of data available to him via computerised information
retrieval systems, with his own tapes and video units, his own
language laboratory and his own electronically equipped study carrel,
he will be freed, for much of the time, of the restrictions and un-
pleasantness that dogged him in the lockstep classroom. We have
reached a dialectical turning point in the technological development
of society. And technology, far from restricting our individuality,
will multiply our choices—and our freedom—exponentially.

Thus the community and the adult world may be deluged with a range of
educational alternatives and possibilities within a few years. When that
time comes teachers will either be seen as having helped to prepare the way,
in developing programmes and the learners' skills, and will be accepted in
the partnership as helpful guides and tutors, or their counter-like stance
in face of such a tide of development will lose them much of the respect
and influence they might have had in what will be an enormous expansion
of learning within the community.

In Education, we spend too much time involved in 'great debates'
about the curriculum, the impact of which becomes little more than merely
grouping different disciplines, or pushing their names about on the timetable chequer-board. There are times when, although we appear to make
major changes, the final outcome is little different. Macro changes in
education will always be ineffective and have little impact unless they are
followed by concomitant changes at the micro level, where the teacher puts
the change into operation with the pupil in the classroom. As a macro change,
comprehensive education still awaits to some extent upon the change in
attitudes and relationships that must take place within the schools and (as
mixed ability teaching is to some extent for certain age ranges, a logical
development of comprehensive education) within the classroom.

Community Education is now becoming another macro-level development. The education offered by community schools and colleges should
be compatible with their other aims. That education (for education is still
the major aspect of their work), must offer more than the mere reshuffling
of titles and disciplines. If it does not at the hidden curricular and micro
level reflect what many of us claim, and all that that implies, at the macro
level, then the other aspects of community institutions may lack a safe and
solid foundation. The adult's increasing capacity to cope with his own life
and the autonomy of his own curriculum, is the rock on which self-supportive, independent, flourishing communities may more certainly be
established.

The School and the Community[1]

Stewart Wilson

The title is a little unfortunate because it implies two separate entities, the school on the one hand and the community on the other whereas I shall try to prove the thesis that the school and the community are inseparable. I shall try to do this in three ways:

1 by showing that what we are doing in many of our schools is not what I feel education should be about.

2 by showing what I feel is wrong with society itself.

3 by showing how the school and the community should come together to build a new democratic society where real social justice, real equality of opportunity and real living are found.

I believe absolutely in comprehensive education as a principle but I am saddened at what I see happening in practice in the name of comprehensive education. Alright—we have some fine new buildings and we do away with the iniquities of the 11 + selection system. But then what? Do we then start to select within those fine new schools so that the child who was in the 'D' stream in the old Secondary Mod is now in the 'G' stream in the new comprehensive? Will our syllabuses be re-written from preface to conclusion so that they try to find out what is relevant and meaningful for our youngsters—or will they have the odd paragraph tagged on here and there to accommodate the so-called high fliers—or the so-called remedials, depending on who gets the Head of Department jobs? Will the CSE examination—which is becoming so well established in the secondary mods and accepted by parents and employers in its own right and by the kids themselves—now have to play second fiddle again to 'O' level in order to prove that 'of course' our comprehensive are as good as the grammar schools? Will the move towards internal assessments under Mode III which gives to teachers their rightful responsibility for assessing what has been learnt from their teaching now be arrested in favour of the safer more traditional, yet totally anonymous examination of Mode I? Indeed will our new schools perpetuate the myth that there are two separate species of pupil—one which has this right to be assessed at all and one which has the doubtful privilege of following 'Newson type courses' but which cannot be entrusted to leave school with the bits of paper which society, rightly or wrongly demands for entry to its rat race?

115

Even more fundamentally do we really still believe that the correct way to teach children is to assemble thirty of them in a classroom, sit them all in rows and then expect them all to be equally interested in what we have to say, to absorb it all in equal quantities, to apply the information given by us in identical ways in their homes or neighbourhoods or jobs—or even to attend our lessons day after day, week after week as a unit of thirty without illness or absence which by the very nature of our teaching puts them at an immediate disadvantage? Would we be so dammed careless with the real status symbol of our society—the motor car? Would we allow it to proceed along the conveyor belt missing out the odd vital piece every now and again?

Whether we like to admit it or not absenteeism is becoming a real problem in our schools—it is becoming a national problem in all walks of life and at all levels of society. Now given attractive learning and working conditions, given a real democratic involvement in what we are doing, given a national programme of health education I am sure we can reverse the trend but children and adults will still fall ill and yet we slavishly allow the classroom conveyor belt to grind on. Recent research has shown that if a school of 1,000 pupils had ninety-five per cent attendance during a week it would in fact mean that 100 pupils had some time off. If the attendance was ninety per cent 200 pupils would have missed time; if eighty-five per cent 300 pupils.

Do we find it totally impossible to treat each pupil as an individual—at least for part of the time? And are we going to continue making the excuses I have been hearing since I first came into teaching that individualized learning situations are alright if one has the time as a teacher to prepare individual work assignments? Colleagues, we have to make time.

And will our new schools get away from the hierarchical structure which bedevils our present school administration? Will headteachers begin to realize that they are not god-like figures able in themselves to give instant answers on issues ranging from educational policy, personnel and staffing matters, financial considerations and a whole portfolio of day to day disciplinary and welfare problems? Will every member of staff—right from the youngest probationer be made to feel that he is part of an educational adventure so that his less obvious energies and talents may be released for the common good—instead of lying dormant and frustrated as happens in so many schools at the present time? Above all, will the young people who will inhabit our new schools be allowed some real say in what we are planning to do with them. How often do we as teachers ever sketch out to our pupils exactly what their course in a particular subject is going to contain each term? How often do we encourage their participation in formulating their curriculum—especially in their early years or in compiling the individual subject syllabus?

I am a great believer myself in the common curriculum at least in the early years in the comprehensive if only as a means of ensuring that no child has severe gaps in his education but it doesn't therefore follow that the component parts must be in identical quantities for each boy and girl.

On the question of pupil democracy isn't it really time we stopped mimicking the old style public school with its elite band of prefects dispensing their instant brand of judgments and justice. Can't we realize that no prefect system in the world will adequately control discipline in the corridors and cloakrooms of our large comprehensive and that the only form of real control is the self control vested in each individual pupil?

And what of the parents and the community around the school? How welcome do we really make our parents in our schools? Oh, I know we have our open days and our parents meetings but in how many secondary schools are parents or members of the public openly encouraged to come into school at any time to see the sort of work we are doing with their children or better still to participate in the lesson itself. How many are encouraged to come in to have school lunch either with or without their children? How many are encouraged to come back into school in the evening—not as part of a formal evening class but just to try out things they have never tried before—to bounce on the trampoline perhaps or hit a shuttlecock for the first time—or play five-a-side or table tennis with their youngsters in the sports hall or to dabble with colour and patterns in the art studios or develop their holiday photographs in the school dark room—or to try out the electric cooker in the HE room to compare it with their gas cooker at home—or to do some turning on the lathe or sharpen their tools on the grinder.

Now I know that many of you would like to say, 'Yes, but we are doing this or we are doing that in our schools already. Some of the things you are advocating are common practice in many of our schools.' But how many schools are there, I wonder, where the Head and his staff have ever really sat down to consider what their total philosophy should be—or if they have, have then published it for everybody in the school and surrounding community to see? I know there are many wonderful innovations taking place in our schools but I feel the whole lot lacks purpose and co-ordination for the simple reason that we have never really stopped to consider what our schools are really for and what their place in our local community is to be.

How many schools are still organized in the belief that the staff is made up of so many specialists? First we have the administration specialists— the Head and his three deputies—and perhaps a Head of Upper School and Head of Lower School for good measure. You know you'll find some wonderful definitions of the roll of the Deputy in the advertisement columns. There was one which referred to the second Deputy as the 'Academic Registrar', no less, whose appointment, and I quote, 'would augment the second tier of the school's management structure'. I just hope there will be somebody left in that school to do the teaching. There are the subject specialists who so jealously guard their own field of operation. We have that new breed of specialist—the House Tutors or Year Tutors or School Counsellors. These are the trouble shooters—the people who pick up the problems—the classroom trucculence or the broken home, the poor attendance, poor time-keeping or the emotional crisis. When will we realize that what we are doing is to re-write the law of Parkinson in big bold capitals. You withdraw more and more majors and colonels from the front line to do the admin and pastoral work with the general behind the scenes, leaving younger and less experienced subalterns and privates to stick it out at the battlefront which in itself creates more and more casualties to be patched up by the men at the rear. It is a ridiculous state of affairs because the one factor which is remaining pretty static while we pile on the superstructure is the staffing ratio. Administrators will trot out the figures eighteen or nineteen, but how many young English teachers or maths teachers or science teachers or geography or history etc. etc. ever teach classes of eighteen?

Is it any wonder that many of our younger teachers must be getting somewhat disillusioned about the education system? As our secondary schools amalgamate under various re-organization schemes and so become larger, and fewer, they are in fact in danger of seeing their chances of total involvement in the school becoming less and less. Obviously they cannot all aspire to senior posts in the large new comprehensive and many of them must wonder at the prospect ahead. Is their week to consist of teaching their classes of thirty or so pupils for thirty-six periods out of forty, leaving little energy or inclination for educational reading and discussion at the end of the day? Are they to see policy decisions kept increasingly in the hands of a select few at the top and even the contact with parents to be the prerogative of the pastoral staff?

I welcome anything which gives increased finance and status to our profession, but *please* make sure they are teachers first and administrators second. I have started by posing what I hope are pertinent questions about our schools because they constitute an area we understand. This is where we operate—the school is our pitch. The area outside the school is less familiar territory for many of us, but I am totally convinced that in fact the two areas, the school and the community, are inseparable. So let us now look at this other area—the community.

Stapylton is fairly typical of any industrial neighbourhood in the north-east. First of all we have the raison d'etre of the area—the steelworks or the engineering works, in this case the Cleveland and Lackenby works of British Steel and the Smiths Dock Shipyard. Further out there is the huge chemical complex of ICI Wilton. It is hard industry with dirty, dangerous and often deafening working conditions. We all know the picture—from the outside.

Then there is the housing. There are still the terraces of nineteenth-century or early twentieth-century houses backing onto the works themselves. Gradually these are giving way to the sprawling new housing estates with their odd blocks of high-rise flats. The process of transfer is a painful one with the old established community with its family loyalties, its neighbourliness, its corner shops, being torn asunder and having its heart ripped out before the new community on the estate has even approached the weaning stage. People are lost. They have lost the security of familiar territory and they have lost the security of family ties—and in their place? A modern house (yes with a high rent); a new shopping centre (half a mile away for some); their kids going to a large new school (along with 1,200 other kids); a brand new social club with Cyril Lord carpets and keg. bitter; the club circuit comedians and pop groups four nights a week.

For some it is a better life. When the money is coming in (especially when both husband and wife are working) the home is like a little palace with fitted carpets, new furniture, a colour telly and the car parked outside. For many it is a constant battle to make ends meet; especially the increasing number who are unemployed and those on social security or supplementary benefits. It is a struggle to supervize or satisfy their children; or quite simply to get any serenity or contentment out of life. And what about those who are left behind in the diminishing rows of terraced houses down by the steelworks? They are often the ones with the least energy or inclination or ability to move; the old, the permanently unemployed, the broken families, the immigrants—and that increasing band of wanderers—the ones who commute from one twilight area to another following the casual job market or their latest sleeping partner or escaping their debts.

I am not dramatizing the situation. There are four million people in this country dependent on supplementary benefits—benefits which set the lowest level at which a person is expected to survive. Four million or one in thirteen—twenty per cent of the population or ten million people are living in poverty. Is this the quality of life we should accept in our society in the 1970s? Can we go blindly turning the educational machine in our schools oblivious to the physical and spiritual deprivation which exists around the school?

The two just have to come together. It is no use our creating some cosy little oasis for ourselves in our schools, oblivious to the desert conditions which often exist outside. It is no use our creating a warm and secure environment for our pupils from nine o'clock to four o'clock and then shut our minds to the fact that the prospect for the other seventy hours is bleak and forbidding. If we have the least grain of social conscience we must be involved in the community outside the school. But, on a far more simple professional plane, if the education we are providing in our schools is to have any real meaning or relevance for our boys and girls it must surely be based initially on the community they know and the environment where they live. These two statements of faith really bring me to the nub of my theme, that the school and community are inseparable.

As educationalists *we must* be concerned with the quality of life in the community. Because if we are not, who is to be concerned? Equally important, who is then in a position to do something? The politician? I doubt it. There are many sincere politicians at local and national level. Every now and again they manage to translate their political power into real practical benefit for the whole community. At national level our Health

Service is perhaps our best example of this. But one single politician serving in his local ward or in his national constituency cannot hope to have the contact with the members of his community that a school of some fifty trained educationalists can have, dealing as they are with the young people in that community for seven hours a day. Nor does he have the £1 million resources at his disposal which we as teachers have in our large modern schools. And if not the politician who else? The planners and developers? Some planners do indeed have a deep concern for the quality of life in our community. But on the other hand it is our planners and developers who have been responsible for our soul-less housing estates and the urban motorways which are poisoning many of our town centre areas with noise and pollution. Our legislators? No laws are ever going to solve the problems of violence and vandalism. These are symptoms of a sick society where we find a community at odds with itself. Certainly the help of all these other agencies must be enlisted—but the responsibility for positive action is *ours* as educationalists.

The School. The main job is to remove all the artificial barriers which have been created over the years in the world of education (for any school which has aspirations to be a real community school.) These barriers are many-fold:

1   the barrier which we have put up around our educational buildings, our schools if you like.

2   the barrier which we have put up to other sections of the community.

3   the barrier which we have erected around ourselves as teachers with regard to our teaching role.

4   the barrier with which we have surrounded the curriculum of the school and the subject syllabuses.

5   the barrier we have put up around the young people in our schools as though they become different animals once they step inside the school.

6   the barriers which often exist between a Head and his staff and between different departments in the school.

Let us look at these barriers a little more closely and see if we can't agree that there is no place in the school for such barriers and that the sooner we knock them down the better. Let us start with the buildings. By what divine right are school buildings only open for approximately seven hours a day for 190 days a year? How much longer can we tie up forty-six per cent of our local Council's annual budget on education alone and yet only allow a thirteen per cent use of our building plant and educational resources? Isn't it time we treated our schools as the public property they are with the public having similar access as they do for public libraries, art galleries and parks? Does it make economic or social sense to see our sports hall and playing fields often lying idle in the evenings, at weekends and in the holidays; to have the excellent meeting and rehearsal facilities we have with our halls and lecture theatres and classrooms even lying similarly empty; to provide our schools with sophisticated kitchens and then have only 190 boilings or fry-ups in them each year? And has it never occurred to us that the vandalism which we all bemoan and which itself is partly a product of boredom and frustration finds it greatest expression in the evenings, at weekends and in the holidays in attacking the large isolated, empty and often darkened public buildings? Johnny wouldn't normally throw a brick through a lit window, especially if his mum or dad were on the other side— or better still if he were on the other side of that window himself.

I often think that as a Head I have the best job in the world—not just because of the job itself but because my position and my master key give me access at the weekends and in the holidays to a sports hall when I can take my own youngsters and their friends to let off steam—or a running track and jumping pit for them to test their athletic ability—or a lathe if I want to do a bit of turning myself or a library if I want to refer to some books—and the same applies to my staff. And I often think—why shouldn't other mothers and fathers have this chance to do their thing when they feel like it? Of course there must be safeguards; of course public property must be properly used. But is seven hours a day for 190 days a year proper use?

And then we have the barrier which we erect around ourselves during the day. It is a barrier which allows in our club members, in other words, our pupils—and often reluctantly, associate members of our club such as parents, advisers, HMIs, probation officers, EWO, the school doctor, the careers officer and so on. Is there no place for the non-member? For the unemployed former pupil, or the over-sixties or the handicapped—or the folks across the road so that they can be in a lively atmosphere where there is something going on, where they can meet and chat and drink coffee or have a meal—or actually participate? And what about the under-fives? Could we not very quickly with our expertise and facilities provide a little fairyland for them—a fairyland of sandpits and paint, of things to climb on and of older girls who read stories?

And what about the biggest barrier of all—our professional training which tells us that we are equipped to teach young people between the ages of eleven and sixteen or eleven and eighteen in a building which shall be called a school. Isn't the community our classroom? Couldn't much of our drama and singing and painting and photography for example happen in the market place? Couldn't much of our maths teaching take place in the bus station or the supermarket or the police record office or the town hall computer department? Isn't the living community the real starting and

121

finishing point for our science and geography, history and environmental studies teaching. Isn't this the real world which our pupils should be looking at and listening to and thinking about? And isn't this the way to interest the outsider, the man-in-the street, in education? Professor Halsey, in his Educational Priority report speaks about an educational exhibition which was put on by EPA schools in a Liverpool department store and which attracted 10,000 people. That's more than the average school will attract to it formal parents meetings in a hundred years.

Is it really impossible for the father who is on a two-till-ten shift to join in a school metalwork class in the mornings—or for the mother who has finished her early morning cleaning job to join the cookery class, or for the young unemployed lad who desperately wants to improve his maths to join the CSE group—or the retired trades union official who has a yearning to learn French to join the first year class in the language laboratory? I know that for most of us this is totally new ground—and there will always be those who say—why don't they join a proper evening class? And the answer is, for the same reasons that the other ninety-eight per cent of our population don't join formal evening classes: either because they can never get out in the evenings; or because they are working in the evenings; or because the evening centre is too far away; or because the subject they want isn't on the syllabus; or because they have to sign on for a six-week or twelve-week course; or because they have to pay a lump sum for the course in advance; or because the people who go to the classes are not their type of people; or because they can't take their children with them; or because they don't want to be taught in a formal way but just want to try something out for themselves; or because their own experience of education as children was an unhappy or unrewarding one and one they don't want to risk again; or quite simply because we in the education camp are competing with the pub and the club. If it is a fact of life that most men and women in this country enjoy relaxing over a drink in the evening isn't it really time we shook off the Victorian tradition of our schools and education centres and allowed drinks to be sold—if only for a couple of hours in the evening?

Right from the start the adult centre should be part of the total teaching resources and tutors part of the total teaching staff and as such just as likely to teach eleven year olds as forty-five year olds—as indeed all staff should be. All staff must be prepared to accept a flexible teaching day which may mean that some teach on a Saturday instead of a Friday or evenings instead of mornings. There is nothing more invidious in the teaching profession in my opinion than the question of payment for extra work done out of school hours. As a profession we want to be paid a decent rate for the job and when one is running classes in the evening then you have time off in the day in lieu. At least that way you may preserve your sanity!

There is a further aspect to this barrier which we have erected around ourselves as teachers which is not only anti-educational but smacking of downright hypocrisy. I am referring to the untrained person, untrained as a teacher that is, being allowed into teaching situations with our pupils. We are perfectly happy—as indeed we should be—to allow a non-teacher like the Careers Advisory Officer to talk to a fourth and fifth form group—often with no teacher present and then to answer pupils questions and guide them in decision-making. Or it may be the local ward Councillor talking about the work of the Council—or the old iron-stone miner explaining how they got the iron out of the Eston Hills—or the trade union official from the steel works explaining the negotiating procedure to a group of senior pupils.

In my book those are teaching and learning situations and they are being conducted by the right people. The common factor if you like is that they have all been arranged and controlled by the trained teacher. Is it then too radical to suggest that we take this a stage further, namely that where we can persuade the expert to come into the classroom or teaching situation they are allowed to assist the teacher? There are skilled craftsmen living near our schools—some of them unemployed—who are only too keen to come into school and assist in the teaching situation under the teacher's direction—or to assist the school in some practical way with small construction jobs or with servicing the school vehicle for example. The question of payment doesn't come into it. For them the satisfaction is in using their skills to the benefit of the school and its pupils, or quite simply, in the case of the unemployed, the fulfilment of having something to do— to feel that they are useful again.

Can't we extend this further? We all know of fit and sprightly pensioners living in the old peoples' flats and bungalows near our schools. Many of them would dearly love to come into our schools where there is a bustle and activity rather than sit in solitude in their bungalows. Could they not help in individualized learning situations for example by looking after the mechanical or clerical side of continous assessment whereby they mark up a pupil's assessment card once a skill has been mastered? Could they not assist with the duplication of work cards—or in keeping the filing or stock systems in order and up to date for teachers who are working under pressure? With the development of Mode III Project work requiring endless amounts of local reference material much of which can be gleaned from local newspapers or local radio, is this not also a sphere of activity for the pensioner or for the man in the wheelchair—or the bored middle-class housewife—or the Duke's daughter for that matter, depending on where your school is situated.

Are we then starting to approach real community involvement? Of course the teacher's role in all this is enhanced. He becomes a real teacher. He is no longer in the position of trying to impose his will on a class of thirty reluctant students. He is teaching in the real sense of the word by guiding the individual work schemes of his pupils. Because the best definition I have seen for the verb 'to teach' is Chambers 'to guide the studies of'. Well he would be guiding the studies of his pupils using every bit of help

123

he can lay his hands on. There is another factor in all this which I think is equally important. By involving all sections of the community in the education process we are breaking down the barriers which so often exist between different sections of the community—between the old and the young for example or the fit and the handicapped or the professional and the semi-skilled.

The fourth barrier I mentioned was the one with which we have surrounded the curriculum of the school and the subject syllabuses. Take English, for example, with its slavish insistence on the written word—when in fact ninety-nine per cent of communication for the ordinary man in the street is by spoken word. This should be the subject which builds up confidence in self-expression in the average citizen and we all know by the very nature of our profession how vitally important this confidence is if one is going to develop proper relationships at home and at work; if one is going to make one's voice heard instead of meekly accepting the other person's point of view whether it be on the shop floor, at the union meeting, in the pub or in the home. Of course, as a society we would all like to write well and with the correct spellings but let us first make sure that we can read well and speak with confidence.

Or take maths. When are we going to stop using text-books which are written and printed in London or Edinburgh and instead make up our own text books or work sheets using the maths which is all around us in everyday life? The first maths book I would like to see our seconday children issued with is the local bus timetable and the local 1:50 000 Ordinance Survey map. With documents like these you can provide children with an endless series of interesting and relevant mathematics problems involving everyday arithmetic and statistics and awaken their curiosity about their own environment.

Or take environmental studies. How many people must there be in this country who know about the lifestyle of the Eskimo—or about the unusual habits of the Australian Aborigine and yet they do not know what it is which makes their own village or town or County Borough tick. To many people their town consists of the street where they live, the road to school or work or to the local football ground, the shopping centre, the pub and for a few, the Church. They have never been taught to look at their town from the point of view of seeing what is good about it—or bad about it—what is lacking or what can be improved. They have never been taught to explore their town and its immediate surroundings; to discover what is old and examine what is new. And still we blurb about the Pilgrim Fathers and the Equatorial Rain Forest. To some children, yes, these may be relevant and interesting—but, let us get our priorities right.

Yet again, how many science syllabuses stress the science of living with health education, the care of the body, safety in the home and a practical understanding of the main services of everyday life as the top priority? Under the heading religion how many children in our schools will hear the

Christmas story for the umpteenth time this Christmas and yet, living in a multiracial society as they do, have no conception of what Reincarnation means to the Hindu or Ramadan to the Moslem? Or how many do in fact know about Reincarnation and Ramadan but have never been taught to understand their own prejudices against their coloured compatriots? And how many can recite the ten commandments but have no moral code of their own?

Or in home economics how many pupils are really taught the practicalities of budgeting for a family of six on a total income of £25; of seeking out the cheapest cut of meat and making it into a meal fit for a king; or of having an eye to the small print on the tins of meat or bottle of squash or packet of biscuits which really shows you which purchase will give value for money? This is practical living for most people.

And in physical education how many hundreds of thousands of secondary school boys and girls change into their football kit or hockey kit every week only to run aimlessly up and down a field making up the numbers so that their more skilful team mates can show off their skills—only to cease healthy physical activity the day they leave school because they were not taught the excitement of individual sports like canoeing or rock-climbing or moorland walking or golf or squash or badminton or skating or real athletics, not just the annual sports day jamboree. Leisure hours can be used to recharge the mind and the body rather than be passed away aimlessly in front of the television or in the bingo hall.

I know there is a great deal of work going on in schools and teachers' centres on curriculum development. But there is a danger with phrases like Nuffield Science, Modern Maths, Field Studies, Social Work, Personal Relationships and ROSLA courses being bandied about so frequently, of our being lulled into a false sense of security and into believing that our schools are hot-beds of research and innovation when in fact much of what is happening in many classrooms is no more than a subtle form of child minding—with the child not enjoying the exercise one little bit.

The fifth barrier concerns our attitudes to our pupils. So long as schools consider themselves as something separate from the community then I suppose you can make a case out for school uniform. But is it really our job as teachers to chase Johnny Smith because he is not wearing his school tie or to frown at Mary Brown because her skirt is two inches above the knee instead of one inch. Aren't the real issues of growing up and coming to terms with life just a little more important? Again so long as one is not liable to see Johnny's parents today or tomorrow or this year even, then I suppose it doesn't matter too much if we belt Johnny across the ear hole if he steps out of line—or whack his backside with a cane. But if Johnny's mum has just come into the building for a session in the pottery studio or if you'll be meeting his dad in the table-tennis league at seven o'clock I would suggest that such a crisis in Johnny's behaviour would be less likely to happen in the first place and that if it did occur you are more likely to prefer

125

to place Johnny's chastisement in the hands of the proper people—namely his parents.

Which brings me to my final barrier—the barrier which often exists in our schools themselves—between the Head and his staff or between different sections of staff or different departments in the school. As I said earlier we have got to get away from the idea that the Head is omnipotent—just as staff have got to get away from the idea that they have no responsibility for the overall educative process in the school or for the basic philosophy of the school. As a staff we are all involved in everything that goes on in a school—or should be. As Heads we must come down from our lofty perch and get involved in the new teaching situations we are creating just as assistant staff must be prepared to accept more responsibility for the general administration of the school. Above all everybody must be involved in formulating the philosophy of the school and once the philosophy has been stated then everybody must support it—or get out. There are too many schools where members of staff or different sections of the staff are diametrically opposed on fundamental issues and we can't carry that into our new comprehensive and community schools. Because on them, these new schools of the future, will rest the responsibility for improving the standards and attitudes in our society, standards which in terms of education and the general quality of life are still abysmally low for millions of people.

The Place: on leaving Sutton Centre[2]

The first principle is the absolutely fundamental one of terminology. Having established the principal of terminology and the phrase community education I wish we could move away from the title 'Schools' and 'Colleges'. One of our first tasks at Sutton Centre—before it opened in fact—was to establish the name Sutton Centre and remove any vestige of the word 'school' from the title. Not only are these establishments so much more than schools both in their facilities and their concept—but the sad fact is that the word school is still anathema to so many people (young and old). Keep it simple, keep it general, that's why I like the word 'Centre'.

The second principle is equally fundamental—namely *the principle of location*. James Stone, our Director of Education coined a lovely phrase when writing the feasibility study for Sutton Centre. He spoke about taking education out of the monastery and putting it back into the market place of life. So let us consider for a moment this fundamental matter of the location of our schools. Since the Second World War it has been customary to locate many of our new schools and certainly most of our secondary schools on the periphery of the communities which they serve. If we examine why this should have been so I suspect that there are really two reasons; the first, the long-held and cherished idea of the school (like Fountains, Rivaulx and Jervaulx if you will) in a setting of sylvan peace—the second, a much more mundane reason that the Standards for Schools Regulations require any school other than a purely infants school to have x acres of playing fields and it has generally been considered convenient for the school, as well as aesthetically pleasing, if those playing fields are immediately outside the windows of the school. To achieve such a situation does of course require the school to be placed on the periphery of the town or housing estate.

If we are right in our views that education must come out of the monastery into the market place then I think we shall have to examine afresh the siting of the schools. Look back for a moment at the siting of the very early Church schools and you will find them at the very heart of the community which they were intended to serve—the old village school on the green with the church alongside. In just the same way the thousands of church schools built in our towns in the 1870 spate of church school building were to be found at the very centre of urban parishes. I think that in the future we shall see more and more schools sited in this way, not sited as separate entities, well satisfied if their own surroundings are attractive and securely fenced off from the world outside but sited with due regard to their interdependency with other community facilities—the public library, the health centre, the sports hall and shopping precinct.

Well, James Stone did just that with Sutton Centre—located it right next to the market place in Sutton. What a location for a community school. But of course, such a location brings its pressures. It exposes a school—it exposes its teachers and staff. Three public rights of way go right through Sutton Centre. People see us as we really are—they see our good moments and they see our bad moments. And if also you add the fact that we have no playground at Sutton Centre (thank goodness)—and of course no adjacent playing fields—our pupils have to take their breaks and their relaxation in the classrooms and tutor areas and coffee bars and so the public passing through the building sometimes see some funny things—like teachers and pupils taking their break together, for example!

Our third principle concerns the provision in the building. The building we are talking about is of course much more than a school providing a strictly educational service. And this is why I feel that James Stone and Henry Swain got the formula so nearly right at Sutton Centre. Their first bold move was to site the youth centre (notice, not a youth club but a centre open to all and any young people) right by the building's main entrance. To the left the theatre—to the right the bunker as the youth centre is called. In other words you aren't isolating young people from the rest of the community. You aren't treating them as lepers or untouchables purely because they can be noisey, boisterous, even uncouth at times, and they rev up their motorbikes—and sticking their centre at the back of the building away from everything and everybody else. They persuaded Social Services that Sutton Centre was the place for the physically handicapped and the aged and so we have a day care centre for these people right in the middle of the complex. They have even persuaded Social Services that Sutton Centre was the ideal location for the Probation Service and their social

127

workers—even for the Registrar of Births, Deaths and Marriages—and so the phrase 'from the cradle to the grave' is rather apt at Sutton Centre. They persuaded the Careers Service to move their Offices right next to the bunker I referred to and the University and WEA that they should have some physical provision in the Centre and so provide the opportunity for integration with other adult education provisions in the Centre. They persuaded the District Council to pool their monies with the County to provide rather extensive and lavish sports and recreation facilities on the same site. Above all, perhaps, they made the building attractive and welcoming. Out went cold corridors and dull classrooms and in their place a carpetted, curtained and brightly decorated building which exudes warmth the moment you step inside.

They failed in only one respect with the building—and in many ways that was a matter outside their control—namely the financing of the building. It has been financed in stages with the result that it is still being built nearly five years after it opened. The first section to open, away back in 1973 was *part* of the school provision and that was very much the classroom part. We had no workshop facilities when we opened and no indoor sport facilities for two years and so, sadly, in the public mind the building known as Sutton Centre was seen as a school providing for school children. This was an unfortunate legacy of the financial provision which took us some time to get rid of. My excitement about Deans Centre in Livingston New Town is that when we open on 17 August[3] all the facilities, even including the landscaping, will be complete. There won't be a contractors hut in sight and there will be as many adults in the building on that first day as pupils. The provision should therefore be as all-embracing as possible—but it should be planned to open as one unit.

But having stressed the principles of terminology, location and provision we move on to perhaps the most crucial principle of all—*the principle of management*. Joint management is doomed to failure because with the best will in the world, if you get two or more people running a centre like Sutton Centre (we have nine separate section heads in Sutton Centre with two others, the Building Superintendent and Catering Manager answerable, varyingly, to all nine) the chances of their always agreeing on fundamental matters of principle and philosophy are negligible. (Our Building Superintendent was even asked recently by one section to store their toilet rolls separately—needless to say he told them what they could do with their toilet rolls!) And even if the individuals on the management team agree, the chances of their parent bodies agreeing are even more remote. Because you then have District Councils arguing with the County Council, Education Committees with Social Service Committees, Leisure Services Committees with the Baths and Laundries Committees and very often, as we all know from bitter experience, ne'er the twain shall meet. The public in Sutton were denied access to our magnificent recreation facilities for over a year because the District Council wouldn't see eye to eye with the County

Council over fire regulations and the handicapped people were penned back into their day care centre by a Social Services Committee which no doubt wished to demonstrate its muscle on the pretext that a building which their people had been using for over a year had suddenly become a high fire risk.

Now I'm going to choose my words carefully because I don't want anything I say to be construed as a criticism, real or implied, of my fellow management colleagues at Sutton Centre. They have their brief to work to— and while I might disagree totally with that brief, I must nevertheless respect their duty to carry it out. But it is no use some sections in a complex like Sutton Centre working to a centre-wide policy and others working purely to a narrow, sectional policy. It is no use some sections seeing the Centre as being open to all sections of the community, the rough as well as the smooth, if other sections are playing safe.

It was this frustration—the frustration of seeing the need for one clear policy for Sutton Centre and the impossibility of ever achieving that on the present management structure which finally persuaded me to accept this new post in Scotland with overall control of the complex and one parent body—the Lothian Regional Council. But even then, leaving a place like Sutton Centre which becomes a way of life, is one hell of a wrench.

In fairness to James Stone he wanted one person—a Supremo as he called him, to be in overall control of Sutton Centre. But the District Council were putting a lot of money into the venture and they wanted 'their' man to be responsible for 'their' part of the building. And if he hadn't conceded that point there wouldn't have been a Sutton Centre. Since then reorganization of local government has led to further devolution and dilution of management. That is why it is so heartening to see the move—as in Scotland—towards a Community Education Council because education must be the umbrella under which the whole structure is financed and managed.

Of course there is so much more to management than the purely professional side to it but this is where we are moving into relatively uncharted waters. I think there is so much at stake in the development success of the community school that we must have the professional hand on the tiller—at least in the early stages. Because as professionals we are paid to manage, we are paid to think, we are paid to take decisions. Having said that—and having established the Art of the Possible then, more and more, we must involve our users associations and our school councils in policy-making and self-help management. Initially such bodies would only have advisory powers but once the community produces its own leaders and identifies its own needs then they must increasingly be given executive powers. So much for the principle of management. We must move on now to what I have listed loosely as educational and organizational principles.

Top of my list among these is the principle of maximum use. These buildings are there to be used fifteen hours a day, seven days a week for fifty-two weeks of the year. The staff—and of course I include the teaching staff—must therefore accept the *principle of the flexible day, the flexible week and the flexible year*. And this means that before long we are going to have to grapple with the problem of the teacher contract. At Sutton Centre there is an unwritten contract between the teaching staff and myself that they work a ten-session week (a session being a morning, afternoon or evening). If one puts in an evening or weekend session then one has a morning or afternoon off in lieu during the week. And we only achieved the staffing necessary to give people this time off in lieu by all working an eleventh session during the Centre's first year—five mornings, five afternoons and one evening or weekend session to prove that pupils and parents and the wider community could and did come back in the evenings for a proper two-hour session in the activity of their choice. Having proved our case we were able to persuade the Director that we should have an extra injection of staff to allow for staff time off in lieu. But it needs to be put on a firmer basis than that. As it stands at present this extra staffing must be at the mercy of cuts in educational expenditure and, of course, staff cannot be held to an unwritten contract although it must be stated that in the five years since the Centre opened not one single member of staff has gone back on it. We must cut out bureaucratic red tape. We must make it easy for people to use our buildings by rent-a-room schemes and pay as you learn schemes.

You will have noticed that I referred to the ten-session week and this brings me to the second major principle in this area—the *principle of the block timetable*. Of course, this isn't something peculiar to the community school because I would like to think that all schools are moving away from the anachronism of the forty-minute period and the forty-period week. Not only is it bad educationally—especially if one is talking in terms of mixed ability groupings and a more individualized approach to teaching and learning—which I assume we are—because then the teacher needs time with the individual and the individual needs time with himself and that is something the forty-minute period doesn't give. Not to mention the sheer waste of time moving from A to B (schools operating a forty-period week can literally waste the equivalent of three weeks of teaching time beginning lessons, finishing lessons and with everybody in transit) and also the wear and tear on nerves and the fabric of the building. But in a community school there is a more fundamental reason for the block timetable principle and that reason, quite simply, is the community. If the community are going to be persuaded to come into our community schools—and here, I particularly mean the educational component then we must rid our buildings of those abominable bells which blare out at regular intervals and the avalanches of pupils sweeping from one part of the building to another. If Mrs Smith and Mrs Jones are really going to be persuaded to join in the art class or cookery class—or whatever, they want to be reassured that it doesn't matter too much if they arrive at 9.30 or 9.50 because the lesson will in fact be going on until 12 o'clock. The block timetable helps to relax the building and de-institutionalize it.

This leads on to the third principle in this section. The *principle of mixed ability teaching*. Again, this of course isn't something peculiar to the community school. It is a fundamental principle I would hope of comprehensive education. But if poor Mrs Jones and Mrs Smith have to start wondering whether they should join the 'A' stream or 'C' stream or 'H' stream in our large community schools we shall kill the idea of adult participation stone dead before it starts. Mixed ability teaching does of course demand smaller classes and I think it is high time in our secondary schools we got back to the principle that teachers are paid to teach—they are not paid to have so-called free periods. If we did that and got our most valuable resources of all—our teachers—back into the classrooms we would have our smaller classes. But in our community schools smaller classes are essential for another reason. Quite simply you can absorb one, two, three or four adults into a class of twenty-four. It is a darned sight more difficult to absorb them into a class of thirty or thirty-four.

Which leads me into principle four in this section—and this for me is a very important one. I believe that as teachers we must undertake a far wider *pastoral role* than we have done hitherto. The community school teacher must be prepared to get in amongst the community—on their home ground as well as in the community school itself—and I mean getting inside the homes to meet the mums and dads so we can start to understand the housing and economic conditions under which our pupils and the wider community are living. This pastoral role isn't just concerned with dealing with a child's behavioural or emotional problems. It is concerned with his or her personal development as an individual and as a member of the community. I would like to add a further extension to this principle, namely that the staff of the community school should live in the community they serve—but that is one I am hesitant about even though I and many of my colleagues do live in Sutton. There are economic factors which may prevent some staff from doing this and the fundamental fact that people's private and family lives are their concerns and it is not up to me or anybody else to dictate to people where they live. But we must be careful about telling people what is good for them without being prepared to accept it ourselves. Like the Heads who sing the praises of comprehensive education and send their own children to private school!

I would like to finish with a final observation. When I appointed my deputies at Deans, to help me draw up the final short list, I sent all candidates a letter with three questions:

1 What do you understand by the term 'community school'?

2 How deep are your own convictions that education must now move towards the community school principle? (Seriously—if you are not con-

131

vinced on this point please withdraw your application now and so preserve your own sanity—and mine!)

3 What do you think your main contribution to Deans would be
  a as an educationalist?
  b on a personal level?

The answers I received filled me with hope for the future because they reinforce my belief that there are many committed teachers in our schools today who so obviously believe in the Principle of Community Education. All they need is the opportunity to put this into practice and for this to happen it is up to us all to spread the gospel of community education as far and as fast as we can.

Notes

[1] Paper presented at a conference of teachers in November 1972 at Hartlepool prior to comprehensivization in the town.

[2] Part of a paper presented at the Stantonbury Conference on Community Education in February 1978.

[3] Deans Centre opened in 1978.

Developments in Adult Education at Rowlinson Campus

Sylvia Coupe

I was asked not to give you a history of Rowlinson Campus and willingly complied. A short background of the present position may be more helpful in putting what I have to say in some sort of perspective. We are a Campus—though heaven knows what that means. That we see ourselves as a focal point for the communities round about may be more meaningful. We comprise a comprehensive school for 1750 students between eleven and sixteen years; a Sixth Form Centre of 250 students; a Youth Centre for about 600; a Sports Centre with a varied flow of children and adults day and night and an Adult Centre with about 2,700 students—some during the day—most in the evening. It is on developments in this last area that I would like to concentrate. At Rowlinson it is all exciting, demanding and developing, but, I believe, it is in the field of adult education the excitement, demand and development are most clearly seen.

One hopes the image of the adult returning to 'school' to do cake decoration, woodwork, dressmaking has broadened and extended. The first and last of the Rowlinson prospectuses will illustrate:

1969	34	broadly practical classes
	8	on languages, mathematics, sociology.

1976/7	68	broadly practical (doubled)
	56	'mind stretchers'—language etc. (a seven-fold increase).

Why this development? I think basically because Rowlinson is able to respond quickly to the needs of the community and to do it with skill. It is able to recognize needs by firstly creating an environment in which the adult feels at home; a quality identified by the Open University visiting Rowlinson to assess a scheme which I shall later describe. At this point it is apt to quote from their report:

> The group was supported by the pleasant, non-threatening environment of Rowlinson which has an unusually flexible and relaxed atmosphere.

Secondly the relationship appears to be an individual one with each student and lastly in creating this environment letting students and tutors alike realize it is one of equality. When all three factors work together there

133

is a partnership of all in the Centre. The image of 'school' held by many adults is changed into an atmosphere in which they (the adults) are at ease and do not feel institutionalized. Tutors are encouraged to establish this good relationship with their own students—a team working together. If one remembers that each adult has some expertize to offer—then what an enormous variety of skills—academic, craftsmanship, and the art of living— are gathered there every evening. Recognition and acknowledgement of this encourages the feeling of equality.

There is another important factor which has helped adult education to expand. The high drop-out rate in adult education classes is often regarded as normal. The assumption, casually arrived at, is frequently that the student is not suitable and has failed. So the student tends to think this too. The good head of centre has to recognize that the failure is ours: we have not met the needs or adapted ourselves to the individual; we have not discussed the content of the course he intends to take early enough with him to see if it is the right one for him. We have found that if we acknowledge our failure the 'drop-out' student will tell us where we failed, *but* communication must be in a language that most people can follow. Beware jargon!

We feel it no longer possible for the head of centre or a tutor to sit alone and design a programme that *we* feel will be suitable. (Though we could doubtless fill courses and have the usual failure rate in this way.) Now we see that our plans must be a team effort—students, staff, head, advisors— preparing the programmes together. This is now done in every subject area. There is a paper on new proposals in Fabric Craft produced by all tutors (embroidery, dress, fashion, upholstery etc.) and students meeting and discussing range and method. There is now in this area an interesting widening of content and much group and team teaching. Each tutor is thus aware of others ideas. A leader emerges and provides link and continuity. There is, naturally, a difference in degree, as for example between Keep Fit and Return to Learning.

In the more academic areas—languages, Return to Learning—there is more and longer discussion in programme planning. Languages well illustrate this. We use, basically, the BBC courses (and the BBC co-operate with us). Our courses are planned for adults. We decided in our discussions that the time factor was one of the stumbling blocks and so now record programmes and work in arrears. This enables the tutor to know his course well, and, if he gets to know his students (as he must at Rowlinson) he can adjust the amount of content and depth in each session. Our discussion also showed that we frequently went too fast in the language area. It was also made clear that the gap of a week was not helpful to many. A supplementary booklet was devised for revision and reinforcement at home.

The enormous help and boost given to language studies can best be illustrated by some detailed account of the development in German. Initially our drop-out rate tended to be high so we contacted all students who had left before completing the course in one particular year. We wrote, telephoned and visited asking 'Why did you leave'? 'Where did we fail you'?

It was found that some in the group (a non-selective one) were thought by the others to be highly motivated and able to give time to study. These tended, after a few weeks, to dominate the group and appeared to show impatience with the slower ones who felt increasingly unsure and inadequate. 'We stopped asking questions—I felt ashamed—I thought myself a drag—and so stopped coming'.

These findings were given to the planning group and it was decided to experiment. Firstly there was to be some intensive counselling of opters for German language during enrolment week. This is possible with us since students do the enrolling thus leaving tutors free to counsel. The highly motivated student was offered an intensive First Year German Course. The class met every night for a two-hour session during the first week, followed by two nights a week for four weeks and thereafter once a week. The aim was to complete the year's course in two terms. The other groups (which contained many of those who would normally have been drop-outs) all meet on the same evening and each group is restricted to eight or nine students thus ensuring a closer relationship, more intimacy and a narrower ability and speed range. Meeting on the same evening enables students and tutors to come together socially—coffee etc.; groups can team up for a time if they wish; visiting helpers can get round etc.

There are, this year, 192 students doing German. 136 enrolled for one of the first year courses and thus far we have lost four. We asked for comments from the intensive course students after the first six weeks.

It has been important to realize how well prepared all work must be. We have adapted all the material, prepared supplementary work, edited tapes, and produced our own texts for additional use at home. Since very little at Rowlinson is done in isolation a member of the school staff (responsible for audio-visual material and Head of Guidance but a tutor in modern languages in the adult centre) has helped enormously with books and recordings. The students have also formed language clubs where they meet over coffee, arrange their programmes, do projects, speak the language, devise slides and arrange to take over some parts of lessons.

To work in this way the Head's attitude must be flexible. Staff need reassuring that they can successfully discuss together and experiment. He needs enthusiasm and imagination or he won't find it in his Centre. He needs to realize every tutor has special abilities and is the better for being allowed to use them. He also needs a listening ear himself and Rowlinson isn't bad at meeting this particular need. We all, Head of Campus, Assistant Heads, Head of Adult Centre, Sports Centre and Youth Centre have lunch together so everyone hears everyone else's hopes and trials. The policy of the Head of Campus and all his Assistant Heads is the open door. One must never be too busy to listen.

The next development which I feel might be of interest, and which we regard as important, I'll describe under the broad umbrella title 'Return to Learning'. It ranges from 'Reading and Writing' (the Adult Literacy Scheme) through to an Open University Course. The recruitment in this area comprises a very wide range of age, ability, education and social background. We recruit largely by word of mouth—though the local radio is willing to help and has encouraged interest by broadcasting discussions between tutors and students at Rowlinson. Our own Campus News Letter, distributed in all centres and the school twice a year, also helps. Our own students do an excellent job in encouraging people, whose past experience in education has been less than pleasurable, to come in.

Preliminary students are much helped by the presence of former students, who have gone through the difficulties, at pre-session meetings where we endeavour to help the would-be student to identify his problems. The help given by former and present students is significant for us since we have found that wherever and whenever possible we must make it viable for a student to put something back—what they then continue to take out seems more valuable to them.

Many students in the Return to Learning Programme have no idea what they really want. There is some vague talk of 'O' levels which many see as their only vehicle. Discussion often reveals a desire to keep pace with the family. We don't start discussion of needs at heavy enrolment time but arrange introductory meetings before this. As soon as the course required is identified the students go along for further talk with the tutor. Those who still don't know continue to chat with Maurice (an Adult Education/Community Advisor for the Sheffield Authority), Robin (our link man in Return to Learning), Jim (Head of Centre), Peter (Head of Campus). Any commitment they may choose to make is thus done with some prior knowledge. We begin, after enrolment, where all turn up again to encourage, help and reinforce, with a five-week module. Come and sample; see how you go; would you like to change? No fee is charged for this sampling course. This year some of our Adult Literacy Students of last year have joined English for Pleasure. We hope we encourage students to see the process as a continuous path, not a series of hurdles.

The Return to Learning programme has led us into a fascinating development with the Open University. For a number of years we have had a group enrolled in Living Decisions and English for Pleasure. Their enquiry was 'What are you going to do for us next year?' We didn't feel we had the resources or capacity to meet their ever increasing needs. Our usual meeting of students and tutors brought up a certain type of dialogue crudely put:

'Where do we go next?'
'What do you want? Have you thought of Open University as an avenue?'
'Oh shut up'
'Why aren't you interested?'

'Don't feel capable—couldn't hold our own with University folk—
don't want to go to the Poly, we are at home here—why can't you do it?
—if it was here I'd come.'

The result was that Peter and Jim met the Regional Officer of the Open
University to enquire about the possibility of the OU enrolling a group of
Rowlinson students with the study centre at Rowlinson. Within three
months it was agreed that such a centre should be tried. Indeed the OU
went further than we had hoped possible. They understood that continuity
of group and environment was important and, therefore, appointed our
tutor Robin Fielder, as their tutor counsellor. There were ten students at
Rowlinson. The OU established two control groups as similar as possible to
the Rowlinson groups. The results of their investigations at the end of the
first year were surprising, even to so positive thinking a place as Rowlinson.

In the control groups there was a forty-four per cent drop-out in this
first year. In the Rowlinson group no one left and all twelve are going on
to do a second year. They have been much encouraged by their results
and are now quite willing to go to the Polytechnic: they were ready, individually, to join new groups and change them if necessary. They had not
been aware that they were 'Special' but, at the end of the year when they
did know, they arranged a night out—'The Guinea Pigs Night Out'.

One could continue. There's much interesting work in the day time—
there are also lip reading and speech therapy groups. But enough is enough
and more than enough is indigestible.

I should not close without mentioning that the success of developments
in further education owes much to the total environment—the true co-
operation of the whole campus in word and in deed. It is no accident that
the Campus Executive includes the Buildings Supervisor and the Catering
Manageress. It is no small help to have *no* caretaker outside a room one
minute after official closing time, jangling his keys! To co-operate one must
be in tune with aims and have as full an understanding as possible—as well
as a knowledge that one's contribution is necessary and appreciated. And
finally the Sheffield Authority throughout our short seven-year history have
had the complete trust and support of our CEO and his colleagues. No
pattern has been imposed and we have been given freedom to respond in
our own way to the needs we have found.

Eleventh Sessions at Sutton Centre as a Community Involvement[1]

Stewart Wilson

I'll start off by defining the eleventh session. There are ten daytime sessions in the normal teaching week in Sutton Centre, five mornings and five afternoons. Anything over and above that we term 'our eleventh session'. Eleventh session may, in fact, mean an evening session; it may mean weekend sessions or it may mean sessions in the holidays. When we first opened we started with twenty-four staff and there is no question that they were dedicated staff and quite willing to give far and above the normal expected amount of teaching time in the week. In that first year we all worked the evening session or on occasions the weekend session as an extra; an extra to our normal full-time ten sessions day-time teaching week.

But I soon realized that you could kill off your staff very quickly this way, being the dedicated staff they were (and still are) and being involved in so many other aspects of developing our Centre such as building up curriculum, writing up our subject syllabuses, developing Mode III CSE and so on. Obviously there is a limit to what people can give, and so I put the case to the Director of Education towards the end of that first year that I must 'spell' staff off, that is give them time off in the day in lieu of their evening or other sessions, and of course if I were to do this—in other words if a member of staff was working one evening session and he had one day time session off in lieu, then effectively I had lost one tenth of my teaching allowance. Boys and girls have to come to school during the day. They haven't got to come to our evening or weekend sessions, therefore I must make sure that I fulfil my obligations to day-time education.

The Director very quickly saw the case and so after the first year we had a ten per cent additional staffing allowance to enable me to give staff time off in lieu. If I can give an example from last year[2], we should have been entitled to forty full-time teachers. To spell all those off for one day-time session is equivalent to spelling off four teachers for a full week and so I was allowed an extra four full-time staff in my staffing.

There has never been any question of our staff not accepting this flexibility, in fact quite apart from it being essential in the running of a community school it can also be very attractive personally. In other words some staff will not come in until Monday afternoon, and their weekend will extend until Monday lunchtime, because they're working say Wednesday evening or Thursday evening or conversely, some staff do not come in on Friday because they are putting in two evening sessions or weekend sessions, therefore they must have two full-time sessions off in lieu of that. There are no timetabling problems in all this because their time off is built into the timetable before the beginning of the school year.

Well now, what exactly can our eleventh session offer? First of all we do direct them at our own boys and girls at Sutton Centre putting on a wide range of courses from extra maths or English to drama, or pottery, for which they can come back to five nights a week.

We also extend this to our feeder primary schools so that younger children who are going to come here eventually can come into—for example —our basic skills sessions. Nor do we draw the line at boys and girls from other secondary schools in the area joining in, if there is room in the classes. We have also been developing our family classes whereby mothers and fathers can come back and join in classes with their children. These classes have been extremely successful.

And then there's a third area where we have been developing namely our 'pay-as-you-learn' adult classes run as part of our eleventh session, whereby adults can come in and do the particular course they wish, being taught by members of our teaching staff. As we operate it they come in for something and pay for what they have that particular evening. Just now it is 35p for a two-hour session which is the going adult education rate in the county.[3]

I would like to give you some idea of the range of classes. On Monday evening we have dressmaking, which is a family activity, Young Farmers' Club; basketball; mathematics and basic mathematics; science; language lab sessions; French; film and video; reading and writing for pleasure; children's theatre; English and drama for examinations; library and Spanish, and that's the sort of pattern you find on most evenings of the week, with the exception of Friday which is a quieter night. And then on Saturday mornings we open our workshops to the community where fathers in particular and mothers if they want to of course—and children—can come in and use all the facilities in the workshops. They pay the normal going rate of 35p for a two-hour session for use of the equipment.

There can be no doubt about the popularity of our eleventh sessions. Last year[4] we had 700 boys and girls on role, and our average weekly attendance at eleventh sessions always exceeded the 700 mark. To bring it down to simple terms that means that every single boy and girl is coming back for at least one eleventh session a week, although of course it doesn't quite operate like that. What it means in practice is that some boys and girls are coming back for two, three, four or even five eleventh sessions. One or two of course are not coming back at all for various reasons, but you can see that it has justified itself. Already this year with 900 boys and girls on the role we are having an average weekly attendance of just over 900.

There are other aspects of community involvement through our eleventh session. There is a video session for example, where the teacher has taken his video equipment and the team helping him out to an old people's home

140

in the locality where there have been certain problems of fitting in to the local community. There he filmed and interviewed people in the community and then they all came together in the old people's home one evening for an open session where they could see the film, and discuss their common problems. The same teacher also more recently ran a video on the problems of vandalism in Sutton. Again he has been able to get out and about with his video unit and interview people and find out how big the problem is and what we can do about it.

I can also think of others which are becoming self-supporting, or self-generating. 'The Coffee Pot' for example, is directed mainly towards the twenty-five to forty age group, especially professional people who perhaps in a working town don't have the normal facilities associated with larger cities where you get a greater cross section of the population.

Some eleventh sessions take on a life of their own. There is the Weekend Rambling Club for example which is extremely popular and regularly turns out forty to sixty members on Saturdays or Sundays. This started as an eleventh session and now is very much self-generating.

Other eleventh sessions are run more on a self-help basis. Use of the language labs for example where adults can now come in and organize themselves. They know which tape they want, put it on and then teach themselves Italian, Spanish or whatever they require.

A further provision which started as an eleventh session was our adult literacy programme. This grew so rapidly from its beginning three years ago that finally we formed a separate adult literacy unit which is now self-supporting through an adult education urban aid grant.

Of course we haven't done it all yet! One area which we would like to see developed is running our own community newspaper. We would like this to start off as an eleventh session getting the community involved along with our own staff and our own pupils. That one is still at the beginning stage.

There's one further completely new development which certainly has grown or is growing out of our eleventh session and that is a 'pay-as-you-use' system of room hire. We are trying to persuade the public that this is their building and so far as we are concerned we would far rather see every single space in it being used every evening and at other times such as weekends and holiday times, rather than lying idle. So we are trying to persuade them that all they have to do is to phone in, check there's a room available, come in, use it, and pay there and then, rather than going through the long lengthy procedure which most Counties operate of having to fill in forms in triplicate and so on and so forth. We operate the system at 5p per hour per person. This is now getting off the ground with different kinds of groups in the town and surrounding area coming in to hire rooms.

To sum up then, what have we really proved through our eleventh sessions system? First of all that it can happen; a teaching staff, given commitment to the community school ideal can be persuaded to work a flexible teaching day, a flexible teaching week and a flexible teaching year. Secondly that children and young people want to come back in the evenings and at weekends and in the holidays to learn. Not just to do the fun things, although of course there's a place for those, but to come back and do some hard graft as well. Thirdly, that adults can work happily alongside young people. This can apply at both simple and more involved levels. First year girls for example are coming back with their Mums to do family cookery, and on the other hand our sixth-formers are doing 'A' Level classes alongside adults in the community. But perhaps most fundamentally of all we are starting to persuade and convince the wider public that a school is their building as well as their children's building and that they have the right of access and a right to the vast range of facilities and interests which a school through its buildings and staff can provide.

Notes

[1] Paper presented at the Community School Conference held in Sutton Centre in February 1977.

[2] 1976.

[3] These are 1977 figures.

[4] These are 1976 figures.

Adult Education and Community Action:
The Northern Ireland Experience

Tom Lovett

The 'troubles' in Northern Ireland have given rise to increased demands for some form of integrated education at primary or secondary level, or a more 'relevant' school curriculum, as a means whereby education can make a positive contribution to the ills of this particular society. Such hopes, for hopes is what they are, may well be exaggerated given the apparent cultural, institutional and community divisions in Northern Ireland. Research indicates that the home and community are much more influential forces in forming children's attitudes and values than the school. If this is so then integrated education can only expect to have a minimal effect on improving the relationship between the Catholic and Protestant communities, given the existing divisions.

Expectations, however, seem to be concentrated on the young despite the fact that certain social, economic and political changes which have taken place in Northern Ireland over the last decade have combined with the commonly experienced effects of the violence in both communities to create a situation in which the Protestant and Catholic working-class are faced with very similar problems, suffering the same difficulties, and attempting to resolve them in a similar fashion. The decline of old established neighbourhoods; the increasing centralization of political authority (particularly since the reorganization of local government and the introduction of direct rule); the growth of large social, welfare and educational bureaucracies have, together with redevelopment and the lessening of traditional social structures, produced a situation in which people in both communities find themselves experiencing the same social problems yet increasingly isolated and cut off from many of the decisions affecting their everyday lives and general welfare.

Given this situation one would expect that the major emphasis should be on exploring the contribution that 'adult' education can make in assisting those intimately affected by these developments, and striving to come to grips with them, thus assisting in building a much needed 'bridge' between the communities. Yet, in the main, adult education in Northern Ireland operates in a very traditional manner and, as elsewhere, caters largely for the middle class section of the population. The organization of adult education reflects a general trend in modern society which results in a concentration of resources (in terms of information, knowledge and expertise) within institutional frameworks which are effectively divorced from the great mass of the population who need them most.

143

This trend is now under scrutiny and subject to increasing criticism by people both within and without the major adult education agencies. The question of social responsibility and social purpose, so much a part of the adult education movement in Great Britain before the Second World War, is now a central debating topic amongst adult educators and has led to a number of community based action research experiments in various parts of the country designed to explore this problem. (Liverpool, Southampton, Keele.)

Adult education in Northern Ireland does not have the same tradition. Neither the universities nor the Workers' Educational Association have been actively involved in the provision of adult education to the working-class section of the population, even to the limited extent that is to be found in Great Britain.

Yet historically adult education has been most effective in catering for the needs of the working-class when it has seen itself as part of a larger social movement amongst that section of the population. The phenomenal growth of community groups in Northern Ireland (there are over 400 according to a recent count) concerned with a variety of issues from the provision of community centres, to seeking greater participation and control in the decision-making process, may not measure up as a social 'movement' in the sense of a coherent and shared social philosophy. Nevertheless in both Protestant and Catholic communities throughout the North certain common attitudes and structures are emerging as people attempt to deal with their social environment. It is one of the most positive developments to have taken place in the country during the troubles, even though it has received very little coverage by the media.

Assistance came from the field officers of the now disbanded Northern Ireland Community Relations Commission—many of whom saw their work in very broadly defined educational terms, i.e. helping people to 'learn through doing' by providing them with necessary information. Adult education—with the exception of these few dedicated individuals—has not taken advantage of the opportunities afforded by these developments at grass roots level to make a significant contribution to the problems facing both Catholic and Protestant working-class communities in the North.

In some respects this is understandable given recent developments in adult education generally in these islands. Increasingly terms such as 'continuing', 'recurrent', 'permanent' and 'community' education are employed to clothe adult education in new garments which however do not succeed in altering the fact that it is still primarily concerned with more education for the already well educated, despite the fact that it is in some respects a 'social' service heavily subsidised out of taxpayers' money. Such terms, are, however, very attractive to the adult education profession seeking as it does to establish its claim to serious consideration in the education world where its status is still quite low. In fact adult education is, like the educational system in general, increasingly contributing to the growth of that very specialization and professionalism which community groups seek to combat. There is less emphasis on its historic concern with social justice and equality yet the conditions exist for that concern to be vigorously and positively interpreted, particularly in Northern Ireland.

The universities have, in the past, contributed significantly to the practical development of that concern. The existence of extra-mural departments in many universities in Great Britain is a testimony to their desire to establish a firm relationship with their social environment and a practical illustration of their sense of social responsibility. Such departments provide an opportunity for the local community to make use of the resources and research of the university. That 'community' has, in the main however, been predominantly middle class and the relationship one that is dominated by, on the one hand their needs and interests and, on the other, a narrow definition of what is and what is not the proper domain of university adult education.

The decision by the New University of Ulster to establish, in 1972, an Institute of Continuing Education at Magee University College, Derry was, given the fact that it was the largest investment in adult education by any university in Western Europe, a practical illustration of its concern to establish a relationship with the Northern Ireland community. The reasons behind this decision may have owed less to a sense of social responsibility, and a commitment to adult education than to more pragmatic considerations. Nevertheless it offered a unique opportunity to explore the problem of adult education and social responsibility and, in particular, the contribution that a university adult education institute could make to the needs, problems and interest of the working-class communities in Northern Ireland in general, and Derry in particular.

The University had (in its own words) 'committed itself to an unusually ambitious and large-scale development of community-oriented education'. Granted this commitment, but given the tendency for adult education institutions to define 'community' in middle-class terms, it was decided by one member of the staff to concentrate some time and effort specifically on working-class communities. This was in fact one of the main recommendations of the Russell Committee on Adult Education, i.e., that universities should engage in work of an informal or pioneer character with the 'disadvantaged'. The term disadvantaged is used in that report to cover the working-class and other minorities suffering from physical and mental handicaps. Its use as far as the former is concerned, implies certain negative connotations and judgements regarding their life-style and general attitudes to education. The term working-class community can be interpreted in a much more positive fashion implying a distinct set of social relationships, values, attitudes and culture common to Catholics and Protestants existing alongside different religious, and historical traditions. The culture and community of the Bogside and Sandy Row have in

145

fact much in common with traditional working-class communities in the North of England.

Such communities, defined in terms of social structure, culture and values, cross the religious divide and, as indicated above, they face common social and economic problems and have reacted to them in a similar fashion in terms of community action. This was the 'social environment' to which it was felt the university had a specific responsibility. The absence of any widely developed further or adult education structure below university level in Northern Ireland presents a situation similar to that faced by universities in England in the 1920s and 1930s. This is particularly true of Derry which has been neglected in this field, as in so many others. However its very traditional, close-knit social structure made the task of establishing a relationship with the various working-class communities in the city less difficult in some respects than in a modern urban environment despite the problems of operating under war-time conditions.

The concept of community education as a framework for the development of a comprehensive and relevant educational service for the Institute's working-class constituency rested on certain broad assumptions:

1 That in order to define the nature of the university's responsibilities in this field it was essential to establish a close working relationship with the communities concerned. This, was made easier by the fact that the 'Institute' was in close physical proximity to such communities—at least on the Catholic side—and the fact that it was regarded as 'neutral' territory even though Magee University College was little used by either community before the Institute was established there.

2 That the establishment of this relationship would bring to light opportunities for assistance of an educational nature which would not necessarily fall into conventional educational modes.

3 That the opportunities for the provision of a comprehensive co-ordinated adult education service for the general population in working-class communities would be greatly assisted by working closely with the organizations thrown up by such communities.

4 That the 'activists' involved in community work in both communities would benefit from the resources and services available from a university institute and vice-versa.

5 That a two-way flow—the university going into working-class communities and such communities making use of the university would greatly benefit both.

These assumptions were based on the results of similar work in other parts of Great Britain undertaken by the Workers' Education Association and a number of University Extramural Departments. The Derry situation is, of course, very different in many respects but the problems and the people are also very similar to those found in Liverpool and Southampton.

The Institute has its own buildings and resources separate from the main university campus. It is right in the centre of a relatively small and compact city, despite the 60,000 population. It is cheek by jowl with communities such as the Bogside and Creggan. It is a new Institution with staff given the opportunity to develop their own interests and, at least initially, not tied to pre-determined programmes and courses. All these features have meant that it had very distinct advantages over similar institutions elsewhere in its attempts to cater for the working-class, despite the absence of any specific funds or action/research. (In fact many of the other developments in this field have depended heavily on such funds and have not grown naturally out of activities and specific responsibilities of the agencies concerned.)

The work has now been in progress for seven years. It has progressed slowly, due to both the difficulty of working within a city in conflict and the problems inherent in working from a university base. Nevertheless contacts were established with many of the community groups in the city and elsewhere in Northern Ireland. Echoing the experience of the community workers employed by the Community Relations Commission, it was found that people were only too pleased that someone, or somebody, was prepared to take an interest in their problems and willingly gave their co-operation once a position of mutual trust was established. Slowly it was possible to open up the resources of the Institute, and other agencies, to the needs of a number of working-class communities not only in Derry but throughout the North. Nothing spectacular has occurred, just a gradual involvement by the Institute in a variety of activities which have confirmed the original assumption upon which the work was based and underlined the potential that exists for adult education to make an important contribution to the problems facing the working-class in Northern Ireland. The work also underlined the need for universities to adopt what the Alexander Committee on Adult Education in Scotland calls a community development approach.

In Derry that approach has taken a number of forms. This has included acting as consultants to various community groups on matters such as social and recreational surveys, community organization, community newspapers, and community radio. In one instance this resulted in the establishment of a neighbourhood resources centre in Shantallow, a new housing estate in the outskirts of the city. This in turn resulted in the provision of a general adult education programme in the area combining the resources of the Institute, a newly formed WEA branch and the local technical college. Over four hundred people were eventually involved in activities held in a number of schools in the area.

147

The resources centre has also assisted in the formation of a number of informal study groups which are not subject based but grounded in the culture, problems and issues facing local people (particularly women). Such groups emphasize a democratic, dialogue approach starting where people are; seeking to increase social awareness and to develop the skills and confidence needed to deal with what appears to many as an increasingly complex and hostile environment. This has, in turn, resulted in demands on the Institute for personnel, information and resources and a number of those involved have become more active in their own communities. Plans are also afoot for the provision of a course on community development for those involved in the variety of community associations in the area. It is hoped to combine an examination of existing skills and insights with a detailed analysis of the social, economic and political causes of local problems. It will also act as a counter to the increasing emphasis on community work as a professional activity, emphasizing instead its essentially democratic nature.

The Institute has also acted as initiator and host for a series of conferences on topics of interest to community groups in the City and throughout Northern Ireland. A series of three conferences on Development in the North West brought together community group representatives and a variety of specialists concerned with various aspects of city and regional development. It afforded an opportunity for one particular community group, the Bogside Community Association, to present its own detailed proposals for the City's development, proposals which were in fact quite influential.

In the summer of 1974 a conference organized by the Institute on 'Politics and Community Action' brought together representatives from community groups, Protestant and Catholic, throughout the North to debate their problems with politicians, civil servants, administrators and professionals from the various statutory bodies in the province. The contribution of the two speakers from the community groups were amongst the most outstanding at the conference for their lucidity and critical analysis. This conference led to a further one in the Institute run entirely by the community groups with the Institute providing the necessary resources. Both underlined the common problems and issues facing the Catholic and Protestant working-class. The very act of coming together on 'neutral' educational territory proved a valuable learning experience for all concerned and led to the eventual establishment of a province-wide organization for community groups.

Other activities have included:

1 assisting the Bogside Community Association in establishing its own educational programme, including informal discussion groups throughout the area on topics of local interest and concern in an effort to stimulate more community involvement;

2   a training course in the Creggan to enable local people to set up their own advice centre (it is hoped that this will lead to a poverty survey in the area);

3   seminars to assist community groups to examine the aims and functions of their organization. This was a very successful learning exercise. It provided an opportunity for those involved to stand back from their everyday community activities and to examine in some detail the aims, methods and organization of their community group in an educational setting away from the pressures of everyday activities.

4   a one-day conference for community groups—Protestant and Catholic —in Derry. This resulted in the setting up of a city-wide *ad hoc* committee which has produced a number of reports on community development, particularly vis-a-vis government policy, for general discussion by all the community groups in the city.

5   a local Radio Action Group involving local community activists set up to explore the possibilities of a community radio service in Derry. Papers were produced and meetings held with the officials from Radio Ulster to discuss ideas put forward by the Action Group. As a result a local radio station was set up in Derry with a full-time producer.

6   a one-week workshop on community action held in Holland. This workshop involved sixteen local Derry people (Protestant and Catholic) engaged in community activities in the city. It was organized on the Dutch side by the Folk High School in Bergen and it involved those who participated in a practical investigation on the ground of community development in Holland in areas with similar problems and divisions to those found in Derry. The workshop was highly successful. It gave those involved a deeper insight and understanding not only of their own community activities but of each other.

7   a weekend workshop on 'Communications and Community Action' involving the use of radio and TV for community groups from Belfast. This proved extremely successful and further workshops are to be arranged with the community groups concerned.

8   the establishment of a number of informal community study groups in Derry concerned with the study of local issues and problems particularly those related to social change. They were very successful and indicated the extent to which aspects of people's lives and culture could be the basis of a social education programme.

9   arising out of the latter eight community education programmes were produced and broadcast on Radio Ulster to discussion groups throughout

the province using local people as discussion leaders.

On a more formal level the Institute has established a one year full-time academic course for adults leading to a University Certificate. This course is concerned to cater specifically for mature students who lack formal education qualifications and has attracted a variety of students from working-class communities in Derry and elsewhere in the North. It is the only course of its type in Ireland and differs fundamentally from similar courses in residential adult colleges in Great Britain in its strong links with the local community. This enables the College to offer the course on a full-time and part-time basis (thus encouraging married women to attend).

It also enables the students to continue with their activities within their own communities and to link this hopefully with their studies. This has a multiplier effect in terms of local knowledge of what the Institute has to offer. Some of the students have in fact been employed as part-time tutors in some of the activities detailed above. It is easy to over-state the significance of the work described. However the indications are that a great deal more could be done by those concerned with adult education in Northern Ireland if they adopted a flexible, outgoing, imaginative approach, concentrating on specific working-class communities.

The major problems facing adult education agencies in Northern Ireland, as elsewhere, are their institutional structure and their conception of social responsibility. Given the divergent, and often opposing, views about the role of adult education within such institutions work with the working-class will only be a small part of their total concern. However, pressure inside such institutions, allied with pressure from the working-class themselves, can play a part in enlarging that concern and opening up their educational resources. This can be seen as a further extension of the 'reform' element in British adult education seeking to provide expertize, resources and facilities from all the providing agencies in a general community education service catering for the wide range of interests and needs to be found amongst the working-class, but not specifically linked to any movement for social change.

The latter is a more radical move and requires a sense of social commitment as distinct from social responsibility, and it is difficult to visualize any of the formal adult education agencies taking on that role. However here in Northern Ireland there is a real sense in which community action is a social movement of some potential amongst the working-class. It would be greatly assisted by the creation of an independent adult education 'movement', concerned specifically with its educational needs, rather than depending entirely on formal adult education agencies. Like the successful Highlander Folk School in the USA such a movement would need to avoid the dangers of elitism and narrow ideology, which have beset previous attempts in these islands to establish a working-class educational movement. If it did so then it would act as a pathfinder for those who are seeking a distinct role for adult education in the field of community action.

Bibliography

ADAMS, FRANK, (1971) *Unearthing Seeds of Fire: the Story of Highlander* USA Quadrangle Books.

Adult Education: A Plan for Development (The Russell Report) (1973) HMSO.

Adult Education: the Challenge of Change (The Alexander Report).

ASHCROFT, BOB and JACKSON KEITH (1974) 'Adult Education and Social Action' in *Community Work One*, JONES, D. and MAYO, M. (Eds.), Routledge and Kegan Paul.

LOVETT, TOM (1975) *Adult Education, Community Development and the Working Class*. Ward Lock Education.

Northern Ireland Community Relations Commission. First Annual Report, 1969.

4

PROJECTIONS

Introduction

The four papers which make up this section barely spread to all the future possibilities in community education and this was not their task. In fact, only Colin Fletcher's paper could be called crystal ball gazing and this has been included both as a means of taking stock and as a focus for the debate which so many contributors seem to wish to initiate. The purpose of the section is to show that community education will continue to develop and will do so largely as the result of initiatives from its practitioners. In deciding what to do next in the light of their convictions and the changing world they show an independence rare in education circles.

Philip Toogood's paper is particularly valuable as a summary of the arguments for community education and for an 'open community education institution'. Community is 'common predicament', he says, and (echoing Keith Jackson) within institutions it 'happens by contrivance where children share a home within the school with each other and their teachers and grow from this into the practice of independent learning'. For this there should be small units, definable space (territory), large blocks of time and a tutor system. He outlines the mini-schools of Madeley Court's Lower School—their purposes, methods and projects. He then discusses the way in which community education confronts problems. Falling rolls present an opportunity to devote more space and more teachers to make comprehensive community schools which, in turn, should seek to provide a forum for the professionals who confront the coming crisis in the welfare state. The problem *within* school education seems especially related to the fact that the role of the head teacher can be an obstacle to democratic change.

Neil Thompson opens with the case for in-service training. It is particularly important for educators to understand the communities they serve and an 'in-house' approach is able to provide a balance between theory and practice. He describes Abraham Moss Centre's two-day course and the background to the local Allied Workers Group. Local studies emerge as particularly important for staff and may lead to subsequent innovations. Nevertheless, challenges to success arise from the time needed for training to be effective and the support required from those outside schools and colleges who shape the education within.

Introduction

Chris Elphick locates community education in community development and defines it as preparation for survival. He gives an account of the National Elfrida Rathbone Society's activity in Liverpool 8 and shows how the projects in art, joinery, landscaping and with local schools are closely related by purposes and 'benefits'. His chance comments are all the more challenging because they show the size of some of the stumbling blocks:

four out of the project team of five are from the immediate locality.

two team members spend half the week working in the nearby comprehensive helping the teachers understand the local community more.

Thus, these projections from the present have at least two practices in common. Toogood and Thompson write of inter-professional groups not to focus upon the people but on the problems of the place. Thompson and Elphick write of managing their own training and sharing it with the community. All three writers etch their projections in terms of increasing awareness, social change and community control. Colin Fletcher guesses at the next and subsequent years because he shares these concerns and because as an observer it is a useful thing for him to do. He sees the period as one of consolidation rather than rapid change. This, he writes, may be a success story when the opposition has been fully weighed up.

154

Tomorrow's Community Education Institution

Philip Toogood

The Case for the 'Institution' of Community Education

The case for an educational institution as opposed to a network in our urbanized form of existence is overwhelming. Society today is the product of industrialization—a highly artificial and contrived state of affairs. It needs within itself, within its fabric of discrete particles of competing individuals and thrusting pressure groups, a coherent network of institutions, or nodal points, where general issues of human development and destiny are made precise and wherein authority is devolved from the general society to the institution to achieve specific objectives. They should be facilitative institutions, democratic but not democracies, authoritative but not authoritarian, unafraid to stand firm in the face of anarchy or in the face of that desire for law and order which would make them servile instruments of the social policy of dictators or demagogues. I support the 'Open' Community Education Institution, at the heart of which is the school.

Community, Education and the Institution Defined

The problems of society today can only be solved when the society has become a community. Community occurs where a common predicament is shared. Sharing requires sympathetic understanding which in turn is the beginning of wisdom or the desired end of education. The educational institution acknowledges that it is in the business of enabling personal change and development in people. It seeks to affect this change by contriving opportunities for reflecting upon experience, by discussion, by abstract consideration, by devising solutions to be applied and once again reflecting on these as they are experienced. The institution protects through its procedures the momentary suspension from the operation of real material constraints and is necessary for that supreme human functioning—the operation of sympathetic understanding in action and commitment. This institutional suspension should not be a withdrawal—in fact the institution should associate itself with the society from which it springs and should include the unemployed, the aged, the young mothers and the young adolescent seeking to enjoy informal social interaction. Nor should the institution remain behind walls but should give an opportunity to people to move out, to find out, to serve, to raise a voice amongst the pressure groups, to act positively.

Edward Thring of Uppingham and Henry Morris of Cambridgeshire Village Colleges

Edward Thring of Uppingham School, one of the few great nineteenth century headmasters to have much of relevance to say to us today, in one of his oracles on education said 'Never rest until you have the Almighty Wall on your side'. What he meant by this was that the institution is necessary and vital to the spread of education in the society, but that the dead hand of 'institutionalization' should not be allowed to dominate the institution. The mark of the successful community education institution is its non-institutional flavour. It sets free but acknowledges the basis of freedom in that interpersonal contract of mutual respect and understanding which makes of the educational institution a network of care and consideration. Henry Morris, in his memorandum over fifty years ago, wrote about the Village Colleges 'lying athwart the daily lives of the people' and spoke of 'no leaving school', of education from 'the cradle to the grave'. No more did he mean that the institution's style of intervention should be authoritarian, but in the very detail he included in his memorandum, in the specification of showers for village footballers, and in the way that in 1929 he was seeking money for 'nursery groups' within the Village Colleges where local mothers could share with the older girls of the secondary school the experience of child upbringing, he was emphasing an enabling style, an education of relevance and of concrete inspiration. Not for nothing was Morris a bitter opponent of Cambridge University. He regarded the University as being 'national' and to that extent separated from the real problems and opportunities in rural Cambridgeshire.

Indeed, what institution other than a Community Education institution could house in one day (as I have known it at Swavesey Village College), an English for adult immigrants class, an antenatal relaxation group for expectant mothers, infant welfare clinic, keep nimble session for the aged, Community Service Interdisciplinary Support Group lunch, family planning clinic, three club groups, twelve LEA evening classes, a packed and sociable youth club attended by over 100, as well as all the normal functions of the secondary school, public library and extracurricular after school activities by the teachers. The Community Association of the Village College used to grant aid transport for youth and old people and gave pump priming grants to preschool play groups and voluntary youth clubs within its catchment area—quite apart from promoting most ventures within the Village College itself. The most distinctive recognition to its non-institutional functioning was given to Swavesey by the Social Services of the area who knew that the close work between youth centre and school would enable children of the most difficult background to join the school and to find their way via the informal structure of the Community Education aspect into a meaningful position in the formal school.

The Urbanized Community School/College of Tomorrow

The urbanized community school of tomorrow should however not only gather around itself groups of adults seeking to learn, to interact socially, to enjoy recreative leisure and to participate in the democratic structures of the internal government of the institution as in many of the Cambridge-shire Village Colleges, but it should also create, in a new way, community within itself. Shared predicament does not happen in the formal school directed by authoritarian, front of class teachers who have come to pass on to the aspirants the crock of culture whose badge adorns their letter headings and in black gown material protects their suits from the stain of chalk. Community happens by contrivance where children share a home within the school with each other and their teachers and grow from this into the practice of independent learning. To this end the contrivance of specialist areas and specialist subject teaching within secondary schools has created the need for a corresponding 'medicational' service of pastoral care partly to repair the ravages of a mistaken curriculum. This specialist preoccupation in the years from eleven to fourteen in secondary schools has led to armies of eager teachers leading herds of largely docile horses to water only to find that they will not drink once they are there. Some do—but very few in the spirit of independent enquiry which is at the heart of all real learning. We are guilty in such a system of presenting what Alain called '*La coupe amère aux rebords enduits de miel*' (The bitter cup with honey smeared rims.) How many would-be scientists have been attracted by the mumbo jumbory of the white coated priesthood of the super-equipped science lab only to be assured by what passes for scientific learning that it is all so special that it is only for an élite who can learn long words and guess the right answers? Children need a small unit to identify with in the secondary school at first; it needs a territorial definition; it needs long blocks of time; the teachers need to be also the tutors; the home must feel welcome. In our large macroschools we need minischools of not much more than 100 children where children and teachers can be people rather than categorized and catechized.

The Micro-community, or Minischool Within the Vast School of Today

The system coming into operation at Madeley Court this year (1978) will set out to do this for the younger children. There follows extracts from the Annual Plan which has now been accepted by the Governing Body and which will now be worked upon by the three main teams of teachers, Support and Evaluation, Heads of Subject Area and Heads of Half Year to produce the institutional framework for the start of the September term.

157

THREE MAIN AIMS OF MADELEY COURT SCHOOL

1 Provide for acquisition of knowledge and skills necessary to the pursuit of a successful and happy life.
2 Promote the attitudes which will help the young person to become a good citizen.
3 Develop in the young people at school that self-knowledge and confidence that helps to make happy adult people.

FOUR MAIN METHODS

1 Comprehensive school . . . to be a school where arbitrary selection is avoided so as to give ready access for young people to opportunities for learning on the principle that each young person is of equal value in the school. Hence the predominant grouping of people should be mixed-ability. Children grow towards the categories in which they are grouped.
2 Community school . . . to be a school where a positive network of personal relationships between teachers, children and parents operates to promote mutual respect and understanding. This community of the school as an institution should be constantly affecting the life of the community within which the school is set: the community should be present within the school on a broad front and the whole tenor of the academic experience of the young person at school should be that movement of the mind from the practical everyday circumstances of community existence to the abstract reflection upon the principles of it and back again to the everyday reality.
3 A place for independent learning—to be a school where young people are brought to learn on their own initiative. The characteristically human part of our reasoning is the problem seeking part of our selves. We seek problems, we suggest solutions, we test these, rejecting and refining and proposing new problems and solutions. Independent learning requires both individual and group work. Individual independent learning requires access to a wide range of resources of all sorts, whilst group learning requires facilities for discussion and personal interaction. In both circumstances the role of the teacher is of crucial importance—to contrive the learning. In this process of teaching the relationship of teacher and pupil is all-important. The best learning-teaching relationship is often co-learnership . . . when the teacher as expert learner is engaging in the process along with the pupil. The promotion of discussion, the provision of autonomous and remedial courses, the fostering of the cohesion and co-operation of the group—these are all additional tasks for the teacher in developing independent learning.

158

4 A place for social fulfilment . . . to be a school where the prevailing ethos is acceptance of the individual—not that uncritical acceptance which allows for the antisocial to ride rough shod over placid and compliant neutrals, but the acceptance which challenges the person to join in, to commit to taking part in the task. Every young person should be accepted and the foundations of their educational development should be built upon who they are now rather than what they ought to be. There should be adequate social facilities for children, parents and teachers so that the informal bonds can be forged firmly early in their time at school.

LOWER SCHOOL—THE HALF YEAR MINISCHOOL

DEFINITION

. . . The six minischools should be set up as corporate entities of 80–100 children in half-year groups of children, having six tutors (ideally four group tutors who are also their teachers for core subjects in the minischool base) and a territorial base. They will do half their timetabled learning in the week in the four main core curriculum areas of sciences, social sciences, English, maths, in the minischool base. The remainder of the week they will come out from the minischool base to do activities which require more specialist equipment, i.e., PE, foreign languages, craft, music, art, and drama. The head of the half-year minischool will be responsible directly to the headmaster for the educational welfare of the children in the minischool and for the operational welfare of the tutors in the minischool team. A member of the support and evaluation team will be the general adviser to the head of half-year group and will represent the overall policy of the school to the head of half-year group on behalf of the head where direct contact is not necessary. The head of subject area will be the subject adviser to the minischool team and responsible to the headmaster for this function. The head of subject area will prescribe the autonomous studies within his subject area, will advise the specialist teacher within the multidisciplinary tutor team on all aspects of the specialist function including special interest studies, remedial and interdisciplinary programmes and the specialist pedagogy. The role of the head of half year will be to advise the teacher on all aspects of the general pedagogy as it relates to that particular half-year group and to direct and lead the team of tutors in the pursuit of the aims of the minischool.

The aims of the minischool beyond the three main aims of the school are more specifically to develop the following characteristics in the pupils (observing the four main methods outlined) . . . .

159

PROJECTS

GUIDANCE PROGRAMME	1 *Independence in personal decision-making*—a guidance programme should be operated to increase competence in decision-making and value-forming in personal, vocational, social and educational fields.
COMMUNITY SERVICE	2 *Awareness of personal identity*—a community service programme should be developed throughout the school.
EXTRA CURRICULAR ACTIVITIES	3 *Enjoyment of life through personal fulfilment*—a programme of extra-curricular activities should be developed.
HOME-SCHOOL LINK → COMMUNITY EDUCATION	4 *Personal stability in growth from family roots*—a home-school link programme should be developed leading into a community education programme and later participation in the school-based youth club.
MINISCHOOL COUNCIL	5 *Autonomy in the goal-seeking processes of the school*—the half-year group council should have specific powers within the half-year group in certain defined areas . . . children should be encouraged to participate to the full.
PRODUCTIVE UNIT	6 *Competence to work productively and co-operatively*—the half-year minischool should seek to become a productive unit in a co-operative sense over as wide a field as possible.

The resource-based independent learning will be the responsibility of the individual specialist teacher calling on department's expertise and resources for learning in response to the curriculum needs of the half-year group. The central team will supervise independent learning when it is timetabled.

THE MINISCHOOL BASE

It is envisaged that each of the six minischools will have a separate base where the children can look after their own things properly and where they can stay on after school under supervision for recreative and study activities, and to which their parents can come during and after school and for parents' evenings. The base will also have places for the tutorial staff, storage of specialist equipment necessary, social area, study areas, paperback book sections, satellite resource sections, display areas, etc. So far as possible it will be kept for the use of the children of that minischool and for those minischool tutors —either with the minischool children or with groups of older children who come to them when the base is not occupied for

160

specialist maths or English lessons (maths/English specialist areas will no longer exist).

THE MINISCHOOL CURRICULUM

The curriculum will be a combination of subject areas which will be interrelated by the method of teaching and by the circumstances of being in one minischool base (for half the time in the week). It will not, in a prescribed form, be an integrated programme. Hence maths, sciences, humanities (history, RE, geography and English) will exist as prescribed separate courses but the unity of the learning experience will be contrived within this variety of subjects through consistency of method, resources used, and the relationship of the teacher with the child. A variety of different timetabling devices may be pursued within the minischool time allocation. Subject areas which are to take place in specialist areas outside the base should try to be present in the bases whenever possible (display, special events, etc.). It may be that facilities for follow-up study independently within the base can be set up as well on occasion. The prescribed curriculum should be interpreted with due consideration to the six aims of the minischool so that these are not simply promoted in the non—'teaching' time of the day, i.e., specific tutorial sessions, etc.

It is important to be clear that the aims of the institution must be interpreted consistently through the whole system. The community comprehensive school which takes this style of facilitative intervention in the society which has produced it, must adopt this style within its most minute dealings in corridors, in playground, assemblies and so on. The network of personal relationships must reflect the ideals of the whole institution. 'Successful' and 'closed' institutions dedicated to 'success', competitive conscience, badges, uniforms, élites, etc., are 'successful' precisely in the measure that they are consistent. The community comprehensive school must also be consistent—true to its ideals.

The Community Education Function of the Institution

The community education function of the school should not be simply a department, like for example, the maths department. Community, shared predicament, should be the pattern of the whole institution's existence. This extract from the Minutes of the Education Committee of Cambridgeshire County Council as the dual youth and adult education structure was reorganized into one community education structure is a model for any LEA wishing to resuscitate its schools with the kiss of life:

To enable and encourage people to . . .

161

1 Take responsibility and interest in small or large community groups.
2 Participate actively in a democratic system.
3 Show compassion for their fellows.
4 Broaden their education and range of interest, and in so doing help them to make the best of their personal resources.
5 Learn how to gain, exert, accept or remove authority.
6 Learn the art of establishing and managing personal relationships.
7 Appreciate the need for personal integrity and sense of responsibility in a society which affords the maximum freedom to the individual.
8 Make the most of their talents and come to terms with their limitations.

It acknowledges that education is in the business of contriving that people form their value systems and learn the art of social involvement in the shared common predicament.

Features of the Contemporary Predicament Leading to Developments in The Community School Today

Certain features of our common predicament cry out for association with community schools. Whether the continuing unemployment will be solved by public works and direct labour; early compulsory retirement; later access to jobs or work sharing in a common agreement to work fewer days a week—solutions which require either a push to the left in politics or a push to the right—there will be a paramount need for education in the society in which these extreme solutions may be operated. There will be a prime necessity for our 'sixth forms' to accept the unemployed youth and to contrive a realistic education. This will be impossible to assimilate successfully unless the style of teaching is geared to creating access to resources, to developing learning skills, and providing for social interaction in school. Similarly unemployed or underemployed or ex-employed adults will need day courses for educational interaction. The shared common predicament (as opposed to the shared particular predicament) can surely only be found in the school for all ages ... which 'lies athwart the daily lives' of the community. As the birth rate goes down we should take advantage of the extra space in schools and extra teacher numbers to create this community education institution as part of a national educational revival—this time based not on maximizing the capital-forming potential of the large institution, nor on the maximum plant utilization principle, nor on the creation of an élite to run the white hot technological society model—but—on the modest model of the shared common predicament which facilitates that conversation 'begun in the primeval forest ....' (Oakeshott *On Political Education*) about the nature and purpose of human existence. There will need to be a tremendous increase in part-time education, in community service; parents and children doing school meals and Meals on Wheels?; in school more world of work contact; of unit-based degree courses and continuing education courses in all fields and at all levels of abstraction to replace the torn fabric of our Higher Education system, rent by the new found discovery that perhaps more education of the élitist, mandarin-creating sort, does not necessarily of itself create wealth but may even prevent its formation by an over emphasis on high technology and on creating a technocracy whose apartness creates the worm in the fruit which eventually eats it all away.

The Special Case . . . Crisis in the 'Welfare' State

Above all the community education institution has to mitigate the harm in our society which is the product of the critical situation of the welfare 'professionalized' provider state. Our consumer society seeks to consume services to satisfy its real and artificial needs. It develops an instrumental attitude towards health, education, care. As in the potentially catastrophically successful automation revolution in industrial production so in the welfare state the successful servicing of needs has perhaps increased the area of need by damaging self-reliance, the dignity of forestalling the emergency and the capacity to cope. The community school which is enlarged to be the community education institution should seek to be a catalytic agent working between the caring professions. It should seek to be a forum for interdisciplinary meetings between the police, the probation service, the social services, voluntary agencies, churches, doctors, teachers, lawyers, etc. Such a local group once set up should have as a secondary function the job of supporting community service by the children. The community education institution so envisaged should seek to educate in self-reliance through community service: the child care course based upon its creche, mothers and toddlers clubs, and its tutor mothers home economics scheme, the community study programme reinforced in the later years at school by practical, regular, voluntary attachment of students to old people's homes, to schools for the physically and mentally handicapped, to individuals in the neighbourhood who are in need.

By What Right Head Teacher?

In all this there is the crucial question of the community education institution's authority to intervene in society in the way outlined above. Here the Taylor Report puts its finger on the sensitive spot. Who are these Head Teachers or teachers as professionals to be intervening in society with decisions, with so-called 'social engineering'? 'By what authority do you say, O Head Teacher, that my child should join a minischool, one of whose objectives is to seek to become a productive unit in a cooperative sense

163

over as wide a field as possible?' Good question. But by what authority does a Head Teacher or teacher seek to teach a child to read and to facilitate this gives access to a school library? Are we not, as a community education institution either on the path to being manipulated by politicians whose purpose is the short term acquisition of power or on the path to being asked to assume a mantle of authority which is far beyond our brief? I suggest there are imminent dangers in both becoming too demagogic or too authoritarian. The key to the situation is in consistent, patient, rational consultation, clarification of aims and above all the recognition that at the end of the day we are about the business of enabling people to take their lives fearlessly into their own hands in fashioning a society of people who respect other people's equal right to freedom and to a sharing of the common predicament. Surely an institutional, but deinstitutionalized, framework is necessary to enable even this debate to be peacefully and positively conducted.

Training for Bridge Building

Neil Thompson

One concern facing the community school or college is the need for a change in attitude on the part of the staff from that of their counterparts in more orthodox settings. Often, where the declaration of objectives on the part of the head or principal is clear, community schools have little difficulty recruiting people with a high level of commitment and with at least a theoretical understanding of the task ahead of them. Once people are in post, however, with the need to put theory into practice, the difficulties assume greater proportions. Mixed-ability groups, shared-use facilities, home visiting, the school or college as a resource for the communities* and the communities themselves as resources for the school or college, are but a few of the relatively recent ideas needing assimilation and absorption. The complexities involved in mastering even one of these areas are considerable, but to face them simultaneously is a task which even the most stout-hearted and tenacious might find daunting. Nevertheless, without a solution, the 'community' door will remain locked and barred. Perhaps most progress has been made with those affairs which are internal to the institution, or which offer resources *to* the communities. Harnessing community expertize and putting it to work *for* the school or college is less widespread. Any failure may arise from a reluctance to accept the dramatic reversal of roles which such a development suggests. The most common implied assumption is that the experts are to be found in the classroom, yet undoubtedly if we are to even partially comprehend our communities, it is from those communities that we must seek the necessary expertise. Nowhere is there a greater need for a radical departure from established norms than in the field of in-service training for understanding the communities we serve.

The value of in-service training has been frequently reiterated in many arenas but has never been more relevant than in today's emergent community institutions. The idea that every teacher should keep abreast of his/her specialisms is far from novel and countless teachers up and down the country regularly meet with colleagues to exchange views, clarify aims and develop ideas. Often, courses organized away from school or college act as stimulants but once embroiled in the humdrum routine of everyday life one has some difficulty in retaining a clear vision of things learnt in less hectic surroundings. In cruder terms, 'when you're up to your ass in alligators it

---

*I believe 'communities' to be a more realistic term than 'community'. Certainly in urban environments, and arguably in all cases, the complexities of modern life are such, that the homogeneous community, if it ever existed, is now largely a myth.

is sometimes difficult to remember that your original intention was to drain the swamp'!

Within most of our schools and colleges there is a wealth of expertise which we sometimes fail to recognize and significantly fail to utilize for the benefit of our communities. In a school with an emphasis on mixed ability approaches, for example, the experience and techniques acquired by the remedial specialist will be highly valuable commodities, but if the expertise is passed on, and utilized with each group and by every teacher, its value will be increased.

To be effective, such dissemination of knowledge and skill requires thought, careful preparation and above all a commitment by the school or college to 'in-house' in-service training.

The special circumstances surrounding each school will vary considerably and training will be of most value if it relates very specifically to the practical experiences of those taking part. Learning through experience is a well-used concept equally relevant to work with young people or adults. It is particularly apposite in the context of in-service training, and an 'in-house' approach if appropriately structured, will allow theory to assume its rightful place and not to dominate.

In-Service Training at Abraham Moss Centre

From the outset at Abraham Moss we have placed a high priority on 'in-house' in-service training and, as much of our teaching is undertaken in teams, we have been able, with general agreement, to release people from their teaching commitment during the working day. Everyone gains and no-one loses from the increased expertise resulting from relevant in-service experiences. The short-term deficit incurred by having one team member absent for the duration of a course, is amply offset by the long-term gain for the team as a whole. Covering lessons for absent colleagues becomes more palatable when it is understood that a reciprocal arrangement will exist in the future. Additionally, when course tutors are drawn from the ranks of the staff themselves many more possibilities for follow-up exist, once theory has been tempered by practice. Similarly, at a later time, if the need arises, refresher sessions at the end of the working day are relatively easy to arrange.

Most staff agree that, as a community centre, we should have very close contact with the local communities in our district, a major part of which is a multi-racial area of social and economic deprivation in North Manchester. Since the Centre opened the Youth and Community Team has developed strong links with groups and key individuals in our locality. As far as possible the Team has attempted to respond sensitively to real concerns and has tried to avoid a 'soup kitchen' approach where Abraham Moss as a major resource decides the menu, cries 'come and get it' and, depending upon the particular variety and strength of our broth, people take it or leave it. In 1974 the Team helped to establish an Allied Workers' Group for the area and, from its genesis, where six people met in the sitting room of one of the members, the group has grown, to include anyone in the district who sees his/her role, private or professional, in a community context. The group has now in excess of thirty-five members and meets at least monthly to exchange views and expand ideas, leading towards a unified approach to some of the developments in this area.

Summer playschemes serve as a useful example of this approach in action. As with many inner city areas, there will be a number of playschemes in the district each year. These will be funded by various organizations and statutory bodies and will rely extensively upon volunteers, as well as upon paid helpers. The existence of the Allied Workers' Group has meant that the training needs of people involved in all playschemes are being met in a unified way. We have a co-ordinated course of five evening sessions and, in addition, a full day workshop arranged with other courses and drawing from the whole of Manchester as part of the City's training programme. Once the playschemes have begun, there will be an emphasis on shared resources and joint projects with each scheme co-operating with the others in whatever ways are appropriate. It is arguable that a pattern similar to this would have emerged in this case without the Allied Workers' Group, but the belief that its existence has hastened the process, is widely held.

It was in this general climate of opinion and activity, twelve months ago, that the Youth and Community Team began to explore one particular area of concern. Considering the Centre as a whole and the communities as resources, a central dilemma was apparent. Many of the developments and groups with which the Team has been involved over the past few years are known intimately to the Team's members and few people besides. Regrettably, there is so far no policy for larger numbers of staff to have a dual role of teacher/youth worker or community worker/teacher.

One of the difficulties in having a relatively small group of people acting as youth and community workers is that knowledge and understanding of the surrounding area have to be disseminated. As with any large organization, communications are sometimes less good than we should like and knowledge which might be utilized in the classroom, whether in the academic or pastoral care sense, is not appropriately spread by news-sheets or memoranda. The centres of interest, groups, personalities, general geography and social and ethnic composition of the district are often most clearly comprehended by visiting and talking with people. A printed sheet at best provides a superficial view and at worst may be unintelligible, whilst talks or lectures would offer only one dimension in a highly complex pattern. Many Centre staff do not live in this area of Manchester, a fact sufficient in itself to widen the gap between the local communities and Abraham Moss. Consequently, there is a clear need to build bridges between those who live in the district and those whose professional responsibilities include a sensitive response to the wishes expressed by the communities. Further, if the classroom is to become a vital place for young people, intimately binding the locality with the learning process, the communities themselves must become major resources in a resource-based learning environment.

With these thoughts in mind the Team decided to offer an in-service training course to Centre staff, largely from the school and college, which would help them to understand, in a meaningful way, at least some of the issues surrounding developments in the district. We hoped that by being participants people would undergo experiences which would ultimately enrich the learning environment for students in the classroom. Additionally, we hoped for increased awareness and subsequent improvement in the welfare services of the Centre as a whole. Our aim was to stimulate and act as catalysts rather than to impart a body of knowledge. The course would be a starting point rather than an end in itself, and if repeated frequently (in the event this has become twice a term) would allow for further staff discussion, leading to extensive developments throughout the complex.

A Two Day Course

Our model was an induction course prepared for workers on a Job Creation, Community Advice, Project a year or so earlier. The experiences we created for this previous training programme occupied five full days. A similar time allocation was considered to be over-generous for the later course, in the context of a Centre already engaged upon a comprehensive training programme, and with the need to provide continuity in the classroom. After discussions at a variety of levels it was finally decided that the course could occupy two full days. No-one regarded this as entirely satisfactory, but it was the best compromise we could find, having taken all our circumstances into account. Agreement was reached with School staff that teams would provide cover for four absent colleagues and the Open College made arrangements for a similar number; one from each of the four departments; to attend. It was generally accepted that course members should behave as if they were training elsewhere with their commitments to normal routines relinquished completely, in order to create a group identity and to give adequate discussion time during meals and breaks in the programme.

Our main difficulty was to prune back the important components to a realistic level without losing too much of value. Similarly, considerable thought went into allocating sufficient time to each contribution, so that the treatment of each topic was not too superficial. The primary needs appeared to be those of putting the district into some sort of geographical and sociological perspective; exploring the pre-school developments currently taking place; examining youth work initiatives at a variety of levels and discovering what direction community developments were taking. Although offering a structured framework, we attempted to avoid a rigidity which might prevent staff from exploring personal interests and concerns. Additionally, it was decided to emphasize that discussion between course

168

members and community contributors would play a vital part. In this way we felt that the course would be dynamic and allow for changes, which a less flexible structure might restrict. A brief synopsis of the course is as follows:

DAY 1: Introduction

A chance for course members to receive handouts and ask questions and for the 'shape' of the course to be explained.

Session 1 9.30 a.m.– 1.00 p.m.	A local resident, Community Development Worker and Town Planner give their views of the district past, present and future. Part of this session is spent exploring the district by minibus and on foot.
Session 2 2.00– 4.00 p.m.	Pre-school needs are explored by visiting a local childminders' resources centre, a day nursery and a playbus and discussing perspectives with the workers at these places.
Session 3 4.30– 6.00 p.m.	Youth Work 1. An investigation of non club-based youth work in the district. Detached work, residential work, an adventure playground and a drop-in coffee bar for young people are considered with the workers from each field.
Session 4 7.00– 9.00 p.m.	Youth Work 2. A view of club-based work with opportunities to visit two local youth clubs speak with young people as well as full and part-time workers.

DAY 2

Session 1 9.30– 11.00 a.m.	Working with mentally handicapped children. A local Community Development worker and mothers involved in a self-help project, show a film and explain their position.
Session 2 11.15 a.m.– 1.00 p.m.	Ethnic minorities. A number of local people from various multi-racial backgrounds discuss their work and its implications for education.
Session 3 2.00– 4.00 p.m.	Community development. The local Social Services Community Development Worker is joined by members of local community groups to explain their involvements in the district.
Evaluation 4.00 p.m.	An opportunity to evaluate the course and discuss its implications.

The Case for Knowing the Place

There is no room for complacency. Content has already been modified, following comments received from participants, and if the course is not to become stale, continued reappraisal will be necessary. By the very nature of things the complexities of community structure will stimulate change, and such changes must be reflected by the programme we offer.

Although the course is now well established, we have yet to fully explore the possibilities which have impinged upon those people taking part. One justification for continuing has been the belief expressed by many teachers, that the experience has added a dimension to their thinking which was previously absent. Despite the fact that many participants have worked in the Centre for a number of years, the opportunity to spend time with individuals and groups from the locality has not presented itself in this way before. Fresh perspectives on the local area are emerging and there are indications that teachers are following up issues which fired their imaginations. If this continues, undoubtedly the quality of work, in and out of the classroom, will be enhanced. The existence of a two-day training session, in itself, will work no miracles, but taken in conjunction with the general desire to offer a worthwhile community education 'from the cradle to the grave', fires previously dormant may now burst into flames.

Nevertheless, the limitations are all too apparent. Community schools or colleges face unusual challenges which may be solved only partially from within. Internal critical evaluation and subsequent action will be vital components in achieving community aims and objectives, but there can be little doubt that the demands on staff are greatly increased. A genuine desire to succeed will not, in itself, lead to success. A new ideal requires new perspectives and new solutions, not only from teachers themselves, but from all those external influences whose contributions shape our community schools and colleges. Until there is more general acceptance of joint appointments, increased staffing, virement budgeting and a host of similar innovations, the infant which showed such promise may well become a sickly adult, destined for premature retirement.

Community Education and the Rathbone Project

Chris Elphick

General Comments

The major focus of community education should be the extension of community participation and control over educational resources. It should not just be limited to schools or relevant social curriculum or associated educational establishments but should include every aspect of education in the community. Community education must also be concerned with the extension of managerial control held by the local community over its neighbourhood schools.

For many years we have been aware of the phrase 'people deprived of education are deprived of the means of translating what they know into thoughts they can think'. Community workers, social workers, teachers etc., have all been looking at ways of tackling educational deprivation. Community education is one of those great umbrella phrases which conveniently means different things to different people. To some it is a new name for play centres, youth clubs and evening institutes, to others it is the development of all-embracing community colleges, 'hypermarkets of corporate life' as Colin Ball called them, and to others it is the organization and process of learning through all the social relationships into which an individual enters at any point in his life-time.

No matter what definition we choose it is difficult to deny the basic links that exist, or that ought to exist, between education in its broadest sense and community work. Community education is that element in community development which most lucidly emphasises the growth in skills of community management.

There is of course, a strong sense in which all community development is educational, in that the awarenesses of the public is sharpened by contact with communally based action and involvement. The education system is inextricably bound up with the rest of everyday life—an educative dimension is unavoidably present in the community, both inside and outside institutions. Without consideration of the educational process it is likely that community development will be lop-sided and simply a transient or short-term success. It is also true though, that the community educator can only operate in the knowledge that, without major reforms in the community context, his endeavours are in vain.

Community workers are today involved in every aspect of community life ranging from employment to money to play. Today there are many community groups involved in a great variety of activities. Within this flurry of activity it is the role of the community educator to identify and emphasize the educational processes present in any community activity. Each time a community group organizes around an issue learning takes place, learning in the most important way—from experience and from each other. Basically community education is preparation for survival.

National Elfrida Rathbone Society

NERS is a large voluntary organization working with educationally disadvantaged children and their parents, supporting community and school-based projects throughout the country, aimed at tackling the problems of educational disadvantage at the grassroots. The society's main objective is to help people make the best opportunity of all important educational opportunities and experiences so that they can meet the challenge of living and working in the real world.

Rathbone operates local projects in various parts of Britain but because of very limited financial resources can only hope to cover a fraction of the need. Rathbone is trying to expand—it is project orientated but with an emphasis on the bringing together of skills and ideas so that they may be properly recorded and analysed and then made available to many more people.

Rathbone in Liverpool

The Rathbone Project in Liverpool was set up in 1974 as an experiment in education in the community. The intention was to place a team of workers in a building which would be developed as a community resource with the aims of:

1 providing a stimulating environment in the centre and community which would encourage the development of personal skills in the context of the real life choices the young people face.

2 providing an informal support service for young people with problems.

3 providing an opportunity for local people, particularly parents, to be involved with the community and its young people; the identification of need and the generation of services and learning experiences for all.

4 communicating proven experiences of method to other statutory and voluntary agencies in the area.

The project was a new departure for the National Society who had, up to this point, largely confined itself to working with educational disadvantage within the school. The project is based in a small part of Liverpool 8, an inner city area of Liverpool. It works with an easily identifiable community and four out of the project team of five are from the immediate locality.

The work falls into four main areas, all concerned with educational processes that exist within the community and all equally concerned with the development of self-confidence, self-respect, individual talents and skills. The four areas are:

1 Community art/drama work including a community darkroom. Much use is made of creative activity as it is seen as an ideal way of developing self-confidence and of especially allowing youngsters to use and expand their imaginative abilities. The project has explored in detail the practical uses of community artists (one of these as a trainee) and a further team member specializing in development of photographic/8mm. work.

2 Joinery workshop—job creation project. This is a scheme employing eighteen people learning and teaching the skills of furniture-making. Skilled craftsmen teach unskilled, formerly unemployed, young people a variety of related skills and they all produce furniture and playgroup equipment for the local community.

3 Environmental improvement project—job creation project. This scheme employs fifteen gardeners and unskilled youngsters creating landscaped garden areas out of derelict land in the local area. They design and build gardens, patios, play equipment, seats; plant flowers and shrubs, etc. Both the joinery and environmental projects bring the youngsters into contact with their community in a different way than they have done before. They are able to see their new found skills being put to use, they can develop a much more imaginative and creative view of their area and other people begin to see them as other than vandals or delinquents.

4 Work with a local community school and general youth work. Two team members spend half the week working in the nearby comprehensive school helping teachers understand the local community more. They are both local people and can not only help teachers develop a greater understanding but can also work with parents and reluctant pupils in the hope that greater mutual understanding will develop. They also carry out aim two from the project's base which is an old terraced house in the middle of the area.

Rathbone is concerned with the identification and development of resources and skills. Drama groups, elaborate playschemes and photography are only a means to an end—the project has to be flexible enough to respond to ever changing community need and must continually reflect these changes. We are working with people imprisoned by their own lack of self-confidence and self-respect. We must try any method of helping people rebuild that self-confidence and reassert their belief in themselves. We have as our goal a new environment in which growing up can be classless— we know, though, that we will never reach this without trying and when we try, we will have to face many pitfalls. The challenge of our work is in how we overcome these pitfalls and stay true to our aims.

Community Education Training Unit

The above unit idea has arisen out of Rathbone's experiences largely in Liverpool and is an attempt to help other people gain

1   a concept of resources and resource development, and

2   develop the educational roles of available resources.

The unit will work in a training capacity with community groups, community workers, local authority employees, teachers etc., with the following aim: to promote the concepts of education in the community through the identification and development of resources that exist in any given community and to evaluate and examine the local, national and international implications of the work of the unit.

The objectives of the proposed unit are stated as follows:

1   the identification of resources and an examination of the ways in which these are used.

2   training of community organizers in the imaginative development of these resources.

3   provision of courses, workshop facilities and information to fulfil particular stated needs and to increase the awareness of groups and individuals.

4   organizing evaluation with this effecting the action of the unit.

The lives of each one of us are a series of educational processes—we are continually involved in learning situations which come out of and because of the community in which we live. This learning cannot be institutionalized or categorized—it is free to all regardless of age, sex, social status, race etc. The real function of community education is to help people understand and develop these processes, to break down the view that knowledge is a commodity which can only be obtained in certain places at certain times, to help people develop skills and talents which can be used for the benefit of themselves and their communities. We must continually be aware of the implications of the development of self confidence and ready access for everyone to tools and resources. If we are going to enable more people to have more access to more information then we must help them use that information. There is always the danger that we may raise people's expectations only to be unable to fulfil them.

Contemporary man has decided not to state his privilege but his right to be part of the decision-making which rules his life and decides his destiny. Any change of power though will be meaningless if it is not combined with an increased awareness by those who are under-privileged—community education is charged with the responsibility of accommodating that increased awareness and of helping ordinary people to develop talents and abilities and to acquire the skills and ideas necessary to begin to affect real change over their lives.

The Forseeable Future

Colin Fletcher

It is an unenviable and possibly odious task to guess the future, one can be utterly wrong and one's biases can give considerable offence. If, however, the future is portrayed as choices and constraints such guesses may help to channel effort and high-light the challenges to what is quite properly a movement.

Institutionally it is likely that policies and commitments in the secondary and adult sectors will continue to be separate whilst the workers in these fields begin to learn a lot from each other. The common focii are broadly those of relevant knowledge; meaningful relationships; lifelong learning; the institution as a joint and jointly controlled resource and the belief that local change is a vital component of social change. The next step, as it were, is to clarify the ideas; yet again for those with some experience and to do so patiently for those with tolerance and ideals but no personal contact.

Community education depends on two near mythological terms:

Community and *Education*

By community one can read either neighbourhood, town, or single class residential area. The term is used as a keep-net for all sorts of activities where there is more than a slight participation between people living close by each other. It may, in fact, be better just to call community education local education and so convey the essential premise that people should be able to control and use public resources. Education is a muddle of goals, laws and establishments that depends upon the economy on the one-hand and the relationships of those involved on the other. What the notion of community education introduces is a heightening of the contradictions of present provision. These contradictions refer to the changing context of education and to the lack of organization to meet them. The 'goals' reveal where and why they will cause disturbance. They are respectively:

1 to encourage a pleasant, enjoyable and more meaningful recreation.

2 to broaden the quality of life of the participants.

3 to fit people for jobs and prepare them for better jobs.

177

4 to facilitate social change, to give the people back what is theirs, to redistribute in favour of the lower paid; to advantage the manifestly disadvantaged.

Casting one's mind through these criteria it would seem that only recreation could be said to be non-controversial, whilst fitting people for jobs is a conventional goal which challenges the others to a greater or lesser degree. For broadening the quality of life is also engendering a critical individual, and facilitating social change is challenging the power structures upon which most of us depend. Generally speaking, community education may be said to be the lever for independence away from old forms of dependence. It comes as no surprise therefore, that many of those in power dislike it and that many of those who are relatively powerless also feel unsure as to the burdens that they are suppose to carry.

Even so, the grass roots may be changing the plant formation. But before discussing possible sources and strengths of opposition it is worth summarizing what has been learned so far. Community education faces the demands of the latter rather than the earlier part of the twentieth century. The debate into which it enters therefore centres upon three related questions:

1 What kinds of men and women will be able to cope with the pressures of the year 2,000 and beyond?

2 Do the keys to success or even survival lie in the individual or the group; and has collective experience and effort been undervalued to date?

3 Do groups and the individuals within them have the necessary social knowledge and intellectual equipment to continue and extend the process of shaping the place where they live?

It is the last question which makes two aspects of education explicit. They are first that community education establishments assume secular interests and involvements: there is almost an awareness of replacing religion and its rituals. Secondly, community education is a commitment to engage in domestic politics; it both reinforces existing groups and encourages the formation of new and rival groups. Community education is therefore an act of social intervention albeit with a discretion that actually begins with the roles people play in education.

A Definition

Community education is engaging in the practices of local social change and has its beginnings in alternating between the roles of teacher, pupil and adult such that each person is all three over the course of time. Some people, of course, begin at the end rather than the beginning. They advocate the desired effects in terms of 'positive discrimination'. This term means that the poorer the community the more it should get. The process of intervention is a conscious commitment to do something about poor conditions. It is no accident that those who concentrate upon the causative process tie their thinking to a community school whilst those concerned with effects think more in terms of adult education. Community education as defined here actually refers to both endeavours and more besides. Nevertheless, the separation of provisions into those which relate to a statutory requirement for all children under an adolescent age and those that relate to the broad expanse of provision for voluntary adults is still made by those engaged in practice. This has allowed community education considerable diversity and to be defined by practice.

The definition of community education advanced here depends upon an awareness of the role of the teacher. The self conception as part social-worker, part evangelist and part nucleus of knowledge and resources should not detract from a close examination of relationships in detail as well as events that are the consequences of intervention. The term intervention may be a clumsy description of the process involved. In the first instance it means to get in between what is happening and what is likely to happen. Sweezy calls this a consequence of being able to see 'the present as history' so that by appreciating how events are caused we do not take a fatalistic attitude and regard the future as being out of (our) control. 'Getting in between' is no easy matter because it involves more than redefining the place and scope of existing institutions. There is redirection and the deter-mination that it takes to push against antagonistic and apathetic inertia. Even then there is the key question of the willingness of people to be so affected; some may feel that the troubles of critical people are largely of their own making and that only infrequently do they actually go out across their own doorsteps to tackle the world outside.

Community: An Issue in Itself

Part of the problem is the need for definition that spreads in application from rural villages, to suburban neighbourhoods, small towns and inner-city ghettos. Most practitioners have thought about the characteristics of their own place and find it difficult to match these with the taken-for-granted ideal of 'people living wholly connected with each other' that the word community may well imply.

It is probably unnecessary to idealize. Instead the Common characteris-tics that are recognizable to the lay eye can be given decisive force: that which people say is important can be made hard criteria. Again the voice from within can be heard to real purpose.

The term community may be an ideology—'a necessary illusion'—but an 'inter-actionist' perspective asks that we confront the problem of what people mean when they *use* the idea. To what things does it refer? What are the material i.e. real reference points? The world of work may be the hub of sentiment, the problem is to know the historical story in which the real things play a part. Changes must be known as people themselves know about them.

From within, that is, there are four headings under which conditions for a community may be grouped. They are a necessary condition and some sufficient, historical and emergent conditions. First the necessary condition; a necessary condition is one which must be satisfied if the term is to be applied. The term community applies to a 'psychic sphere'; a place is our *space*. A community reflects upon itself; people say 'it is ours'. This demands an us and them. Strictly speaking a line is cast between us and the rest. The line is placed around a geographical space by social sentiment and the space is often an elbow in a valley; an estuary to the sea, or the fording of a river. In saying 'us' and 'our place' the person indicates a common character born of common experience. Since the date of settlement personal fortune has been bound up with collective fortune. 'Lived together, laughed together, and loved together, "they say", and we've fought each other, abused each other, then ignored each other'.

Secondly, there are the sufficient conditions; sufficient conditions may not all be satisfied or well satisfied. It will be evident that these conditions blend with that which is necessary; they are manifestations of co-operation, collaboration and conflict. There could be collective constructions. Men and women have built houses and churches; subscribed to halls and memorials. So, too, there may be collective symbols; when groups make music, play games and organize festivals, carnivals and galas. For example:

We can remember the depression mind. We can remember no work. The men in this village built the swimming pool entirely without pay. They brought their own picks and shovels. The women came with a penny for a packet of five Woodbines. When it was done children came from all over the area to learn how to swim. It was the first—a little village like this.

In all probability a community had more simple economic purposes than it serves now. The setting was conducive to commerce or work. It was a place to which those from scattering settlements could come for trade, or it was a place which gave shelter; water-power; and raw resources and it was not as cosy as it sounds. Men were serfs, and often they were evicted for great tracts of land to be enclosed. So, too, there could be a clear sense of hierarchy of masters and men with a great social distance between them. The community may have been self-sufficient; it may even have been 'run at a profit', but it did not possess the means of accruing vast capital. More often than not most surplus was devoted to making homes into palaces and subscribing to the building of places of worship and education. The capital from 'within' went to establishing service industries, but the major industry or agriculture was developed by outside capital. What may have been an island has long since been a peninsular. Major industries began that were dependent upon processing or manufacturing for sales well beyond the scope of the community. The original economic beginnings passed out of scale as well as possession. The ownership and consumption ceased to be local.

This brings us to 'emergent conditions'. A community may be distinct, but only its name is likely to be unique. Strangers have come in the wake of capital: 'foreign' owners, managers and workers. What is a condition of strength for the community becomes a weakness: whoever can afford to live in it and pay its prices can stay. Now strangers can settle and make their fortunes. Such strangers are accommodated, used and virtually incorporated. But they remain strangers, and can be held responsible for squabbles and disputes.

In a sense to be the same 'old' community the same people should be in power. The pecking order is still the same. Whatever the setting, those who are powerful patronize those less powerful who do 'the doing'. And all this suggests, of course, that the community organizes its own life for itself; there is a marked inability to cope with formal or legalistic procedures. A community is anti-democratic because the 'same people' make all the decisions in different capacities. Furthermore the community is an anti-progressive force because of its efforts to maintain the hierarchy. This is not to say that the *whole* community is either anti-democratic or anti-progressive; only that part of it which represents the whole: the 'leading families' and 'men of influence', and only then when they wish to be.

A defensive tone is to be anticipated. Since the 'influx of foreign capital' the community has lost whatever internal holistic symmetry it had achieved. Now there are laws to challenge custom; principles to ensnare practices. And, perhaps naturally enough, these very emergent conditions are part of the community itself as well as a reason for becoming more vociferous in its own praises. For those who have always lived in the community it is not the darkness of its eclipse that is frightening but the harsh glare of having to make everything explicit. The emergent condition of all communities is how they cope with that which exposes them.

Criteria for a community: a summary

1   The necessary condition of a sense of identity which may be recognized by:

    a   a distinctive name

    b   a distinctive dialect or vocabulary

    c   the use of landmarks as boundaries with neighbours whether the latter be regarded as communities or not.

2 The sufficient conditions of:
   a a population of three and four generations
   b established churches, chapels, clubs and institutes; also greens, ponds, common land; plaques, war memorials and squares (These details barely begin to list the 'noble pile' of relics).
   c established teams; festivals; fairs.

3 The historical conditions of:
   a evidence of the 'original' economic activities.
   b evidence of 'classes'.
   c evidence of infra-structure activity, e.g.: market; brickworks; housing associations and service industries.

4 The emergent conditions of:
   a 'Strangers' incorporated in on-going activity.
   b Resistance to changes in 'sense of identity' matters. e.g.: through postal codes; telephone exchanges; road signs and demolition of 'part of the local heritage'.
   c a struggle to make sense of the requirements of recently arrived 'industries' with the part takeover of older 'native' industries by the newer national and international combines.

This summary is meant to serve both those who would come to know their 'hosts' and those who would make communities. In the latter a contradiction can quickly be sensed in a wealth of progressive effort being directed to encouraging the emergence of the new but potentially classbound and conservative collectivities. In fact, because social classes are one part of the definition it is possible to underestimate the consequences. Conventional education largely collaborates with the working, middle and upper classes in their own terms; although the collaboration with the working class may be in terms of aspiration rather than actual achievement. Community education in actual communities can be cavalier about reproducing the classes and cut across the established order of relationships and non-relations. Respectability, at least in the English scene, is a somewhat anxious demand and a spontaneous, critical, collective faculty may well be its natural enemy. This is just one facet of the constraints within the community itself.

A Beginning to the complexities of a single issue

The chief issue is the relation between the 'host' and the 'foreign bodies'. The criteria of a community indicate that a degree of incorporation takes place; the strangers take their place in interest networks and power formations. In Geoff Brown's evocative phrase 'experts are parachuted in on a community to tell them how to run their lives'. The crudeness of this attitude depends largely upon the class resonances given to it. If the paratroopers are firmly middle class and the territory is as firmly working class then there can be the sense of taking civilization to the barbarians. And when this is understood by the locals their resentment towards condescension is increased because they are proud of what they have achieved over the years. It can seem that muck is being thrown at memories.

Nevertheless, this 'us and them' can be too categorically expressed. The charity-supported community education enterprises are, paradoxically, less 'suspect'. Their aims are less grand; most of those working for them do so as part sacrifice and look poor; they work alongside the people rather than draw them in through the turnstiles of concrete-clad peoples' palaces. But they are a small proportion of the whole effort and what follows largely refers to the State sector.

It would seem a fact of community education institutions that many of the staff recruited could have done well anywhere. The proportion holding degrees, honours and having been student leaders is significantly high. To put the matter directly, genius has been bought and brought. Genius means being able to recognize and draw upon the seeds of suggestion of genius in others. Genius is therefore a part of being genuine, it is that part which others can both believe *and* trust so that they can realize themselves; 'In each his special genius' may be the motto.

Put in context, communities have seen successive waves of emigration of their own geniuses. It is probable that educational creaming and occupational careers have removed the brightest post-war children to the four points of the compass. In exchange, as it were, for its loss the community has an importation of the genius of the other areas. Such centres are therefore a compensation for loss; 'barbed' somewhat by young people being able to command salaries which would certainly have retained the community's own geniuses had they had the opportunity.

Thus, there are the consequences of a 'transfusion of intellect'. Some 'host' areas have been the target of many post-war compensation programmes. To some, at least, a community education establishment is the latest in an alphabet soup of relief programmes that makes the formula read:

$$CDP + EPA + GIA = CE$$

Where   CDP   is   Community Development Programme.
        EPA   is   Educational Priority Area.
        GIA   is   General Improvement Area.

Some go so far as to argue that the provision of community education is little more than a cost-cutting exercise on the construction, maintenance and use of buildings and that the gains to the community are considerably less than the gains to authorities sponsoring them. Community education is more than an incidental cost-effectiveness as the joint or multiple use of buildings is built into the provision. In this way the community itself may be strained to find that 'the school', 'the adult education centre' and the 'college' are not identifiable and rather smaller than when they were separately provided. They may feel they are getting less rather than more than they bargained for. The establishment may be both more foreign and less substantial than they had hoped.

The Intra-mural Issues

The early days are those of a siege mentality. Bigger yet though are the issues of running community education establishments because they have the problems of paralleling old with new practices. The designation as a community education initiative encourages new thinking and 'progressive' workers; it is easier to be progressive within such places. Therefore the problems are not those of being a black sheep or a sore thumb (that is of individual strain) but those of making collective sense; of managing change and relinquishing the security of formal insularity. In the school this may take the form of representing compulsory attendance as voluntary choice. In adult education the effort could be that of reaching out to those who would not normally 'come' and doing so with a heavier diet than recreation.

Within too, are the constant small frictions of not having your own place and many matters depend too heavily on the personalities which lead them. Each is in turn responsible to bodies not conversant with the new animal and so has to contain innovation at the same time as plan it. Thus the problems of the front-line workers can be increased if whoever runs their section does not have the support of their governing body. Concealment from the governors is not usually an above average problem; but community education asks for more than the docility of a partial understanding. It is necessary to educate superiors into first principles because their active support is being sought. They may, as political animals, be unwilling to exceed the average involvement and responsibility. Nothing makes community education flounder quite as much as sheer lack of interest locally and the bright lights of national publicity meeting in what would have been the school yard.

'But if that doesn't work we'll try something else'—all community education establishments need careful attention at the design stage. They become 'so and so's baby'. With such a high degree of identification the school or college is accorded an invaluable invisible asset namely 'laboratory status'. 'Laboratory status' is the prestige of being where rules are bent, broken and remade in order to try new arrangements and provisions. The point is simple: no precedent can be argued from the laboratory to the applied production establishments. Consequently the material resources and staffing ratios are better at first and this is held to cause friction in the teaching profession itself.

More importantly here, though, laboratory status guarantees an element of change when change itself is a defensive advantage. All schools and colleges change it is true. But not all want to change as much as they do and few form *ad hoc* bodies continuously to re-examine and recommend major structural changes.

A cliché which relates to this as defence is 'momentum as cover'. Usually the term would apply to industry where one is always told 'we are just undergoing a big change at the moment, could you come back in a year or so's time?'. The experience in industry is to oscillate between federalism and centralism—between departmental empires and a strict accountability 'to the top'. Each 'pure form' has its advantages and disadvantages. The advantage of federalism is greater initiative and involvement but some heads of sections can take too great an advantage. The advantage of centralism is to reduce costs but it also encourages irresponsibility with too many simple saying 'it's not my job'. Change is very often away from federalism towards centralism or vice versa and often handled as guesswork.

Each community education activity has its own catchment but the extent and expense depends upon 'user-numbers'. Clearly, though, it would be a mistake to expect to quickly make 'a community' and misleading to suggest that all neighbourhoods, villages, 'mixed areas', and 'small towns' possess the willingness to understand what is being attempted. The role of the teacher as adult (which is far too mechanical a way to express alternation) is to engage with parents, colleagues in youth and community work and local action groups as they see fit there and then.

Education comes back as it were, to the strains upon the teacher as conventionally understood. And so using old languages we have to try to understand new practices.

The Teacher and what is taught

Put at its simplest, community education practice means that whilst the job itself can be worrying there is also a worry about the boundaries that should be placed around work. The following quotation indicates some of the thoughts of one front-line flack-catcher:

'We have a definite problem in thinking about what we are doing. There are so many day to day problems to be solved and we find that we are eating and sleeping the Centre. There are no props you see, no dais; blackboard, cap and cane. You are always in the middle of the class. You put yourself at risk all the time. It's a real strain. Another thing we find it hard to think about is what it all means. We all work after hours—some of us do little else. But that's just letting yourself be exploited by the system. And we are feeding the system its workers too. We say that their education is to make the most of their leisure but how can it be with such jobs? We've so little time to reflect, to get a thorough theoretical analysis of the whole thing. Most of us know that we need a multi-

185

dimensional consciousness that has yet to be expressed. You are being exploited simply by working for nothing on a problem that's so big. We have to act in a vacuum—to act as if what was going on out there is less important than the thing we are trying to do.'

In sociological jargon this account may be typed as 'role strain'. The term does not really say very much because the tension is between the person and the job as a whole. It could be a case of being thoroughly honest in social commitments and worrying about being swallowed up by the job. This worry happens to many white collar workers between twenty-five and thirty-four years of age anyway, it is taking the whole firm home and trying never to let go of the controls in case anything goes wrong. In community education it means living, eating and breathing the job and having to get far, far away from it for some of the time.

It is, however, possible to express aspects of the job itself sociologically because a third component is being placed alongside what in old language is a dichotomy. The separation made is between expressivity and instrumentalism: between self-development and the learning of occupationally related skills. It is held that these two purposes are related to different parts of the human personality: expressivity refering to belief and love and instrumentalism refering to practicality and calculation. The *new* third component is participation—the purposes of an alert and active citizen. It could be phrased perhaps as 'a career with the world itself' for the content of curricula implied is little less than eco-consciousness—a grasp of how the world looks and works.

Community education may only be different from schools and colleges in putting participation *equal* in status to expressive and instrumental 'goals'. It requires therefore a committed staff and a higher level of articulate agreement than is felt to be present in many staff rooms. A teacher usually 'comes to' community education because she or he wants to join with others with similar ideas. The strain is therefore collective because the conflicts between the staff(s) are an added burden and the more traditional forms of allegiance either to political party or trade union may be the biggest divisive matter. By this it is not meant that class or trade loyalties are in themselves divisive but that it is so hard to relate the strata which they describe to the common ground on which it is hoped that the alternation between pupil, teacher and adult takes place.

Human capital and social investment

The preceding discussion has concentrated upon some of the recurring and major problems which lie within community education and may be regarded as self-limiting factors. At a time when teachers' unions regularly withdraw 'goodwill' as part of their salary disputes, it would take a renegotiation of their contracts to insulate community education from the effects. So, too, there may be little enthusiasm expressed at national level but the quiet, essentially English, revolution continues and is clearly favoured by a growing number of Local Education Authorities. Moreover, institutions are rarely consistent, they can encourage and discourage at the same time; it is why they should encourage which concerns us here.

Community education is more cost effective than traditional education; there is a better use of plant by it being shared and by encouraging spontaneous, as well as programmed, usage. Community education also allows a consolidation between secondary, adult and youth services such that shared premises, resources and administration save expenditure which could otherwise be 'cut'. As for the initiatives it encourages, local authorities could see these as precisely the kind of response they wish to make to 'falling rolls' (the probably temporary decline in child births). A community education commitment would allow them to ride out the trough without dismembering their services. Many will no doubt look to developments in Scotland since the Alexander Report, in the hope that the lessons can be learned quickly enough to be useful. No doubt, too, community schools look attractive propositions because they have so many principles relating to style and do not seem to be discouraged by size. 1,500 pupils in a comprehensive may be too many for an effective education but this is probably because so many solutions are sought in terms of form rather than content. Whom do these hierarchies really help? Human capital is wasted, pupils, teachers and adults 'vote with their feet'. In industry absenteeism has been described as 'strikes in miniature' and this description could well apply to truancy and declining enrolments in secondary and adult education. Yet again, community education could be 'sold' not as a good thing but as a cure for certain ills. It may be unrealistic to expect more noble motives than these.

All this can be furthered by letting the virus out of the laboratory. The 'product mix'—of adults, youth, school, recreation and so on—may not have been tested and proved but at least some of the guesswork has been eliminated. What has been learned at conferences is that community education does not really depend upon lavish centres with sparkling staff. There are steps which can be taken to extend the hours; extend the age ranges, relocate into the community, learn from and with the community and make pleasant, purposeful relationships. There is nothing magical about the term community school or college and many institutions have developed great distances along these lines without adopting the title.

The virus is only likely to lead to a minor epidemic, though, until there is the free exchange of developed resources which show *how* the community is *in* the curriculum, which provide frameworks for sustained and systematic community studies and which demonstrate how new criteria and time-scales for educational work can be understood. The latter is the most important of all, perhaps, it implies a priority upon the lifelong learning commitment and voluntary involvement of a diverse population.

Containing the spread, as it were, is the tradition in teacher training.

To be sure, community education may be referred to as 'interesting' but the implications for teaching are rarely referred to. The qualities needed to be a teacher of all age groups are actually part of the realm of 'mixed ability teaching' and yet few courses acknowledge this. But then again student teachers could show so much interest in the topic that courses are developed in which their teaching practice experience changes the minds of their trainers.

Thus, it is unlikely that authorities and others with community education commitments will starve them of funds and other forms of approval. As links are then established between these commitments and those responsible for teaching teachers, models and methods will become more accessible and contribute to the debate on falling rolls and an ageing population. That I do not see the challenge of community education being taken up on any substantial scale does not mean that it cannot or will not happen.

5

A SELECT BIBLIOGRAPHY ON
COMMUNITY EDUCATION

A Select Bibliography on Community Education

Peter Haywood

A. Community Education—General Works

ALBERT, T.: 'Opening up the doors' in *Times Educational Supplement*, 3222, 4 March 1977, pp. 20–21.

APTER S.J.: 'Applications of ecological theory: toward a community special education model' in *Exceptional Children*, 43, March 1977, pp. 366–73.

ARMSTRONG, R.: 'New directions in community education' in *Community Development Journal*, 12, April 1977, pp. 75–84.

ARMSTRONG, R. and DAVIS, C.T.: 'Community action, pressure groups and education' in *Adult Education*, (NIAE) 50, no. 3, Sept. 1977, pp. 149–54.

BRIGHTBILL, C.K. and MOBLEY, T.A.: *Educating for Leisure-centered Living.* (2nd ed.) Wiley, 1977.

CARR, N.: 'Community learning groups in New Zealand' in *Adult Education*, (NIAE), 50, Jul. 1977, pp. 84–90.

CLUNIES-ROSS, E.: 'Educational technology in adult and community education' in *Community Development Journal*, 9, Oct. 1974, pp. 206–11.

CONWAY, J.: *Understanding communities* CONWAY, J.A., JENNINGS, R.E., MILSTEIN, M.M., Prentice-Hall, 1974.

DAY, P.: 'Community development and adult education—some comments' in *Adult Education*, 44, Jan. 1972, pp. 308–11.

DUFTON, A.: 'Community what?' in *Aspects of Education*, no. 15, 1972, pp. 13–14.

EGGLESTON, J.: 'The search for Shangri-La' EGGLESTON, J. on community work in *Times Educational Supplement*, 3256, Nov. 4, 1977, p. 22.

FAIRBAIRN, A.: 'Adult education in a community context' in *Adult Education*, 43, Nov. 1970, pp. 219–28.

FREEDMAN, A.: 'Changing ethics, changing schools, changing jobs' in *Adult Leadership*, 23, Oct. 1974, pp. 104–8.

HAWORTH, J.: 'The Community Concept, 6: studies in design Towards a more genuine sense of involvement'. HAWORTH, J. in *Education*, 145, 14 March 1975, pp. 281–2.

HEAD, D.: 'Education at the bottom' in *Studies in Adult Education*, 9, Oct. 1977, pp. 127–152.

HIEMSTRA, R.: 'Community adult education in lifelong learning' in *Journal of Research and Development in Education*, 7, Summer 1974, pp. 34–44.

HIEMSTRA, R.: 'Educating parents in the use of the community' in *Adult Leadership*, 23, Sept. 1974, pp. 85–8.

HIEMSTRA, R.: 'Educative community in action' in *Adult Leadership*, 24, Nov. 1975, pp. 82–5.

HUTCHISON, R.: 'Three Arts Centres' A study of South Hill Park, the Gardner Centre and Chapter. Arts Council of Great Britain, 1977.

JONES, P.: *Community Education in Practice—a review.* Social Evaluation Unit, 1978.

JOR, F.: 'The demystification of culture' Council of Europe, 1976.

KOGAN, M.: *The challenge of change* Ed. by KOGAN, M., POPE, M. NFER, 1972.

KRACHT, J.B.: 'Feelings about the community: using value clarification in and out of the classroom' KRACHT, J.B., BOEHM, R.G. in *Journal of Geography*, 74, April 1975, pp. 198–206.

LAWSON, K.H.: 'Community education: a critical assessment' in *Adult Education*, 50, May 1977, pp. 6–13.

A Select Bibliography

LEONETTI, R.: 'Outreach classroom' in *Adult Leadership*, 25, 15 Sept. 1976.

LEVI, P.: 'Old invited to share lessons' in *Times Educational Supplement*, 3100; 25 Oct. 1974, p. 9.

LINLEY, P.M.: 'An experiment with a community workshop' in *Adult Education*, (NIAE), 50, No. 3, Sept. 1977, pp. 167–170.

LOVETT, T.: 'Community development—a network approach' in *Adult Education*, 46, Sept. 1973, pp. 157–65. The role of adult education in community development projects.

LOVETT, T.: *Adult Education, Community Development and the Working Class*\Ward Lock, 1975.

McGEENEY, P.: 'Community involvement and educational change' in *Forum* 14, Spring 1972, pp. 45–7.

MENNELL, S.: 'Cultural policy in town' Council of Europe, 1976.

MIDWINTER, E.: *Patterns of community education* Ward Lock, 1973.

MITSON, R.: 'Comprehensive education within a community centre' MITSON, R., HOLDER, M. in *Forum*, 16, Summer 1974, pp. 88–91.

MOON, R.: 'On the community bandwagon' in *Times Educational Supplement*, 3052, 23 Nov. 1973, p. 4.

MORGAN, C.: 'The community concept 2: origins and development Growth of a multi-purpose, hybrid monster'. MORGAN, C., in *Education*, 145, 14 Feb. 1975, pp. 176–7.

MORRIS, L.: 'A practical approach to community education' in *Adult Education*, 49, Nov. 1976, pp. 228–233.

OSCARSON, J.M.: 'Community involvement in accountability' in *Journal of Research and Development in Education*, 5, Fall 1971, pp. 79–86.

PAGANO, J.O.: 'Linking a community of learners with a community of scholars' in *International Review of Education*, 23, no. 2, 1977.

REE, H.: 'Educator extraordinary' in *Times Educational Supplement*, 3049, 2 Nov. 1973, pp. 22, 75. Extracts from the author's life of Henry Morris.

SIMEY, M. 'Let's put politics back on the agenda' in *Adult Education*, 49, Nov. 1976, pp. 223–227. Role of politics in community development.

SIMPSON, U.: 'Education and community development' in *Trends in Education*, no. 20, Oct. 1970, pp. 39–46.

SINGLETON, J.: 'Schools and rural development: an anthropological approach' in *World Year Book of Education*, 1974, pp. 117–36.

STOO, P.: *Village and Community Colleges*, Association of Adult Education, 1972.

TALMAGE, H.: 'Evaluation of local school/community programs: a transactional evaluation approach' in *Journal of Research and Development in Education*, 8, Spring 1975, pp. 32–41.

TOMLINSON, M.: 'Professional attitudes towards community education' in *Scottish Journal of Adult Education*, 4, No. 1, Autumn 1978, pp. 11–21.

TOTTEN, W.F.: 'Community education, best hope for society' in *School and Society*, 98, Nov. 1970, pp. 410–13.

Two views on community schools 1. U.S.: seeking to involve everybody STEPHENS, E. 2. Britain: close relationships with parents. WOLPE, A.M., in *Times Educational Supplement*, 3037, 10 Aug. 1973, p. 4.

UNESCO: 'Buildings for school and community use: five case studies' 1977.

YARWOOD, J.: 'Informal community education' in *Adult Education*, (NIAE), 46, Jan. 1974, pp. 319–23.

B. Schools, Community Colleges and the Community— Great Britain—General

ARMSTRONG, R.: 'The educational element in community work in Britain' ARMSTRONG, R., DAVIES, C.T., in *Community Development Journal*, 10, Oct. 1975, pp. 155–61.

BALL, C.: 'Hypermarkets of corporate life' in *Times Educational Supplement*, 3105, 29 Nov. 1974, p. 2.

BARBER, D.: 'The college and the community: new dimensions' in *Coombe Lodge Reports*, 9, no. 16, 1977, pp. 581–583.

BETTY, C.: *Focus on the community school* Copyprints Ltd, 1971.

BOYD, J.: *Community education and urban schools* Longman, 1977.

BRIGHOUSE, T.: 'Community school that looks like a horseshoe of houses' in *Education*, 142, 28 Dec. 1973, pp. 660, 663.

BROWN, P.: 'The community school: how large a role?' in *Forum*, 18, Autumn 1975, pp. 25–8.

BULLIVANT, A.: 'Neighbourhood comprehensive school' in *Comprehensive Education*, no. 18, Summer 1971, pp. 27–31.

COLLINS, L.: 'Working to change a multi-racial cultural desert' in *The Teacher*, 28, no. 9, 27 Feb. 1976. p. 6.

D.E.S. Community service in education. (Education Survey, 20) 1974.

DICKSON, A.: 'How every school and college can become a citizenship training centre' in *Community Development Journal*, 12, Jan. 1977, pp. 15–21.

DICKSON, A.: 'The school and the community: Curriculum and community: how can they be combined' in *Community Development Journal*, 8, April 1973, pp. 93–8.

EUSTANCE, R.: 'Schools and the community they serve' in *Trends in Education*, no. 3, Sept. 1975, pp. 33–8.

FAIRBAIRN, A.: 'New methods and aids in community colleges' in *Times Educational Supplement*, 2936, 27 Aug. 1971, p. 30. Educational technology requirements.

FLETCHER, C.: 'Community education 77' Sutton Centre, 1977.

FORRESTER, D.: 'School and community: provision for joint use and sharing in a changing world' HACKER, M., FORRESTER, D., RATTENBURY, P., in *Architects Journal*, 163, 26 May 1976, pp. 1032–58.

FREWSTER, M.: 'Alternative within' in *Times Educational Supplement*, 3095, 20 Sept. 1974, p. 31

GAZEY, P.: 'Community education in England and Wales—an assessment' Nottingham Adult Education Diploma, 1977.

HARVEY, B.: 'The community college' University of Nottingham in *Forum*, 15, Spring 1973, pp. 92–4.

HATCH, S.: 'The role of the community school' HATCH, S., MEYLAN, S., in *New Society*, 21 Sept. 1972, pp. 550–3.

HOFFMAN, M.: 'Reality of vision' in *Times Educational Supplement*, 3094, 13 Sept. 1974, pp. 24–5.

MIDWINTER, E.: 'The school and the community' in *Comprehensive Education*, no. 18, Summer 1971, pp. 31–6.

MITCHELL, G.: 'Whatever happened to community education?' by MITCHELL, G., RICHARDS, J.K., in *Comprehensive Education*, no. 35, Winter 1976–77, pp. 20–23. Administration by local education authorities.

NUT 'Community Schools' in *Secondary Education*, June 1977, vol. 7, no. 1.

PARRY, D.A.: 'Village and community colleges' University of Nottingham Adult Education Diploma, 1972.

PARTINGTON, G.: 'Community school and curriculum' in *Forum*, 18, Summer 1976, pp. 94–7.

PEDLEY, F.H.: 'Community development and the primary school' in *Trends in Education*, no. 33, May 1974, pp. 41–2.

POSTER, C.: *The school and the community* Macmillan, 1971.

PYKETT, P.: 'Schools and youth service in the community: the result of a survey' Church of England Youth Council, 1970.

SALTIEL, H.: 'Community colleges: the concept and the reality' (THESIS, M. Phil., University of Nottingham, 1976).

SCOTTISH EDUCATION DEPARTMENT: 'Professional education and training for community education' HMSO, 1977.

STAPLETON, M.: 'School without walls' in *Forum*, 14, Summer 1972, pp. 94–7.

STOCK, A.K.: 'Community colleges in the United Kingdom' in *International Review of*

Education, 20, 1974, pp. 517–20.

SYLT, E.: 'Community education concepts and practice' University of Nottingham Adult Education Diploma, 1973.

THURSTON, W.: 'The community school concept: a personal view' in *Journal of Applied Educational Studies*, 2, no. 2, Winter 1973, pp. 32–52. Community schools in an EPA.

C.   Schools, Community Colleges and the Community— Great Britain—Specific Centres

AITKEN, R.: 'The community concept 9: Coventry. Combating loneliness in the big city'. in *Education*, 145, 23 May 1975, pp. 574–5. The Sidney Stringer and Ernesford Grange Centres.

ALBERT, T.: 'Choking off innovation: Sutton Centre' in *New Statesman*, 17 March 1978, p. 348.

BENJAMIN, J.: 'There's the Hubb' in *Times Educational Supplement*, no. 3141, 15 Aug. 1975, p. 16. The Holbrook Hubb Community Centre, North East London Polytechnic.

BLACKMORE, P.: 'The community concept 8: Rochdale. From the known gradually to the unknown' in *Education*, 145, 18 April 1975, pp. 439–40.

BOWEN, F.: 'The Cambridgeshire village college: a cultural centre for rural life' in *Aspects* of *Education*, no. 17, 1973, pp. 98–110.

BRACKENBURY, J.: 'Change in process at Impington Village College, Cambridgeshire 1957– 1972' in *Ideas*, no. 23, Oct. 1972, pp. 17–22.

BRACKENBURY, S.: 'The development of a community education service in N.E. Nottinghamshire' University of Nottingham Adult Education Diploma, 1974.

CAMERON, S.: 'Six pronged drive to bring the people in—Coventry community education project' in *Times Educational Supplement*, 3031, 29 June 1973, p. 8.

CARTER, W.G.R.: 'The community concept 5: Sheffield. Earning a title through popular response' in *Education*, 145, 7 March 1975, pp. 250–1.

'Community Clasped: Abraham Moss Centre, Manchester' in *Architects Journal*, 161, 7 May 1975, pp. 964–7.

Community colleges. 1. Cambridgeshire. TURNER, B. 2. Leicestershire. DUNN, A., in *Education and Training*, 14, April 1972, pp. 118–22.

COOKSEY, G.: 'Stantonbury Campus: the idea develops' Dec. 1975—in *Ideas* no. 32, Feb. 1976.

CORBETT, A.: 'ILEA gets into the community game' in *Times Educational Supplement*, 3046, 12 Oct. 1973, p. 7.

CROALL, J.: 'Changing the priorities on the street where they live' in *Times Educational Supplement*, 3158, 12 Dec. 1975, pp. 18–19. The Rathbone Project in Community Education.

D.E.S. Abraham Moss Centre, Manchester. (Building Bulletin, 49).

DEVON (County). EDUCATION DEPARTMENT: 'Sharing and growing: a short account of the growth and activity of community colleges in Devon' 1977.

ELSEY, B.: 'The school in the community' ELSEY, B., THOMAS, K. University of Nottingham, 1976.

EVANS, J.: 'A bold experiment in community catering' in *Education*, 147, 11 Jan. 1976, pp. 517–518. Abraham Moss Centre.

FAIRBAIRN, A.N.: *The Leicestershire Community Colleges*, (NIAE), 1971.

GARTSIDE, P.: 'Local radio and community education' in *Visual Education*, Nov. 1977, pp. 25–27.

GRIFFIN, K.J.: 'An appraisal of innovation and controversy at Countesthorpe College 1970–3' University of Nottingham Diploma in Education, 1973.

HACKER, M.: 'Cheetham Crumpsall centre' HACKER, M., BOOTH, C., MITSON, R., in *Times Educational Supplement*, 3018, 30 March 1973, pp. 36–7.

HAGEDORN, J.: 'Long before Taylor . . . [a study of Belfield Community School]' in *Junior Education*, December 1977, p. 5.

HALL, J.: 'The community concept, 3: Manchester. Forging links with a social system' in *Education*, 145, 21 Feb. 1975, pp. 202–3. Abraham Moss Centre.

HANSON, D.: 'Community centres in County Durham: their functions as educational institutions and agencies for social control' in *Durham Research Review*, no. 28, Spring 1972, pp. 635–43.

HART, P.: 'The background, interests and attitudes to the curriculum of a group of rural children attending a Cambridgeshire village college' in *Aspects of Education*, no. 17, 1973, pp. 111–25.

HARTLEY, D.: 'Community education and the Leicestershire colleges' University of Nottingham Adult Education Diploma, 1974.

HILL, F.: 'School-community centre for Bristol' in *Times Educational Supplement*, 2962, 25 Feb. 1972, p. 8.

HOLROYDE, G.: 'Teamwork fits the bill for a community enterprise' HOLROYDE, G., in *Education*, 146, 5 Sept. 1975, pp. 239–41. Sidney Stringer school and community college.

JACKSON, J.: 'The Strone and Maukinhill informal education project, a Greenock experiment' in *Scottish Journal of Adult Education*, 2, no. 2, Spring 1976, pp. 4–7.

KENT. COUNTY. EDUCATION COMMITTEE. 'Schools and the community'. 1969.

LOVETT, T.: 'Adult education 1. The uses of working class culture' in *Education and Training*, 13, Sept. 1971, pp. 298–9, 316. W.E.A. work in association with Liverpool E.P.A.

LOVETT, T.: 'Community based study groups—a Northern Ireland case study' in *Adult Education*, (NIAE), 51. no. 1, May 1978, pp. 22–29.

LOW, G.: 'Monkstown: an experiment in overcoming obstacles' in *Education*, 28 Oct. vol. 150, no. 18, 1977. Community education.

MCHUGH, R.: 'A case study in management: Sidney Stringer School and Community College' Open University, 1976.

MACK, J.: 'A people's classroom' in *New Society*, 39, 3 March 1977, p. 450. The Strone and MauKinhill Informal Education Project, Strathclyde, Scotland.

MAKINS, V.: 'The story of Countesthorpe 2. Dividends of change' in *Times Educational Supplement*, no. 3129, 16 May 1975, pp. 17–19; no. 3130, 23 May 1975, pp. 18–19.

MEDLICOTT, P.: 'Community dream: Abraham Moss Centre, Manchester' in *New Society*, 8 May 1975, pp. 339–40.

MINCHIN, M.F.: 'Countesthorpe College—problems and possibilities of radical innovation' University of Nottingham Diploma in Education, 1975.

MITCHELL, S.: 'Small Heath School and Community Centre, Birmingham' in *Architects Journal*, 168, 20 Sept. 1978, pp. 521–35.

MOON, B.: 'Stantonbury Campus' Open University, 1976.

MORGAN, T.: 'The community concept, 4: Gwent. Sharing means more than joint use', in *Education*, 145, 28 Feb. 1975, pp. 228–9. School based leisure centres.

MORRIS, G.: 'Cambridgeshire continues its community tradition' in *Education*, 149, 24 May 1977, pp. 369–370.

NETTLETON, J.A.: MOORE, D. *School and community: adult centres in Cumberland.* (NIAE), 1967.

NIXON, R.: 'The community concept 7: Walsall. The local patron pauses for self analysis' in *Education*, 145, 21 March 1975, pp. 326–7.

PARKER, D.: 'The development of a community school' Whitesmore School, Chelmsley Wood. University of Nottingham Adult Education Diploma, 1974.

POULTON, G. and RANDLE, L.: *Threshold of consciousness: an outline of the New Communities Project, 1973–76.* Dept. of Adult Education, University of Southampton, 1976.

QUEEN'S UNIVERSITY OF BELFAST: 'Carry on learning: report of an experimental project in community education' D. & B. Rowlands. Community Education Project, Queen's University Belfast, 1977.

RADCLIFFE, D.: 'Community values and non-formal education' in *Literacy Work*, 7, no. 1, Spring 1978, pp. 37–44.

RENNIE, J.: 'The Coventry Community Education Project' in *Ideas*, no. 32, Feb. 1976, pp. 68–71.

A Select Bibliography

SCOTT, G.: 'Giant hope at a giant school: Stantonbury campus in Buckinghamshire' in *Times Educational Supplement*, 3102, Nov. 8, 1974, p. 12.

STEVENS, A.: 'Efficient full time education: Balsall Heath Community School' in *Times Educational Supplement*, 3104, 22 Nov. 1974, p. 22.

STONE, J.A.: 'The community concept, 1: Nottinghamshire. Sutton brings school to the market place' in *Education*, 145, 7 Feb. 1975, pp. 150, 152.

STONE, J.: 'The family arts centre, Kentish Town' in *Where*, no. 104, May 1975, pp. 126–9.

WATTS, J.: 'Community school: Les Quennevais school, Jersey, England' in *Times Educational Supplement*, 2918, 23 April 1971, p. 110.

WATTS, J.: 'Countesthorpe: a case study' in *The curriculum: research, innovation and change: proceedings of the naugural meeting of the Standing Conference on Curriculum Studies*. Eds. TAYLOR, P.H. and WALTON, J. Ward Lock, 1973, pp. 146–60.

WATTS, J.: *The Countesthorpe experience: the first 5 years* Allen & Unwin, 1977.

WATTS, J.: *Profile: Countesthorpe College* [2] Countesthorpe College examines its aims, in *Where*, no. 79, April 1973, pp. 108–14.

WEST, L.: 'Community schools—adults and children: a Cumbrian AAE perspective' in *Adult Education*, 49, March 1977, pp. 367–373.

WESTERN, S.: 'Community college, priv. print, [1976?]' Predominantly concerned with Ivanhoe Community College, Ashby de la Zouch.

WHITE, R. and BROCKINGTON, D.: *In and out of school: the ROSLA Community Education Project*. Routledge and Kegan Paul, 1978.

WILLIAMS, G.: 'Managing community education: a Leicestershire case study' in *Adult Education*, (NIAE), 50, no. 6, March 1978, pp. 370–375.

WORTHINGTON, J. and SHEEHAN, A.M.: 'Community school at Ballincollig, Southern Ireland' in *Architects Journal*, 167, 22 March 1978, pp. 545–7.

D. Community Education—Abroad

ALBERT, T.: 'Officially free' in *Times Educational Supplement*, 3188, 9 July 1976. Community schools in Australia.

CHESTERFIELD, R.: 'School-community integration in rural Brazil' CHESTERFIELD, R., SCHÜTZ P., in *Community Development Journal*, 12, April 1977, pp. 112–121.

Community school centre act: 'proposed' in *Intellect*, 102, Dec.l1973, p. 146.

Conference. Education and community in Africa. Edinburgh, 1976. *Education and community in Africa*. Ed. by K. King. 1976.

CORMAM, L.: *Community Education in Canada: an annotated bibliography*, (OISE), 1975.

COURT, D.: 'East African higher education from the community standpoint' in *Higher Education*, 6, Feb. 1977, pp. 45–66. Role of Dar Es Salaam University in community development.

CSLEA: *Metroplex Assembly: an experiment in community education*. 1965 (USA).

GARRETT, D. and HALL, I.: *A Community College for the Rotorua Region*. New Zealand Dept. of Education, 1975.

GRAN, B.: 'Education and the integration of leisure activities and pupil welfare: a case study from Malmö, Sweden' GRAN, B., KJELLMAN, L. Department of Education and Psychological Research, School of Education, 1976.

HABERMAN, M.: 'Assessing faculty's community service' HABERMAN, M., QUINN, L., in *Adult Leadership*, 25, Jan. 1977, p. 140—[United States].

LITWAK, E.: *Schools, family and neighbourhood* [United States], Columbia U.P., 1974.

LOEWENBERG, F.M.: 'Utilization of schools for community centres in Israel' in *Community Development Journal*, 10, April 1975, pp. 126–31.

McROBIE, A.: 'Community projects bring back adults into classroom' in *Times Educational Supplement*, 3103, Nov. 15, 1974, p. 14. New Zealand.

NEW YORK (STATE). UNIVERSITY. *Division of School Buildings and Grounds*. Designing the central school plant as a community center. 1948.

ORATA, P.T.: 'Barrio high schools and community colleges in the Phillipines' in *Prospects*, 7, no. 3, 1977, pp. 401–412.

RAHMAN, H.: 'Urban community development project—a case study from Bagladesh' in *Community Development*, 10, Jan. 1975, pp. 38–43.

SARAN, M.: *For community service: the Mount Carmel Experiment* Blackwell, 1974.

SARWONO, S.W.: 'Study service. An experiment in higher education and community development in Indonesia' in *Community Development Journal*, 10, Oct. 1975. pp. 166–170.

STEPHENS, E.: 'US: seeking to involve everyone' in *Times Educational Supplement*, 3037, 10 Aug 1973, p. 4.

WASS, P.: 'Policy issues for community development in Africa: lessons from Botswana' in *Community Development Journal*, 10, Jan. 1975, pp. 14–23.

CONTRIBUTORS

Contributors

Eric Batten One-time teacher in a South-East London comprehensive. Subsequently taught at London College of Printing. After part-time post-graduate study under Jean Floud and Basil Bernstein, appointed as research associate to Manchester University under Stephen Wiseman to conduct a follow-up study of the Manchester Plowden Sample at secondary school level, published 1975 with M.E. Ainsworth as *The Affects of Environmental Factors on Secondary Educational Attainment in Manchester: A Plowden Follow-up*; Schools Council Research Studies, London MacMillan. Subsequently appointed Lecturer in Sociology at Manchester. Keenly interested in the analysis of processes of educational disadvantage and concerned at both a practical and theoretical level with the potential of community education as a means of modifying these processes.

Peter Boulter Director of Education for Cumbria. Educated at Loughborough School and the Universities of Leeds and Leicester, graduating with a BA Honours Degree from Leeds in 1955 and gaining a Post Graduate Certificate in Education at the University of Leicester in 1956. After teaching for three years at the Grammar School, Burton on Trent, entered educational administration in a training post in Birmingham under the guidance of Lionel Russell. Later appointed to more senior posts in the counties of Devon and Warwickshire before becoming Deputy to Gordon Bessey in Cumberland in 1971. In 1974 appointed Deputy in the reorganized County of Cumbria and in 1975 appointed to present post as Director. He is married with two young sons which helps him to maintain his interests in ski-ing, squash and tennis. He has a keen interest in drama and opera and all forms of music and, as one might expect from a Director of Education in Cumbria, spends much recreational time in the mountains, fell walking and maintaining associated interests of ornithology and geology.

Sylvia Coupe Formerly Assistant Head at Rowlinson Campus, Sheffield, is now retired. She was head of Burngreave Girls' Secondary School for ten years until Comprehensive reorganization in Sheffield, September, 1969.

Sara Delamont Born 1947. Read Social Anthropology at Girton College, Cambridge, and then did a PhD in Education at Edinburgh University. Lectured in Sociology at Leicester University School of Education, and is currently Lecturer in Sociology at University College, Cardiff. Research interests in classroom observation, curriculum change and women's studies. Author of *Interaction in the Classroom* Methuen, London, 1976; and *The Nineteenth Century Woman* Croom Helm, London, 1978 with Lorna Duffin.

Christ Elphick Trained as a teacher/social worker and then worked as a teacher/housemaster in a residential community home in Co Durham for two years. Moved to Liverpool and had seven years experience of community development in one of the inner city areas, Liverpool 8. He was involved with a variety of experimental projects and took a particular interest in the fields of community art/community education as they relate to the process of community development. Helped to establish the Rathbone Project in Liverpool in 1974–5 and worked with that project until leaving to establish Cetu in 1976–7. At present a team member of Cetu. He has been involved with various national initiatives such as the Arts Council's Community Arts Committee of which he was a founder member, the joint Gulbenkian Foundation/Arts Council study into the relationship between Community Art and Community Development and the BBC's Community Programmes Unit. He is author of

Contributors

several documents and articles including a booklet 'Community Celebration' a unit on Community Education for the Open University, articles in *Youth and Society* and a chapter on Community Arts and Community Development for 'Boundaries of Change in Community Work' (due to be published in September 1979).

Colin Fletcher Studied Sociology at Liverpool and has since been engaged in research on 'Managers' at Aston University, 'Doctors' at University College, Swansea, and 'Industrial Relations' at University College, Cardiff. In between research contracts he has taught Sociological Research Methods at University College, Cardiff and Birmingham Polytechnic and is currently Senior Research Officer, Department of Adult Education, University of Nottingham engaged in a five-year contract concerned with the development of Sutton Centre. His writings include *Beneath the Surface: An account of three styles of sociological research* (Routledge and Kegan Paul), *The Person in the Sight of Sociology* (Routledge and Kegan Paul) and numerous papers.

Peter Haywood He is librarian for education, University Library, University of Nottingham.

Keith Jackson He became active in adult education during National Service in the Royal Army Education Corps where he learned very rapidly how the educational system had failed to develop the talents of so many in the British working class. After graduating from Oxford in Modern History he undertook a tutor training year with the Oxford Delegacy for Extramural Studies, serving his apprenticeship in the Potteries of North Staffordshire. Five years with the Workers Educational Association included a period in South Wales and then the North Staffordshire District where he was mainly concerned with trade union courses and the development of a joint LEA/WEA adult education centre, Tawney House in Longton. In 1968 he moved to Liverpool University Institute of Extension Studies (then the Department of Adult Education and Extra-mural Studies) as Lecturer in Social Science with special responsibility for Community Development. During the next ten years, during which time he became Senior Assistant Director and Head of the Social Studies Division in the Institute, he worked with a number of community projects seeking to establish a programme of adult education for the urban working class which might match day release courses for industrial workers in its combination of practical value and educational breadth. In 1978 took up the post of Senior Tutor and tutor with responsibility for Local and Community Studies at the new Northern College of Residential Adult Education in South Yorkshire. He has written various articles on the relationship between adult education and community development, and on working-class adult education.

Arfon R. Jones Head of Sidney Stringer School and Community College; was previously Deputy Head of Pastoral and Community at Sidney Stringer, Senior Lecturer in Education and Community Studies at Northern Counties College of Education, Newcastle-upon-Tyne, and Education Officer in Uganda.

Tom Lovett From 1969–1972 worked with the Liverpool Educational Priority Area Project. He was seconded by the Workers Educational Association to explore the role of adult education amongst the working-class population in Central Liverpool. Since 1972 he has been working at the newly established Institute of Continuing Education in Derry, N. Ireland. Most of his work there has been concerned with providing various forms of educational support and resources—including the use of local radio—for social and community groups in Ulster. In 1977 he obtained financial support from a number of sources to set up a Community Action Research and Educational Project. He has published numerous articles on community education and community action, and one book (based on his Liverpool experiences), *Adult Education, Community Development and the Working Class* Ward Lock, London, 1975.

Ron Mitson Former Head of Codsall Comprehensive School, is now Principal of Abraham Moss Centre, and joint author of *Teaching from Strength*, Heinemann, a book on team teaching, and *Resource Centres*, Methuen.

Wayne R. Robins He is project director SNAP (Schemes in Neighbourhood Action and Participation) C.F. Mott Foundation, Flint, Michigan

Alan Simpson Married with two young children. He has been a community worker in Raleigh Street, Nottingham since the Nottingham Areas Project for which he worked was established in July, 1974. In June 1978 the County Council withdrew the Urban Aid grant and he, together with six colleagues, became unemployed in August 1978—the price of success.

Neil Thompson Trained as a mechanical engineer and, after graduating from Nottingham University, worked for Imperial Chemical Industries in the North East. Since then he has worked in schools in Bermondsey, Bristol and Staffordshire. He has been Assistant Principal at Abraham Moss Centre, Manchester since April, 1973.

Philip Toogood Taught at Wyndham School Egremont, then spent eight years as Warden of Swavesey Village College, and is currently Headmaster of Madeley Court School.

John Watts
1953–58   English Department, Sawston Village College, Cambridge
1958–64   Head of English, Crown Woods School
1964–69   First Head of Les Quennevais School, Jersey
1969–72   Lecturer at the London Institute
1972–   Principal, Countesthorpe College.
Author of the schools' series *Encounters* Longman; *Interplay* Longman, *Teaching* David and Charles.
Numerous textbooks published.
1974–75   Chairman of The National Association for the Teaching of English.

Wyn Williams Married with four children ranging from sixteen to six. He has just left teacher training to join the community education team of the Open University Post-Experience Unit. He was the elected Project Secretary for Nottingham Areas Project August 1976–August 1978.

Stewart Wilson He entered teaching in 1958 after spell in the Royal Navy and industry. He has held senior posts in secondary modern, grammar and comprehensive schools before taking up first headship on Teesside in 1966. Opened Sutton Centre, Nottinghamshire's first purpose-built Community School in 1973 and moved to Scotland in 1978 to open Deans Community High School, which is one of the two first purpose-built community schools to come into operation north of the border. He has been an ardent advocate of comprehensive education in the 60s and its logical development into community education in the 70s and 80s. He has campaigned for many years for the Common System of Examining at 16+, for mixed ability teaching, block timetabling, the opening of educational premises for 360 days a year, joint adult and student classes—and the abolition of corporal punishment. He claims he preserves his sanity by walking in the hills and savouring the delights of Newcastle Brown Ale.

INDEX

Author Index

Index

Subject Index

Index